THE LONDON DISCOUNT MARKET

THE
LONDON DISCOUNT
MARKET

W. M. SCAMMELL

ST. MARTIN'S PRESS

New York

1968

© *W. M. Scammell 1968*

Published by
ELEK BOOKS LIMITED
2 All Saints Street
London N1

First published in the United States of America
by St. Martin's Press, Inc. 1968
Library of Congress Catalog Card Number: 68-8999

Printed in Great Britain
by Unwin Brothers Limited
Woking and London
(2418J)

CONTENTS

TABLES

CHARTS

To and for K.

PREFACE

AUTHORS ENJOY writing prefaces. They are the last step on a long road and the writers' relief and sense of emancipation at reaching the end is invariably marked by the largesse of thanks and benediction they shower on friends, colleagues, secretaries, their wives, their families and others whom they have exploited, plagued and pestered along the way. If an author does not become human in his preface he is incapable of humanity, for only then is he relaxed and, in his relief, off guard.

The writing of this book has been enjoyable, but somewhat protracted by changes of scene and circumstance. It was suggested to me while I was teaching at a British university in which peace and time for research were plentiful. It was written during my first year at a growing Canadian university in which all features of the academic life were plentiful save time and leisure. But, though delayed, I think the manuscript gained detachment by the increasing preoccupation with North American financial institutions and ideas. Two periods of peace allowed me, propped in my customary place in the library of the British Museum, to produce the necessary mound of untidy paper covered with characters beside which the Dead Sea Scrolls were a model of legibility but which my good-humoured typists, Barbara Vitols, Rosemary Rogers and Mary Lane reduced to order. The problems of British monetary policy and of the institutions which make and implement it were fascinating to me when I lived in Britain. Since living in North America the fascination has been tinged with some pride in the model which Britain has given for centralised banking systems the world over.

The formal thanks with which authors encumber their prefaces are more than a convention. A book is really a joint product in the production of which many participate. This book could hardly have been written but for the excellent work of the late Wilfred King on the London Discount Market. I had hoped to discuss many things with him but I arrived in London too late, only to read of his death on the day of my arrival. His writings are, however, a mine of information. Specifically my thanks are due: to my old friend, Professor E. V. Morgan who suggested to me that I should write the book, and read, with his customary perception, the final manuscript; to a number of executives in the discount houses, who patiently devoted much time to what, to them, must have been tedious explanation; to my friend and colleague Parzi Copes who, in a memorable first semester and in the intervals of running a department of

9

2,000 students with four faculty, devoted time, energy and ingenuity to getting me time and travel money to write and spend my study leave in Britain; but most of all to my friends in the U.K. (particularly J.J. and A. and K. & J.) whose hospitality sustained me during the three cold winter months in which I wrote the first draft. I am indebted to Mr. W. M. Clarke of the Committee on Invisible Exports for much useful information on the inter-bank loan market.

It is unnecessary to thank my wife, as is customary, for deprivation of my company and support. It is known to our friends that she not only tells me what to write but mows the lawn and does the washing-up while I write it. Besides, she did the index.

Simon Fraser University   W.M.S.
Vancouver, B.C.

Part I

Chapter 1

INTRODUCTION

'Lawyers like to complicate matters;
We like to simplify them.'
The New Yorker

THIS BOOK is concerned with the evolution and activities of the London discount market and with certain other branches of the money market which are closely connected with it. Our task has ample justification. The London discount market was the first of the world's markets in short-term monetary assets, and therefore something of a prototype for such markets in other countries. It consists of firms and institutions so grouped and related that their relations in their everyday working form a pattern that is a major part of the monetary structure and policy of the United Kingdom. Finally, it provides in one group of its institutions, the discount houses, a distinct commercial and financial service, important in its own right apart from the rôle it plays in the general financial pattern, which imparts by its nature and operations a distinctive character to the market, moulding it in certain ways and ensuring its development along certain paths. The formative rôle which the discount houses have played in this process makes them important, as does their uniqueness. The fact that they are unique, that they grew up for one purpose, commercial bill discounting and broking, and now fulfil other and wider purposes; and that a controversy exists as to the wisdom or otherwise of retaining them in their present form—all this ensures that in the pages which follow they play a major part and are the main focus of attention.

This raises a point of definition which must be cleared up at the outset: the distinction between 'discount market' and 'money market'. We must be consistent about the use of these terms. To the writer it seems that the discount market is clearly the market which exists for the sale of two sorts of credit instrument—the commercial bill of exchange and the Treasury bill; that this market consists of the discount houses, the commercial fraternity who discount bills, the acceptance houses who guarantee them, the clearing banks who buy bills 'second hand' from the discount houses (or who discount them for their own customers), the Treasury who, as the authority issuing Treasury bills, form the supply source for the largest amount of any credit instrument dealt in by the discount market; and finally those various other groups who tender for and rediscount Treasury bills and the clearing banks who not only act as their final resting place until their maturity but who also supply the working money capital to the discount houses which enables them to operate. This is a formidable group but it is homogeneous and it consists only of those institutions concerned with buying, selling and holding commercial and Treasury bills. Yet another must, however, be added: the Bank of England which is the ultimate controller of the market and which manipulates it for its own ends.

The money market is wider and somewhat less homogeneous. It consists indeed of the discount market which is its most important part. But it also includes subsidiary and quite separate markets for the provision, holding and dealing in forms of short-term monetary asset other than bills. It includes such additional features as the supply and price of short-term loans from banks, the market for short-term bonds and, since the 1960's, two other important and in a sense rival markets: the market for short-term loans by the banks and others to local authorities; and the new market for inter-bank loans which exists among the overseas and merchant banks. The money market is therefore much more than a matter of discounting bills. Conditions and interest rates in these other markets certainly affect and influence the discount market but such markets exist separately from it. They would have arisen even if the discount market, in its present form, did not exist.

This book will be concerned primarily with the discount market but it will, for two good reasons, make frequent expeditions into the wider territory of the money market: first, that it is difficult and undesirable to disentangle the discount market from the broader aspects of the money market in general; and secondly, because the writer is interested in examining the discount houses and the money market in relation to the broad questions of monetary policy and monetary control. He sees the discount market primarily as a link in the chain of monetary command and only secondarily as a functional group. The limiting title for the book is justifiable because at least two aspects of the money market are not dealt with at any length, namely short-term loans to local authorities by the banking system and the inter-bank loan market. To imply in the title that the book is a treatment of the money market would be to indicate a greater coverage than the book in fact has. Better to sail under a smaller flag but to be somewhat expansive and presumptuous in so doing than to hoist a great and imposing banner on too slight a mast.

Our main task then has two distinct aspects: first to examine the history and activities of the London discount market as a set of functional institutions, as dealers in bills, Treasury and commercial, and as operators in certain markets—a group of firms performing certain specialised services for the public and private sectors of the economy; and secondly, to see this group of firms as a part of the wider system of monetary and banking control, to examine their relations with other financial institutions and to assess the part played by them as an integral section of the monetary system.

The British monetary system is unique in the special rôle within it which the discount market has acquired. We shall trace the development of that rôle, considering how and when its main features emerged; how, for example, the development of a market in call loans enabled the discount houses to alter their character, how their relationship with the Bank of England shaped the discount houses' evolution and enabled them to play a part in the system of credit control; and how, in the twentieth century, new functions emerged which enabled them to survive in conditions far different from those which had brought them into being. By stressing one dominant aspect of the discount market, its place in the system of monetary control, we have provided ourselves with a central theme which serves to give both history and analysis unity and continuity. To write a history of the discount houses, divorced from their wider implications in the monetary system and devoid of their relations to other monetary institutions, would be unnecessary and, for author and reader, intolerably dull. But for the adoption of this wider view a price has to be paid. It is necessary in each part of the narrative to trace not only the evolution of the discount houses but also of those financial institutions with which they have been and are in constant contact, the commercial banks and the Bank of England. Indeed, it is the relations of the discount houses with these other monetary institutions which is our primary interest. For this reason the book must sketch in a background of facts and comments which has been traced elsewhere, for which the writer makes no claim to originality and which may already be familiar to many readers. For this there is no help. One may often take the same route for different purposes, till the same ground for different crops, love the same woman for different reasons. In dealing with the development of the commercial banks, the policies and activities of the Bank of England and changes in the financial environment at large we shall try to touch only on those aspects which have relevance to the activities and processes of the discount market.

Here, however, we find ourselves face to face with a further problem. To embark upon any worthwhile discussion of the place within the British monetary system of the London discount market brings us perilously close to a number of problems which are, and probably long will be, the subject of high debate. Any examination of the centralised banking system as a whole and in general terms involves the central problem of control of the money supply; of how, for purposes of inflating and deflating the money supply, the lines of central bank control run; where are the pressure points, and indeed, even, what does the monetary supply mean and of what does it consist? Clearly into this uncertain country we cannot venture too far. We cannot afford the space for considering these controversial matters; still less can we afford the diversion from the main stream of our purpose which their consideration would involve. We have no alternative but to seek some firm ground of orthodoxy on which to base ourselves. Such a ground we have chosen. From the days when monetary theorists saw inflation and deflation in terms of expansion and contraction of the money supply (defined as bank notes, coin and immediately usable bank deposits), and monetary control as resting on variation of bank deposits geared to the maintenance of the commercial banks' cash ratio, to the day when a Keynesian generation says that effective demand is conditioned by the general liquidity situation of the monetary system, was a long step. It brought us to the new orthodoxy to which the Radcliffe Committee in 1959 gave its blessing. Yet this in its turn was to be questioned, and a new phase of controversy in monetary policy began with Radcliffe. This debate was a dual one, centred initially on the general question of the money supply itself, its relation to general liquidity and the contribution of both to stabilisation policy; but latterly swinging to the problem of identifying the actual means whereby the monetary authorities may control the money supply. All this we have ignored in this book, not because these controversies are irrelevant or because we are unaware of their existence, but because we are uncertain of their outcome and of how far any current theory of the monetary mechanism might be from its realities. It is sufficient for our purpose to accept the intellectual situation as we might have found it in the early sixties when the arguments of Radcliffe had been digested and in great part accepted. The picture of the central banking system thus provided is adequate for our needs.

There is another though minor reason for following the broad open path. A purely functional history of the discount market comes perilously close to being a history of individual firms. The discount market is and always has been relatively small. Throughout much of its history its units were partnerships, private firms and even sole traders of whose activities no detailed record (often no record at all) remains. Now, with its twelve firms, the market is smaller than ever, and although larger firms, public companies and published balance sheets place more of the picture before us, this only covers recent years and it is still a very indeterminate picture. Some day when, within one of the older discount houses, a writer and historian of talent emerges, a good and useful book may be written from the inside, which records the experiences of a firm and which catches the spirit and activities of Lombard Street more felicitously than this one can hope to do. Such a book would be valuable and complementary to the academic studies which have appeared. Perhaps in the quieter period after three o'clock, when the books are balanced and the overnight money is secure, a little historical research and literary effort would be a useful relaxation for some discount house director before he catches the 5.30 at Waterloo. For the present this writer, because of his interests as an economist and because he is looking at the market from the outside, can only hope to stand back and attempt a projection of the market's history and function as an integral part of the British monetary system.

Finally, the writer makes no apology that the method of this study is historical. The discount market is only a century and a half old but it is only against its historical development that it can be truly understood. What it has emerged from, what it is tending towards, is of the essence in understanding it.

B

Part II

'Economics seems to apply to every nook and cranny
of human experience.'

Robert A. Mundell

Chapter 2

THE BILL OF EXCHANGE

'A bill of exchange is a commodity that is subject to rises and
falls in value. That's a deduction from Jeremy Bentham's theory
of interest. He was a publicist who proved that people were
very silly and stupid to disapprove of moneylenders.

Honoré de Balzac, *Eugénie Grandet*

I

SINCE THE WELL-KNOWN legal definition of a bill of exchange is sooner
or later an inevitable quotation in this chapter it is perhaps as well to
begin with it. It occurs in Section 3 of the Bills of Exchange Act 1882
and tells us that 'a bill of exchange is an unconditional order in writing
addressed by one person to another, signed by the person giving it,
requiring the person to whom it is addressed to pay on demand, or at a
fixed or determinable future time, a sum certain in money to or to the
order of a specified person or to bearer.'

Interesting and important points of mercantile law are at once raised
by the definition. For example, since the definition describes a bill as
'unconditional' the insertion in it of any condition, any implication that
it is not a mere request, or that it is a requirement for anything other than
money, invalidates it as a bill of exchange. The time factor is important.
The order must be to pay 'on demand or at a fixed or determinable
future time.' When payable on demand this may be stated on the bill,
as when it is said to be payable on presentation, at sight, or at some
period after sight.[1] Alternatively no time for payment may be stated,
in which case the bill is assumed payable on demand. If not payable on
demand the bill must stipulate that it is payable at a fixed period after
date or sight or on the occurrence of a specified and certain event.

Once a bill is drawn the person ordering payment is called 'the drawer'
and the person who is required to pay 'the drawee.' The person stipulated
to receive payment when the bill matures is 'the payee.' The bill is accepted
when it is signed upon its face by the drawee, who then becomes 'the
acceptor' and thus signifies his willingness to meet the requirements of

---

[1] In this case the drawee inserts the due date when he accepts the bill.

the bill at its due date.[1] The drawee may, if he so wishes, refuse acceptance or he may give either a general or qualified acceptance, the former assenting without qualification to the order of the drawer, the latter being conditional, partial or local. For example, the drawer may accept for only a part of the sum stated on the bill or he may agree to pay only at a certain place. Such a qualified acceptance is a variation of the bill as it was drawn and the drawer has the right to refuse the qualified acceptance, regarding the bill as dishonoured by non-acceptance.

There are precise statutory requirements both as to the presentation of a bill for acceptance and also the circumstances under which a bill may be treated as dishonoured by non-acceptance. Once accepted and once the acceptance, if it is qualified, has been agreed to by the drawer, the bill becomes a negotiable instrument so that title to it passes with delivery. If the bill is a bearer bill this means actual delivery, while in the case of a bill payable at a stipulated future date this means endorsement followed by delivery. Another important legal quality attaching to a bill as a negotiable instrument is that any person to whom it is assigned holds it by independent title. If he takes it in good faith and for value received he takes it free from all defects of title or grounds of defence which may have attached to it from a previous party.

The main convenience of a bill of exchange as a medium of payment derives primarily from the fact that by it credit is given by a seller to his customer for whom the customary 'period of credit' becomes the period of the currency of the bill. The seller may retain the accepted bill until it is paid on maturity but, more likely, he will sell the bill either to a bank or discount house, receiving its face value less discount on the bill at current discount rates.[2] Financing a transaction by means of a bill thus gives virtually immediate payment to the seller while giving a period (i.e., the currency of the bill) to the buyer before he makes payment.

A second advantage of a bill is that it may, as a negotiable instrument, be passed from hand to hand. For example, the seller may use the accepted bill in order to settle a debt of his own by endorsing the bill[3] and passing it as payment to his own creditor.[4] If the creditor decides he needs immediate cash he can discount the bill. Alternatively he can hold it

---

[1] In fact three further 'days of grace' are given for payment.

[2] The fact that he has to pay discount on the bill in order to get his money at once is probably immaterial to the choice between a bill and normal cash payment. If the payment is made promptly by the customer the seller usually allows discount for prompt payment.

[3] If it is an 'order bill.' A bearer bill does not require endorsement.

[4] Always assuming that his creditor will accept it as payment, for a bill of exchange is not legal tender. Its acceptance, however, in such a case is acknowledged commercial usage where the parties are known to one another.

to maturity or use it after endorsement to discharge a debt of his own.

The advantages of the bill of exchange operate most strongly in foreign trade where the period required to complete a transaction is often long and where fairly long credit is normally given. Here the foreign importer may defer payment by accepting a bill of long maturity while the home exporter may, on this promise of receiving money at a future date, provide himself immediately with liquid assets. For each party, payment occurs at the time of optimum convenience, for the seller after the goods are despatched, for the buyer after they are received and perhaps even after they are sold.

Although both 'inland' and 'foreign' bills are similar in principle the dominance of the latter and the existence of the organised discount market in London, in which bills of graded quality change hands, led in the later nineteenth century to the specialised activity of Acceptance Houses.[1] The merchant banks, which in Britain handle much of the acceptance business, accept bills on behalf of clients for commission and thus provide bills of unimpeachable quality which may be discounted by the drawer at the best going discount rate. The Acceptance House for its part must provide, from the proceeds of its commissions, the credit intelligence service which enables it to vet the credit standing of those on whose behalf it accepts bills.

Generally, the Acceptance House gives its service to foreigners in the form of an Acceptance Credit whereby the House agrees to accept bills on behalf of a client up to a given amount. It is common for such an arrangement to be made for a foreign client by his own bank which reimburses the Acceptance House on completion for the value of the bill plus the Acceptance House's own commission. This arrangement is known as a Reimbursement Credit. For its part the Acceptance House must satisfy the Bank of England, to which by process of rediscount many of its acceptances find their way, that its liquidity and assets structure are appropriate to its business and adequate to ensure the credit standing for its acceptances upon which the maintenance of such a business depends.

One other definition and distinction is required to conclude this rather dreary excursion into the legal field—the distinction between a bill of

[1] Acceptance Houses had their origin in merchanting firms of high credit standing whose acceptances could be discounted at 'fine' (i.e., low) rates of discount by the holders of the bills. If the acceptances of such a merchanting house could be discounted at 3 per cent when the acceptances of an unknown firm could only be discounted at 5 per cent it became worth while for other firms to pay a commission to the merchanting firm to accept bills on its behalf for any commission less than 2 per cent. In effect these merchanting firms lent their credit standing to other traders for commission. They came to specialise in this, gradually abandoning their trading activities.

exchange and a promissory note. They are often confused and the fact that Treasury bills, which now form the bread and butter of the bill market, are in fact promissory notes, makes distinction no easier. In fact the promissory note is similar to the bill only in its negotiability, in the rules which govern its endorsement and in the fact that it is defined in the Bills of Exchange Act 1882. In that Act Section 83 gives the definition of the promissory note, the first clause of which distinguishes it from the bill. It is, we are told, 'an unconditional *promise*[1] in writing made by one person to another. . . .'[2] Herein lies the difference: the bill is an order to pay; the promissory note is a promise to pay. Thus the Treasury in issuing a Treasury bill engages to pay 91 days hence the sum mentioned in the bill. Once issued the bill becomes a negotiable instrument passing from hand to hand until paid by the Treasury at the completion of its currency.

Apart from the Treasury bill the promissory note is little used nowadays. A bank note is legally 'a promissory note made by a banker, payable on demand' but this is a somewhat recherché way of looking at the commonest item of legal tender. In some countries, for example Canada, promissory notes are used by commercial banks as documentary proof of personal loans. In this case they give to the personal loan, which is usually for the finance of consumer spending, a precision as to amount and repayment which the more flexible English overdraft does not possess. Readers of the eighteenth century novel and of social and political memoirs will be familiar with the use of promissory notes as 'end of evening settlement' for gambling debts. Charles James Fox and his like were proficient in their use for this purpose. For all the author knows the note in this form may well have its modern exponents.

II

The bill of exchange has a long history as a credit document. There are references to 'bill-like' documents[3] in early Babylonian and Egyptian records. Cicero in letters to Atticus spoke of the transfer of money in terms which implied the use of a bill and there is implicit reference to bills in the Roman legal codes. How the bill came from the ancient world to the modern is a matter of speculation but it is possible that the medieval

---

[1] Author's italics.
[2] Thereafter the definition follows similar wording to that of the bill.
[3] One of the main difficulties in tracing the history of credit instruments is that of classification of the instruments.

bill of exchange came from antiquity via Byzantium.[1] Its immediate predecessor as a credit instrument was the letter of credit which was freely used by popes, kings and princes and of which early examples dating from 1191 and 1199 are extant. The bill, in its first discernible modern form, was in use in the twelfth century in Genoa. It was in use in the same period in Florence and Amalfi, and there is evidence that bills were common in medieval England, where the first statutory reference to them was in 1379. The Venetians, it is known, used them widely in the thirteenth century. Pirenne[2] quotes a German writer who refers to the Fairs of Champagne in the twelfth century as 'the money market of Europe'[3] and asserts that it is in the organisation of credit at these fairs in the twelfth century that we must seek the origin of the modern bill of exchange. These very early bills were in fact promissory notes taking the form of a promise by a debtor to pay at a stated future time for value received. The development of the medieval bill of exchange seems, indeed, to have been a slow process, by which a confession of indebtedness and a promise to pay slowly evolved to a new form of credit instrument. In the 1300's the draft, in a new form, appeared and in the following century the acceptance of the draft by the drawee became established practice. From Italy the use of bills of exchange spread to England and Flanders and from there to the trading towns of Germany. From 1550 to 1650 the practice of endorsement of bills of exchange became widespread and added to their security so that they began to circulate almost as money.

By the sixteenth century bills were known and used over most of Western Europe. Speaking of the sixteenth century Tawney tells us that there was a 'considerable class of financial specialists and a highly developed financial technique' and that 'Antwerp, Lyons, Frankfurt and Venice and, in the second rank, Rouen, Paris, Strasbourg, Seville and London, apart from their importance as centres of industry and as markets for public loans, formed together the departments of an international clearing house where bills could readily be discounted, drafts on any considerable city could be obtained and the papers of merchants of almost every nationality changed hands.'[4] By the seventeenth century legal

[1] Henri Pirenne in his *Medieval Cities* says '. . . the rapid and early fortunes of the Venetian merchants is undoubtedly to be found in the close relationship which bound their commercial organisation to that of Byzantium and through Byzantium to the commercial organisation of antiquity.' Cf. 1925 edition, Princeton University Press, pp. 79–80.

[2] Cf. *Economic and Social History of Medieval Europe*, p. 101.

[3] Cf. L. Goldschmidt: *Universalgeschichte des Handelsrechts*, p. 226.

[4] Cf. *A Discourse on Usury*, Thomas Wilson, p. 63 of the introduction by R. H. Tawney, London, 1925.

decisions and statutory references to bills began to appear and it is apparent that their use in foreign trade was widespread. Richard Malynes, the mercantilist,[1] gives an account of the use of bills by the merchants of Hamburg, Amsterdam and the great trading cities of Europe, but expressly states that domestic bills were not used in England. Bills of exchange seem to have been at this time solely for foreign trade. If Malynes was unaware of the domestic use of bills, so much so as to deny their use in a work on the law merchant, then such use, even in the seventeenth century, must have been very limited. The domestic bill was to have its day in England but in the seventeenth century that day had not yet come. One reason for the tardy use of domestic bills in Britain may well have been the slowness with which financial organisation developed in London. London in the sixteenth century had neither the financial resources nor organisation of such cities as Amsterdam, Antwerp or Lyons. The Royal Exchange was not completed until 1571 and few of the great financial houses which maintained widespread agencies in Europe did so in London. It was late in the sixteenth century before English finance began to reproduce the institutions of the continental financial centres. Even the financial business continued to be largely in the hands of Italians, a fact which irked Cecil in 1553 when he was preparing a plan for controlling the exchanges and led him to remark, somewhat earthily, that a tight hold must be kept upon the Italians who 'go to and fro and serve all princes at once . . . work what they list and lick the fat from our beards.'[2] Some fat remained however. There had been a great expansion of foreign trade during the early 1500's, particularly of the export of woollen cloth. Many merchants had grown rich on the trade. They knew the markets and with their surplus capital they began to finance trade as well as carry it on. The developing sequence of dealer, merchant, financier, banker, was followed until 'rich old merchants' of the woollen trade 'occupied their money by exchanges.' By the third quarter of the sixteenth century foreign trade finance had become sufficiently profitable to form the main business of a special group of dealers and discounters. The discounting of bills by means of which the merchant received his money a 'great while before it is money indeed' had become a normal financial usage in foreign trade. Moreover, usages were hardening and becoming more complex. The first case concerning bills on the English law books was in the reign of James I.[3] The practice of endorsement appeared. All early bills had been made payable to a man

---

[1] Cf. his *Lex Mercatoria* of 1622.

[2] Historical Manuscripts Commission. MSS. of the Marquis of Salisbury, Part I, pp. 162–4, quoted in T. Wilson, op. cit., p. 64.

[3] Martine v. Bome, 1603, Cro. Jac. 6, cited in *Byles on Bills*.

or his assigns and occasionally to bearer, but late in the sixteenth and early in the seventeenth century the practice of making bills payable to order and transferring them by endorsement became prevalent.

There was then a growth of a class of financial intermediaries. From early Tudor times there had grown up a group of 'procurers' and 'inducers' whose main activity was that of arranging loans for merchants and for impecunious noblemen. It is probable that, for many such brokers, activities were varied, including not only brokerage but exchange business and some discounting. One notable group of brokers was that of the 'money scriveners'. Originally scriveners in the literal sense, writing bills and other legal documents for clients they quickly acquired knowledge of the creditworthiness of clients and progressed to brokerage, bringing borrower and lender together for commission. No doubt many of these early intermediaries lived on the fringe of legality. The Usury Laws were severe upon any excesses by them and Acts of 1623 and 1660 laid down maximum legal rates of interest and commission. But that evasion was frequent and rates of interest often exorbitant is clear from many references in contemporary pamphlets. The weight of criticism levelled at such intermediaries in the sixteenth and seventeenth centuries is indicative of their growing importance.

In England the bill of exchange had been regarded with disfavour and suspicion since the fourteenth century. It carried the taint of usury and was frowned upon both by theologians and jurists. So called 'dry exchange' (cambium siccum) was another name for finance bills raised for loan purposes. These were opposed by the church, which allowed ordinary trade bills but only with some sufferance, suspecting that they often concealed usurious practices. Thus, in practice, bills were tolerated only and were permissible only between merchants—a restriction which had two main effects: first, it meant that they were used almost solely in foreign trade where their advantage was great and evident; and secondly, financial operations in bills were virtually precluded since a discounter of a bill could not legally be a party to it and had no rights as an endorser.

In 1697 domestic bills became legal in England. Their use increased quickly and from then until the middle of the nineteenth century such bills were much used to finance domestic trade and credit. Concurrently with this development of the inland bill came changes in the functions of bill brokers and intermediaries. Until about the middle of the eighteenth century these acted mainly between merchants but from then onwards a class of true bill brokers emerged who acted either between bankers and merchants or between banker and banker. The rise of the country banks, which was also taking place at this period, completed an assembly of the elements of a real money market through which surplus money in one area moved more or less easily to another. The actual nature and organisation of this market need not detain us at this stage for it will be dealt with in a later chapter.

What is worth noting here, however, is the very widespread use to which, with the aid of these institutional arrangements, the domestic bill attained in the early 1800's. Good acceptances circulated widely in the district where the parties were known, becoming virtually a supplement to currency in the area. Bills became the normal media of payment of trade debts and discounting bills with a bank the normal method of obtaining bank accommodation.[1] The bank overdraft was as yet virtually unknown and bank loans were, with the new country banks, much less important than bank discounts. It was, in fact, one of the primary tasks of the banks to exchange customers' bills for cash or for drafts on a London bank, and as bills were often drawn for quite small amounts and were very numerous, a great daily volume would pass to the banks. Since much of this paper was not negotiable outside the area in which it was drawn, it was only with the endorsement of a bank that it could be discounted in the London market and have wider currency. Such endorsements were freely given, and these or bank bills accepted by banks (or their London agents) for their customers would be used as currency in many trades and in many market towns.[2] The difference in the quality of such bills was evidently enormous although it is likely that the shakier bills had only a very limited currency and had that probably only in a local area. They differed too, usually as between trades, in their tenor. Some took as much as two or three years, others a few months. In such circumstances the services of a shrewd, experienced assessor was necessary before discounting could take place. King tells us that '. . . the bill brokers, although they gave no guarantee, rendered negotiable vast numbers of bills which otherwise could not have been placed at all, and even with the finest paper there could have been no really extensive discounting without the bill broker as the vital link between the place of origin and the place of discount.'[3]

In 1815 the stamp duty on bills was increased in a way which militated against their use for amounts under £20, but, subject to this, they remained the modal form of payment in inland trade until late in the century. As a result of the growing number of legal enactments and the

---

[1] Cf. *The Bill on London*. Gillett Brothers Discount Co. Ltd., London, 1952, p. 15.
[2] Cf. W. T. C. King, *History of the London Discount Market*, London, 1936, pp. 30-32. Cf. also *The Bill of Exchange and Private Banks in Lancashire*, 1790-1830, T. S. Ashton. Papers in English Monetary History. Oxford, 1953, Chap. 3. This paper gives an excellent account of the rise and fall of the domestic bill in Lancashire.
[3] Ibid., p. 33.

case law governing their use, the English law on bills was codified in the Bills of Exchange Act of 1882, by which bill transactions are now governed.

From about the time of the 1857 crisis the number of inland bills began to decline although this was not immediately apparent because of the growing volume of trade. But after 1870, when trade declined with the great depression, the diminution in their number became considerable. The main reason for this decline lay in the changes taking place at that time in the structure of the banking system. The old unitary banking system of the first part of the nineteenth century was giving way to a concentrated banking system working through a branch network. This made easy the transference of liquid funds from district to district and enabled the old 'equalising function', performed by the country banks and their practice of rediscounting, to be superseded. The overdraft and bank loan became common as means of financing short-term trade credit and their use grew as a result of their flexibility and convenience. Apart from this, changes in the structure of business itself—a shortening of periods of trade credit, a preference by firms for cash settlement and a growing measure of competition—made the bill of exchange less attractive as a medium of payment than formerly.

A further influence on the reduction of the number of inland bills after 1857 was that, after the crisis of that year, rediscounting by country banks virtually ceased. Although this did not at first diminish the number of bills it reduced the flow of rediscounts from the country to the London market, and while this reduction was for a time mitigated by the efforts of the London bill brokers in actually seeking bills in the provinces, by 1870 the accumulation of forces making for the decline of the inland bill was irresistible. The last quarter of the nineteenth century saw a steady reduction both in the use of the bill for domestic trade and in the holdings of such bills by banks and discount houses. By 1914 the volume of domestic bills was insignificant. The domestic bill had had its day but around it had grown up in the discount market an institutional framework which was to service the vast increase in overseas bills, the growth of acceptance business and the great period of 'the bill on London' as an unimpeachable document in foreign trade.

The year 1870 marks the climacteric in the development of the overseas bill. Up to that time large numbers of bills were drawn in the process of foreign trade but there was as yet little internationalisation of the London money market. It was not yet subject to foreign influences. Wide interest rate differences often existed between London and West European capitals without much effect and, with New York still three weeks away in communication, bank rate differences with that city were of little importance. Many of the major banking houses of the city of London had long had a foreign tang about them. Their acceptances had for years circulated in the money markets of the world, negotiable not only by reason of the names upon them but because through the London discount market they could quickly be turned into sterling, which in turn was fully convertible into gold. But after 1870 the tempo of change quickened. International financial intelligence was improving; foreigners made increasing use of the London capital market and international influences grew swiftly. Most notable was the great expansion of first class acceptance business, stimulated mainly by the influx of foreign financiers, which followed the Overend, Gurney crisis of 1866, and by the establishment in London in the last quarter of the century of offices for numerous foreign banks who brought business to the London accepting houses. This business was enabled to grow virtually untrammelled by competition, for the joint stock banks, the only potential competitors, were of the opinion that acceptance business should be left to the new merchant banks who understood the merchanting aspects of foreign trade, had their connections abroad, and were better equipped than they to shoulder the risks involved. This attitude was modified in the early years of the twentieth century but not before it had enabled the merchant banks to specialise and to build up an impregnable position in the acceptance field. Indeed, the rise of the merchant banks at this period had dual significance for the discount market: not only did they perform the function of bill acceptance which, by hallmarking bills, aided the discount market, but by causing the new joint stock banks to turn away from bill business in general they cleared the way for the specialist tasks of discounting, sorting and grading which the discount houses were to perform. Had the joint stock banks entered the acceptance business at this early stage in their development there is little doubt that their activities would quickly have widened to include discounting and the whole gamut of bill dealing, to the inevitable ultimate exclusion and extinction of the discount houses.

By 1900 we find a discount market no longer dealing in domestic bills but now concentrating on foreign trade bills, many bearing the acceptance of one of the great merchant bankers, and withal more than doubling its net discounts between 1890 and 1913. It is not possible from the meagre statistics to dredge any information as to the number of foreign bills discounted, still less the proportion of these bills which covered trade in goods not touching London or a British port although financed by British acceptances. Nevertheless, the amount of such bills must have been enormous. The great strength of sterling in 1914 when the threat of war brought a repatriation of short-term funds to Britain indicated London's position as a short-term creditor. It is clear that the expansion of overseas bills in the pre-1914 period was more than sufficient to offset the decline of the inland bill. What must not have been apparent at the time was the importance, for the future of the discount market, of the appearance in 1877 of the Treasury bill which was in time to become the dominant form of short-term paper.

The interwar period was one of decline for the commercial bill and both the inland and the overseas bill appeared to be sinking to a position of secondary importance (cf. Table I, below). The former lingered in the trades closely connected with importing but were in rare cases to be seen in the home trade; the latter declined secularly before the competition of other media of foreign trade financing while fluctuating also with the ebb and flow of trade in prosperity and depression. Neither recovered in the thirties from the trough of depression.

The classic commercial bill for the finance of overseas trade never fully recovered from the sharp interruption of the 1914–18 war during which its use had contracted to vanishing point. By the end of that war the amount of Treasury bills was far greater than that of commercial bills in the portfolios of the discount houses and banks. In the twenties,

TABLE I

ESTIMATED AVERAGE BILL CIRCULATION IN THE INTERWAR PERIOD
(£m.)

Year (April–March)	Commercial Bills	Treasury Bills Issued by Tender	Total
1922–23	429	490	919
1923–24	480	466	946
1924–25	583	456	1,039
1925–26	633	466	1,099
1926–27	493	501	994
1927–28	508	502	1,010
1928–29	563	505	1,068
1929–30	519	512	1,031
1930–31	440	467	907
1931–32	328	485	813
1932–33	247	571	818
1933–34	245	558	803
1934–35	253	443	696
1935–36	259	505	764
1936–37	276	580	856

Source: Compiled from Table in Paish's Appendix I to Part II of T. Balogh's *Studies in Financial Organisation*.

the volume of overseas bills rose steadily but they did not regain the 1914 level.[1] The growing use of telegraphic transfers and bank drafts for financing foreign trade transactions and the increasing size of business units, often with branches abroad to handle overseas payments, was having its effect progressively throughout the period. When it came, in 1929, the depression brought greater contraction to the commercial bill and between 1929 and 1933 the volume of trade bills fell by more than 50 per cent. Moreover, the period 1933–39 brought only a small recovery, for much of the trade of the later thirties was through bilateral channels and did not give rise to discountable bills. In 1939, the interwar peak, overseas bills were roughly equal to the total of Treasury bills outstanding from the tender.

It might be helpful at this point to summarise the types of bill to be found in the discount market in the later thirties.[2] We can divide these into two main groups, each group in turn subdivided. The main groups were: bills which bore one name only; and bills bearing two or more names. The first group, the so-called 'one name bills' were of two main types: British Government Treasury bills; and the promissory notes of local authorities, public bodies and foreign governments. The second group, the so-called 'two (or more) name bills' was more varied and had several subdivisions. These were: (a) bank bills, accepted by British banks or acceptance houses; (b) fine trade bills; (c) acceptances of non-British banks; (d) foreign agency bills; (e) ordinary trade bills; and (f) bills drawn in sterling by foreigners on foreigners and payable in London.[3]

Of the one-name bills the Treasury bill was dominant and will be discussed at length later in this chapter. In view of its success as a short-term government borrowing medium it is not surprising that, in the thirties, promissory notes issued at a discount and similar to Treasury bills came to be used in imitation of it fairly widely by local authorities, public agencies and foreign governments. At any time a quantity of public and semi-public 'bills' of this kind were outstanding in the market. Much of this paper was of unimpeachable quality but the Bank of England would not accept such bills as collateral for advances and rigorous criteria were laid down to which they had to conform. The total value of such bills was not great. In 1930 the estimate of a witness to the Mac-millan Committee was that it amounted to no more than £20m. In the later thirties, however, local government bill borrowing and bill issues by

[1] Cf. W. T. C. King, *The Banker*, March 1947, p. 172.

[2] For a much fuller description and classification see T. Balogh, *Studies in Financial Organisation*, p. 148.

[3] This classification of bills is still largely valid but the relative strengths of the various categories have changed greatly over time.

public corporations became more frequent and it is thought that £30–35m. of such bills may have been outstanding in the market at any time during that period.

When we turn to two-name bills, i.e., to bills of exchange proper as distinct from financial promissory notes, we find that while there were six types which might be found in the market, there were only two of these which were eligible at the Bank of England for rediscount or as collateral, namely bills accepted by British banks or acceptance houses and fine trade bills. These bills were preferred and were discounted by houses at finer rates since the houses were in a position to use them should the market be forced into the Bank.

By the Second World War it seemed clear that the raw material of the bill market had undergone a fundamental change. It had looked patiently since 1918 for a revival of the commercial bill, but the commercial bill turnover was now so shrunken that no longer was the market an institutional adjunct of the finance of foreign trade but, rather, with its large Treasury bill holding, an appendage of the banking system and of national debt administration, in which the old machinery of commercial bill acceptance and discounting with its essential shrewdness and expertise lingered on as a sometimes lucrative historical survival beside the largely automatic processes of the new era.

TABLE II

HOLDINGS OF COMMERCIAL BILLS, 1960–65
£m.

	London Clearing Banks	Discount Market	Total
End of 1960	166	117	283
1961	250	183	433
1962	269	189	458
1963	311	249	560
1964	420	302	722
1965	451	339	790

Source: Midland Bank Review.

Such a view seemed even more justified in 1945 and for some years thereafter. The hopes of the market that there would be a resurgence of the commercial bill—hopes which had still been nurtured in the thirties with the Bank of England's efforts to preserve the discount houses[1]—were dead. The large issues of Treasury bills and the lucrative

[1] Cf. pp. 214–216 below.

C

market in short-term bonds, both stemming from the deficit finance of the war and early postwar periods, seemed to promise a living for the Houses—a living which was often ample[1] but which was also dangerously uncertain.

As late as 1952 the opinion of the market was that the commercial bill had gone for good.[2] Then came swift and unexpected change and this conviction was confounded by events. During the fifties borrowing on commercial bills more than doubled, while in the first half of the sixties the doubling was repeated. In 1953 bills discounted by banks and discount houses were approximately £200m., in 1960 they were £300m. and in 1965 nearly £800m. In March 1965 commercial bills came to exceed Treasury bills as a discount market asset. Table II shows the course of this remarkable expansion. A nearly threefold expansion in the value of bill holdings (even allowing for price increase) was remarkable. In the credit restriction of 1965 an event took place which would have seemed outlandish even a decade before, when the Bank of England, reviewing the credit supply, found it necessary to ask the discount market to limit its intake of bills of exchange and the clearing banks to limit their acceptances and bill purchases. The discount houses had become, it seems, sufficiently important as credit suppliers to fall within the Bank's orbit of control by moral suasion.

Although no figures exist to analyse this great increase in the use of the commercial bill there is little doubt where the main weight lies. The same forces as before are still at work to bring about the secular decline of the classic self-liquidating trade bill, drawn for finance of foreign trade and secured by documents of title to goods in transit. It is in finance bills, drawn for the supply of short-term credit and often renewable, that the new growth has been concentrated.

A number of influences have worked to produce this new flowering of the commercial bill. Two are dominant and have been prime movers; a number of others have contributed. Of the dominant influences the greatest has been the search by trade and industry during the recurrent periods of credit restriction for forms of borrowing to replace the bank overdraft. This has produced a proliferation of finance bills of which Law distinguishes three types:[3] bills drawn by finance companies and accepted by banks who are given a lien on the merchandise sold; bills

---

[1] So ample that in 1957 a manager of a leading discount house was able to tell the Bank Rate Tribunal, 'I am the Market in certain short bonds.' Cf. Minutes of Evidence, Ques. 8979.

[2] Cf. Richard Law, 'The Resurgence of the Commercial Bill', *The Bankers' Magazine*, December 1965, p. 341.

[3] Cf. Law, op. cit., p. 343.

drawn against stocks of goods in warehouses; and bills drawn against goods in transit.[1] All such bills may involve acceptance credits and their size often means that a number of acceptance houses group together to accept them as a consortium. Finance bills of this type are drawn by some of the largest public companies in Britain and they are now a staple of the discount market.

The second dominant influence in the growth of the 'new bill business' in the fifties and sixties has been the drop in Treasury bills. These climbed to a high level in 1950, fluctuated around this level for a decade and then fell off steadily in the sixties as the deficit in the public sector declined and the successive credit restrictions called for low liquidity of the banking system.[2] Any threat of a drying-up of this life-giving stream was certain to make the discount houses specially receptive to new ideas or innovations in bill business which might replace the Treasury bill. The clearing banks, for their part, were glad to encourage the new bill business not only because their own bill portfolios were threatening to shrink for want of Treasury bills but because the margins on commercial bills were higher and raised the revenue on the bill portfolio. Meanwhile, the authorities did not, at the outset, express any adverse views on the use of bills to meet a demand for credit which was spilling over a supply contracted by shrinkage of bank overdrafts. Indeed the Governor's letter to the London Discount Market Association of May 1965 calling for a curtailment of bill lending was in itself a recognition of the new rôle of the market as a credit supplier on a wider scale than up to that point.

A number of other factors have helped to develop this latter-day bill business. In 1961 the *ad valorem* bill stamp of 1/– per cent was abolished[3] with a resultant saving of 0·2 per cent per annum on a three months bill. The shorter the bill the greater the saving and the number of short bills has certainly risen, contributing to turnover in a market in which quick turnover and small margins are good business. A second contributory factor has been the sharp competition and fall in acceptance commissions, which Law estimates were ¾ per cent lower over the decade of the fifties.[4] This competition came mainly from acceptances done by foreign banks in London and, as bank acceptances came down, the classic acceptance houses were forced to follow. The abolition of the stamp duty and the fall in acceptance commissions together did much to increase the competitiveness of bill finance relative to its main competitor the bank overdraft. The increased competitiveness (together with the credit

---

[1] Such bills are secured generally by goods in transit but not by specific shipments with invoices and documents of title.

[2] Cf. Table III on p. 39 below.

[3] It was replaced with a flat duty of 2d. per bill.   [4] Cf. Law, op. cit., p. 342.

squeeze) has enabled the bill to erode the bank overdraft and attract two main classes of borrower: the hire-purchase financier, whose alternative source of funds is to borrow, often expensively, by deposits from the public; and the large company which has been wont to rely on overdrafts to finance working capital.

It might have been expected that the 'new bill business', much of which is in competition with the most lucrative form of clearing banks' lending, would have provoked opposition from the banks. That it has not done so is certainly due to the fact that throughout most of the period of the later fifties and the sixties the banks have been fully lent, and while they have no doubt been saddened to see frustrated overdraft customers finding accommodation elsewhere and to see new alternatives to the overdraft arising, they have at least been placated by the flow of good margin bills which have been forthcoming to enrich the liquid assets of their balance sheets.

All this new business in bills would not have been possible, however, had it incurred the displeasure of the Bank of England. The 'eligibility' of such bills, that is, the extent of their acceptability at the Bank itself, either as formerly for rediscounting or as in recent usage as collateral,[1] is of crucial importance to the discount houses who will not deal in any volume of bills which are not eligible. The criteria which the Bank of England is applying at any time have, therefore, direct influence on the quality and type of bills which the market will deal in. These criteria have been sensed rather than known. To be eligible at the Bank a commercial bill must carry two good British names, of which one must be the acceptor. All hinges on the Bank's idea of what are 'good British names'. Until recently these appeared to mean the names of a shortish list of banks and acceptance houses. Fine trade bills were not eligible. In 1964 and 1965, however, there were signs that the Bank's eligibility criteria were being liberalised. It began to accept fine trade bills as margin on collateral and to sample the market's trade paper (as it already does for bank bills) by buying parcels of bills from the market at a small premium on the bank bill rate. Good trade bills have come to be offered to the Bank as 'eligible' paper and this has greatly enhanced their status and future prospects.

Our account of the history of the bill of exchange ends, therefore, on a note of sober optimism which would have been out of place even a decade ago when the commercial bill seemed to be a historical survival.

---

[1] The obtaining of 'last resort' help by rediscounting at the Bank is now virtually obsolete because of the Bank's requirement as to tenor of the bill. The modern practice is to borrow for a week from the Bank against the security of short bonds, Treasury bills or eligible paper.

The return of the commercial bill opens up interesting prospects for the discount market and reveals many of its problems in a new light. Above all it gives to the discount houses a chance to exercise once more their old skills of selection, vetting and grading. A recent writer aptly summed up their position when he wrote: 'The Treasury bill is admirable bread and butter; commercial bills are a good deal more trouble, somewhat more lucrative and a very great deal more interesting.'[1]

III

The Treasury bill is the main vehicle of short-term government borrowing. Central to government debt policy, it accounts for approximately 40 per cent of the bills held by the clearing banks. But for the discount market the importance of the Treasury bill has declined. With the revival of the commercial bill and the great business now done by the discount houses in short bonds the Treasury bill has since March 1965 sunk to third place among the short-term paper circulating in the money market. In a normal day £20m. to £30m. of these bills are turned over. At peak periods the figure is higher. By regulating the volume of such bills held by the banking system the Bank of England exerts its main influence on bank liquidity and on monetary policy.

The Treasury bill is a relatively recent financial innovation and was created as a conscious act of financial policy. During the early 1870's large advances to local authorities combined with the British government's purchase of Suez Canal shares resulted in a great increase in the floating debt. The Exchequer Bill, which had been until that time the only vehicle of short-term government borrowing, had fallen almost into disuse. Since the 1830's the market for such bills had been unreliable and the bills were not easily convertible. As other more marketable stocks became available the public, the banks and the Bank of England avoided holding the bills. By the 1860's the Exchequer bill was used only for issue to government departments and the only other means by which the government could borrow short-term was from the Bank of England through Ways and Means Advances for Supply Services or Deficiency Advances for Consolidated Fund Services.[2] There was little to be said for the revival of Exchequer Bills but clearly a more flexible form of short-term borrowing was required to meet the needs of growing government expenditure.

[1] Cf. Richard Law, op. cit., p. 347.
[2] Supply services represent expenditures requiring the annual sanction of Parliament; Consolidated Fund services represent payments made under a standing authorisation.

For these reasons it was decided to replace the Exchequer Bill by some more convenient form of short security. The then Chancellor of the Exchequer, Sir Stafford Northcote, consulted Walter Bagehot,[1] who advised the creation of a short security 'resembling as nearly as possible a commercial bill of exchange . . . issued under discount and falling due at certain intervals.'[2] This advice was acted upon and under the Treasury Bills Act 1877 the Treasury bill was created as a 'government promissory note, issued by tender under discount and having a fixed currency not exceeding twelve months.'[3] This marked the extinction of the Exchequer bill which was progressively withdrawn and ceased to exist in 1897.

Use of the new Treasury bill in the nineteenth century was restrained. Until 1902 it could only be used for Consolidated Fund borrowing. Issues, of which there were only three or four a year, were never greater than £5m. and the total outstanding issue was small, never rising above £20m. From 1899 private (i.e., 'through the tap') issues were made to the National Debt Commissioners and when, in 1902, power was given, and renewed annually in the Appropriation Act, to use Treasury bills for Supply borrowing, the volume increased. The size and number of issues rose and the total outstanding reached £41m. in April 1910.[4] Although these figures were very small compared with what was to follow in the interwar period and later, it should be remembered that borrowing for Supply bills had to be paid off entirely within the financial year of issue—limiting the Treasury bill, at this stage, to being an instrument of very short-term finance and precluding the idea of a semi-permanent float of bills which was later to be accepted as normal. In fact, up to 1914, the Treasury bill provided a small but valuable supplement to the market's commercial paper.[5] It did not prevent external trade bills from continuing to dominate the market nor did it compensate for more than a part of the decline in domestic trade paper. To an observer at the time there would have been no perceptible warning of the transformation to be wrought in the next sixty years, although all the elements of that transformation were already present, even to the foreign use of Treasury bills as a means of holding sterling. This practice, by making foreign-held money more liquid, increased the vulnerability of the British reserves in times of crisis but it had beneficial effects also, for from the movements of such mobile

---

[1] Bagehot besides being a literary figure was a leading financial pundit of the day. His *Lombard Street* appeared in 1873, *Economic Studies* after his death in 1880. He was editor of the *Economist* from 1860 to 1877.

[2] Cf. King, op. cit., p. 276, quoting a letter from Lord Welby to the *Economist* in 1909, cf. *Economist*, 1909, p. 1045.

[3] Cf. King, op. cit., p. 276.   [4] Of which £36·7m. had been issued by tender.

[5] In 1914 Treasury bills accounted for only 2 per cent of the national debt.

funds in and out of the country in response to interest rate differentials it came to be realised that bank rate changes were a highly effective form of balance of payments control. The full realisation, which took place in the decade before 1914, of the importance of bank rate policy and its effect on the balance of payments and the reserves owes something to the growth of Treasury bill finance.

By the end of World War I the Treasury bill had become the leading means of government short-term borrowing and the dominant form of short paper in the money market. The statutory requirement that bills for supply purposes had to be liquidated in the year of issue was dropped in 1914 and there was no obstacle to growth of the issue. By the end of the war the bill issue was no longer temporary borrowing in advance of revenue, but part of the permanent debt, though held in renewable short-term securities. The system became one in which maturing bills were repaid by the issue of new bills and the permanently outstanding volume of bills formed the main part of the national debt. The war period also brought experiments in the method of issue. After April 1915, the method of issue by tender was, for a time, changed for one under which bills were made available 'on tap' to all applicants at rates

TABLE III

ESTIMATED AVERAGE BILL CIRCULATION IN THE INTERWAR PERIOD
(£m.)

Year (April–March)	Commercial Bills	Treasury Bills Issued by Tender	Total
1922–23	429	490	919
1923–24	480	466	946
1924–25	583	456	1,039
1925–26	633	466	1,099
1926–27	493	501	994
1927–28	508	502	1,010
1928–29	563	505	1,068
1929–30	519	512	1,031
1930–31	440	467	907
1931–32	328	485	813
1932–33	247	571	818
1933–34	245	558	803
1934–35	253	443	696
1935–36	259	505	764
1936–37	276	580	856

Source: Compiled from Table in Paish, op. cit.

of discount which were announced and varied from time to time. The rates to be paid for various terms of bills were published and were evidently settled by reference to rates in the London money market and in other key money markets such as New York.

The wartime growth of the Treasury bill issue inspired some misgiving. In June 1915, Reginald McKenna, as Chancellor of the Exchequer, was disturbed at 'the difficulties arising from the rapid and frequent maturity of the bills' and at 'the undesirability of borrowing "bankers' money" rather than public money.'[1] There was also a fear that, if holders of the bills did not renew them as they matured, the Bank of England would have to meet the government's needs by 'Ways and Means Advances', then regarded as a menace to war-time monetary discretion in that they expanded the credit base.[2] There were half-hearted attempts to fund Treasury bills by allowing the Treasury bills to be accepted in payment of subscriptions for long-term government loans.

By 4th January 1919 the floating debt amounted to £1,545m. of which £1,098m. was in the form of Treasury bills.[3] In 1921 outstanding bills reached £1,121m. During the twenties the Treasury bill, despite periods of vigorous funding, retained its important position. (Cf. Table III.) The amount of Treasury bills (including tap bills) outstanding was stabilised at £500–£600m. of which 25 to 30 per cent were usually tap bills.

In April 1921 the method of issue of bills was changed and formalised. The regular weekly tender was resumed, three months became established as the modal period of currency, there was to be a minimum figure of £50,000 for any tender and applicants were at liberty to choose the day of the week from which bills were to run. Apart from maintaining the practice of issuing bills through the tap to non-official holders (so-called 'additional bills') which was continued until 1925[4] and then abandoned, the tender was beginning to assume its modern form. During the remainder of the twenties the volume of bills remained fairly constant. Budgets were usually balanced, but the bill issue reflected the Exchequer fluctuations in yearly revenue and expenditure so that a marked seasonal pattern emerged, the government borrowing on bills during the first

[1] Cf. House of Commons Report, June 21 1915. Col. 952 quoted in 'The Treasury Bill: an Economist's Invention', *Midland Bank Review*, February 1961, p. 5.

[2] Such a view was understandable in view of the wartime expansion not only of Ways and Means Advances and Treasury bills but also of the currency circulation.

[3] Cf. 'The Floating Debt, 1914–39, and Its Effect on the British Banking System—Part I. The Floating Debt Since 1914', F. W. Paish, Appendix I to Part II of T. Balogh's *Studies in Financial Organisation*, p. 191.

[4] These bills were issued at rates slightly higher than those of the previous week's tender.

three quarters of the year and reducing the bills outstanding during the high revenue season in the fourth quarter.[1] A factor also important and full of significance for the future—it was in these years that Treasury bills established themselves as important liquid assets of the banks and came to constitute an essential element in the control of bank liquidity. From 1931 with the coming of a free exchange rate for sterling a new force came to act on the volume of Treasury bills offered, namely the purchases and sales of gold by the Exchange Equalisation Account.[2] This together with new borrowing and some repayment of long-term loans caused wider fluctuations in the Treasury bill tender in the thirties than in the twenties. Nevertheless, the growth of the Treasury bill was restrained and was not sufficient to compensate for the decline in commercial bills which was concurrently taking place.

During the thirties the formal arrangements for the tender and the issue of Treasury bills were gradually established. Until 1934 the clearing banks joined in the tender for bills, competing with the discount houses and with outside applicants. Their presence in the tender at a time of cheap money produced a degree of competition which had the effect of forcing bill rates to very low levels. The clearing banks on their part were often unable to obtain as many bills as they would have liked, but for the discount houses the competition was a disaster, for they found that the rate on Treasury bills was barely above, and indeed often below, the rate at which they obtained their call money from the banks.[3] It was clear that such a state of affairs would, if it continued, soon spell the ruin of the discount market and in 1934 a series of steps was taken by the clearing banks which established a *modus vivendi* for the various interests in the market. The banks reduced their lending rates to the discount houses to $\frac{1}{2}$ per cent provided such loans were secured by bills; they agreed to take bonds as security for loans of 1 per cent; they agreed that they would not buy bills in the market at less than their own lending rate; and they agreed not to participate in the tender for Treasury bills but only to buy such bills from the discount houses when at least a week

[1] According to Paish the authorities at this period saw the desirable normal limits for the total of its bills in the hands of the market 'as between £400m. and £550m.' Cf. Paish, op. cit., p. 194.

[2] The Account was established in February 1932.

[3] The clearing banks would not lend on call save at the rate agreed among themselves of 1 per cent below bank rate. In 1932 when bank rate fell to 2 per cent the discount market was paying 1 per cent for call money while the rate for bills fell at times as low as $\frac{1}{8}$ per cent. Apart from the critical position in which this placed the discount market it created also the absurd situation that the clearing banks were lending to the government on bills at $\frac{1}{4}$–$\frac{1}{2}$ per cent while refusing to lend to the discount market at less than 1 per cent.

of their life had run. These arrangements were an improvement from the discount houses' point of view but they had unpleasant effects as well. The bill rate rose but, with interest rate differentials still narrow, it became imperative to expand the bill turnover. The main weight of demand for bills fell upon Treasury bills and the tender now became fiercely competitive as houses sought to procure them. The tender demand rose until it was several times the number of bills on offer and, in self defence, the discount houses resorted to a syndicated bid in May 1935. This 'imperfection' of the market has remained and is a striking feature of the existing arrangements. The only further modification of the tender system came in the Second World War in 1940, when the tender issue was increased sharply and an agreement was made with the discount houses whereby the syndicate undertook as a group to cover the entire tender applying for the whole issue at their agreed rate. This they were able to do because of the support of the so-called 'special buyer'[1]

TABLE IV

HOLDINGS OF TREASURY BILLS
OUTSIDE THE PUBLIC SECTOR, 1951–65
(£m.)

	London Clearing Banks	Discount Market	Overseas* Official Holdings	Other	Total
End of 1951	791	628	1,171	112	2,702
1952	1,182	705	861	241	2,989
1953	1,338	607	1,069	282	3,296
1954	1,199	615	1,021	541	3,376
1955	1,271	652	961	679	3,563
1956	1,275	523	927	643	3,368
1957	1,403	585	821	579	3,388
1958	1,185	594	891	764	3,434
1959	1,215	635	958	722	3,530
1960	1,017	574	923	975	3,489
1961	1,106	533	1,076	596	3,311
1962	1,067	502	1,023	450	3,042
1963	996	529	1,045	496	3,066
1964	764	453	1,100	374	2,691
1965	784	484	1,027	357	2,652

* Central Monetary authorities from 1963.

Source: 'The London Money Market', Midland Bank Review.

[1] This term is applied to the discount house (at present Seccombe, Marshall and Campion) which acts as Bank of England agent in the market when the Bank buys or sells bills.

who stood ready to supply the banking system with the cash required to underwrite such a task. The consequence of this highly convenient system was that the second war and the period of inflationary finance which followed it saw a huge expansion of the Treasury bill issue. By October 1951, outstanding Treasury bills amounted to £5,550m. of which the banks held £1,200m.[1] Table IV shows the holdings of Treasury bills outside the public sector during the fifties and early sixties. It will be observed that Treasury bill holdings reached a high level in the later fifties but that the sixties saw a steady decline to a level which leaves holdings of the bills lower than at any time since the war. Treasury bills issued through the tender fell by nearly a third between 1960 and 1966. This decline has been the result of a fall in the deficit in the public sector and successive credit restrictions which have called for a reduction in the liquidity of the banking system. Moreover, official funding policy in recent years has helped to swing the weight of borrowing to marketable securities.[2] This account of the history of the Treasury bill since its inception must end, therefore, by recording a marked decline in its relative importance in the discount market, though of what duration this decline may be it is too early to say.

It remains to describe the arrangements under which nowadays Treasury bills are issued each week. Each Friday the Treasury in the *London Gazette* invites tenders, to be sent to the Bank of England on the following Friday, for an amount of bills, usually between £100m. and £300m. which will repay, in part repay, or exceed the bills falling due in that week for repayment. Bills are predominantly of 91 days' currency although some for 63 days are occasionally issued. According to the

[1] The fifties brought two minor technical developments to the Treasury bill: in 1950 the term of bills was altered from three calendar months to ninety-one days—a change which had the advantage of bringing regularity to the weekly pattern of tenders, issues and maturities. In 1955 it was decided to issue in the last months of each year some bills of sixty-three days currency which would mature in the final quarter of the fiscal year (i.e. January to April) during the bumper revenue period.

[2] The following table shows the changing composition of the national debt since 1960:

Composition of National Debt (£m.) 31st March				
	1960	1964	1965	1966
Treasury bills	5,202	4,418	4,672	5,122
Marketable securities	14,946	18,162	17,792	17,846
National Savings	3,293	3,720	3,823	3,650
Other	4,292	3,926	4,154	4,636*
Total	27,733	30,226	30,441	31,254

* Rise due to external borrowing from IMF.

amount of bills offered the floating debt may be increased, maintained at its existing level or reduced—the increase or decrease being in accord with the government's short-term financial needs.

The bills are intended for large-scale lenders—this being ensured by the minimum outlay of £50,000 and the large units in which the bills are issued.[1] In appearance they resemble a large bank note and they bear the legend: *This Treasury bill entitles* . . . . *or order to payment of* ONE HUNDRED THOUSAND POUNDS *at the Bank of England out of the Consolidated Fund of the United Kingdom on the 1st day of June 1966.* The Bill is signed by the Secretary of the Treasury. When a name is inserted in the name-space the ownership of the bill is transferred by endorsement: if the name-space is left blank the bill is payable to bearer.

Tenders are made for the purchase of the bills at discount, a would-be buyer offering, say, £98 10s. per cent for the purchase of a bill (or bills) for which at repayment he will receive full face value.[2] The rate of discount is determined on each issue by the forces of supply and demand—the supply (usually of £100m. to £300m.) being determined by the government's short-term borrowing needs arising from the phasing of revenue and expenditure, the demand by the many factors which condition the demand for short-term paper.[3] Among the tenderers for Treasury bills certain distinct groups are clearly discernible.

---

[1] Units of £5,000, £10,000, £25,000, £50,000 and £100,000.

[2] As an approximation the discount on a three months bill of £1,000 can be shown by the following diagram:

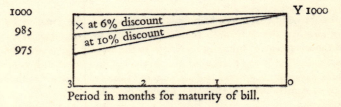

Period in months for maturity of bill.

If the annual rate of discount for such a bill is 6% then the market price three months prior to maturity will be £985 and if lenders think that 6% is an appropriate rate of interest they will bid 98·5% at the tender. After allocation at this price and up to maturity the value of the bill will rise as indicated by the slope of XY to reach £1,000 at maturity. In fact the line will not be straight as is indicated for simplicity but, because of compound interest, will follow either a convex or concave path according to whether it is a long or short bill. For discussion of these matters see W. Manning Dacey's *The British Banking Mechanism*, London, 1962, chap. 5.

[3] Such factors include the liquidity preference of investors for short-term paper rather than long, the level of short-term interest rates, the size of such balances in the hands of industry and financial institutions, the outflow or inflow of funds from abroad, etc.

The most important group is that of the twelve discount houses. These tender as a group—settling their tender price beforehand in accordance with their own borrowing costs[1] and their judgement of the probable size and quantity of tenders from elsewhere. The discount house tender also implies a readiness to take up all bills allotted at the tender price— even up to the full issue for the week.[2] One of the conditions under which the market is allowed by the Treasury to tender as a group is that they must 'cover the tender'. The Houses name the day in the following week on which they will pay for their bills.

A second group of applicants for bills may be the so-called 'overseas banks'. These are the London offices of foreign banking houses, who frequently have large sterling balances which they may wish to hold in fairly liquid form. Such balances vary greatly in amount. They may vary according to the ebb and flow of foreign trade and with the banks' and their clients' views of how long or in what form it is advisable to hold balances in sterling. A strong balance of payments which has created optimistic views on the future strength of sterling may result in a strong demand for Treasury bills from this source. At other times, when sterling prospects seem poor, demand may virtually dry up.[3]

But apart from balance of payments considerations the size of the so-called 'outside bid' will vary in the longer run with movements in interest rate differentials within the British economy itself. From Table IV (page 42) it can be seen that 'Other' holdings of Treasury bills outside

[1] To determine these the discount houses must take a view as to the probable level of bank rate (and by inference of the *Money at call rate*) during the period of currency of the bills for which they are tendering. Since they must earn their living by lending at rates marginally higher than those at which they borrow any anticipated change in bank rate (or of course the call rate which is determined by bank rate) must influence their calculations. Within the group the quota of each discount house is based on the capital and reserves of the house and is weighted by a variable multiplier which means that the houses with the small capital resources can go for a larger proportion of their capital and reserves than the larger houses.

[2] This is an important aspect of the discount house tender. It means that the Treasury is assured that all bills offered will be taken up and also that, providing there is any outside bid (and there always is some) the tender exceeds the bills offered. It may, on occasions, have the discount houses in a difficult situation. For example, on Friday July 21 1961, it was known that, with a serious crisis, a 'package deal' of measures was pending which would probably include a rise in the bank rate, which was then 5 per cent. Outside bidders, in the uncertain conditions, abstained from the tender and the market had to take up 66 per cent of the bills. On the following Tuesday bank rate went to 7 per cent and the houses were taking up their bills at a loss of 2 per cent. Cf. H. F. Goodson, 'The Functioning of the London Discount Houses' in *The London Discount Market Today*, Institute of Bankers, London, 1962.

[3] The main indicator which the discount market has of the probable demand for bills from the overseas banks is the strength of sterling in the foreign exchange market.

the public sector rose nine times over the decade of the fifties under the influence of a higher rate on Treasury bills than the clearing banks would pay on a deposit account: while the same holdings fell sharply again in the sixties as interest rates for available funds in certain other and newer markets (notably the market for local authority loans) rose to exceed the yield on Treasury bills.

A third group in the tender is that of the financial institutions—insurance companies, building societies, savings banks, investment trusts, hire-purchase companies and the like—whose steady demand for investment paper may often lead them, when greater liquidity is required, to hold Treasury bills.

Finally, large industrial or commercial firms, wishing to use Treasury bills as a means of holding temporary surplus cash, join increasingly in the tender but the extent of their participation is irregular and unpredictable. These last two groups have joined in the defection from the Treasury bill market to the local authority loans market in recent years.

One group which is conspicuously absent from the tender is that of the clearing banks. Although the largest single holder of Treasury bills, they do not participate in the tender,[1] obtaining their bills later in their currency by purchasing them from the discount houses.

From this diverse group the Treasury offer is then matched each week by a demand for bills which always exceeds in amount the bills offered[2] —the tender consisting of two broad sectors of demand: the tender at their own agreed rate of the discount house syndicate for all bills offered; and the outside offers of various financial intermediaries and a limited general demand for various amounts of bills at various prices. Thus to obtain bills the outside buyers have to offer at prices higher or at least equal to the price of the discount house syndicate. All tenders must be lodged with the Bank of England by one o'clock on Friday; the Treasury officials go to the Bank to open and consider the tenders and before 2 p.m. on the Friday afternoon to which tenders relate the Bank of England announces the results. All offers more favourable to the Treasury than the syndicate offers[3] are accepted in full: the discount house syndi-cate gets the rest. Once the allocation has been made the Treasury an-

[1] This is not strictly true. All private persons, firms or undertakings who wish to tender for bills must do so through the agency of a bank. The clearing banks only come into the tender, however, as agents of their own customers—never as principals. The Bank of England usually submits an 'inside tender' on behalf of overseas central banks.

[2] The demand for the bills is certain to exceed the bills offered since, in theory, the discount houses bid for the whole of the tender. The excess demand is therefore the amount of the outside bid.

[3] That is all offers which would buy the bills at a higher price than the discount house syndicate has offered. The higher the price the lower the rate of discount.

nounces the average price at which it has placed the week's issue. Bills may be taken up and paid for on any weekday in the following week.

The amount of bills allotted to the syndicate differs each week according not only to the 'outside' demand for bills but also to the degree of success which the discount house syndicate has had in estimating the size of the outside tender price. An ill-considered attempt to reduce their bid might result in the market receiving few bills that week. The allotment to the discount market may vary between wide limits—from as high as 90 per cent to as low as 10 per cent.[1] For example, if we take the tender of September 24 1965, £190m. was offered and £333·8m. in applications was made. Twenty-five per cent of the bills allotted went to the syndicate whose rate was 5½ per cent. The average rate on allotment was £5 9s. 10·47d. and the total amount of bills outstanding £2,570m.

TABLE V

DISCOUNT MARKET ASSETS, 1955–65

End of	Treasury Bills		Government Securities		Commercial Bills		Total including other assets
	£m.	% of total assets	£m.	% of total assets	£m.	% of total assets	£m.
1955	652	61·0	307	28·7	45	4·2	1,068
1956	523	54·8	294	30·8	85	8·9	954
1957	585	61·2	223	23·3	84	8·8	956
1958	594	56·4	321	30·5	70	6·6	1,053
1959	635	56·2	322	28·5	118	10·4	1,130
1960	574	48·0	440	36·8	117	9·8	1,197
1961	533	43·8	449	36·9	183	15·0	1,216
1962	502	40·1	488	39·0	189	15·1	1,251
1963	529	40·5	442	33·9	250	19·1	1,305
1964	453	35·3	438	34·1	301	23·5	1,283
1965	484	33·3	500	34·4	339	23·3	1,455

Source: Midland Bank Review.

On the day of issue (whether to discount houses or to outside buyers) a newly issued Treasury bill is known as a 'hot' bill. Such bills, even when only one day old, may often be purchased by clearing banks for their own customers. After seven days have elapsed clearing banks may start buying bills for their own portfolios but most discount house bills stay with the houses for about a month, after which they find their way in

[1] When the discount houses receive only a small allotment of bills they have, as the saying goes, 'missed the tender'. Within the syndicate each discount house gets an allotment in proportion to its tender. In early 1957 the discount houses fell as low as 10 per cent in their allocation.

increasing numbers to the banks, usually in batches of similar size and maturity dates. Very few Treasury bills remain with the discount houses until maturity but some are held for a good part of their currency in order that they may serve the houses as collateral for call loans.

Such is the system whereby Treasury bills find their way to the market. We may conclude this discussion of the bill by noting the sharp change which has occurred since 1955 in its relative importance as a discount market asset. As will be seen from Table V the Treasury bill has declined from a position in which in 1955 it accounted for 61 per cent of total discount market assets to one in which in 1965 it was 33 per cent; with government securities varying in relative importance, this decline in the Treasury bill has been offset by the rise of the commercial bill from 4 per cent of total assets to 23 per cent. The Treasury bill has thus shifted from first to second (and latterly even to third) place in the assets hierarchy. The proportion of public sector assets has fallen from 90 per cent to less than 70 per cent in ten years.[1] Figures taken for particular dates are misleading because of frequent fluctuations, but Charts I and II demonstrate very clearly the secular changes taking place in the distribution of discount market assets.

It is a far cry from the credit documents of the twelfth century Champagne Fairs to the London discount market of the 1960's. No country has evolved such elaborate machinery for dealing with bills as has Britain. The process of evolution continues.

The changes in the relative strengths of the Treasury bill and the trade bill profoundly affected and are still affecting the character of the London discount market in the twentieth century. It may well be that, with the resurgence of the commercial bill in the sixties, fresh and important changes are afoot. From a market in commercial credit titles, with all that that involves in knowledge of trade and commerce, the discount market evolved to a market in government-created short-term paper with great significance in fiscal and general economic policy. It is now acquiring a new and refurbished commercial image.

Markets in short-term paper exist in many of the great financial centres of the world—in New York, Montreal and Sydney—but they are more logical, more tidy and uncluttered than that of London. What is unique in the London market is that it carries into the new conditions and the new functions much of the paraphernalia of the old. Its quaintly archaic air is that of the type of business which formed and moulded it but which is now vestigial. It is arguable that in this it demonstrates the

[1] There was a sharp rise in security holdings in 1960 (£440m.) to nearly double the 1957 value (£223m.) but apart from this the relative variation in bonds was less than for other assets.

British genius for flexibility, adaptation and the tolerance of change. It is equally arguable that it is clumsy, dispensable and ripe for modernisation. We shall, it is hoped, be better able at the end of this book to answer this question: it is, however, undeniable that the London discount market can only be seen and understood in the light of its historical development. To this we will turn in Chapter 5.

D

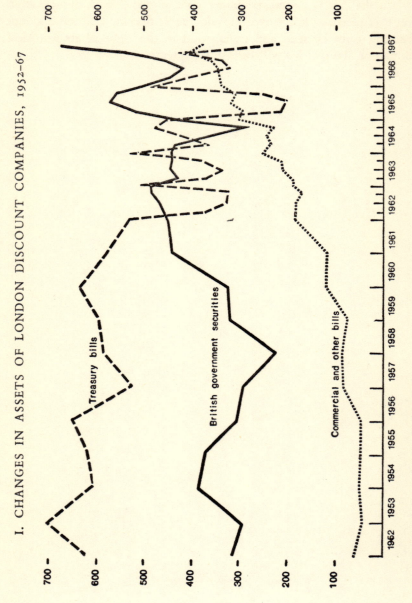

I. CHANGES IN ASSETS OF LONDON DISCOUNT COMPANIES, 1952–67

Reproduced by courtesy of the Bank of England.

II. PROPORTION OF ASSETS HELD IN VARIOUS FORMS, 1952–67

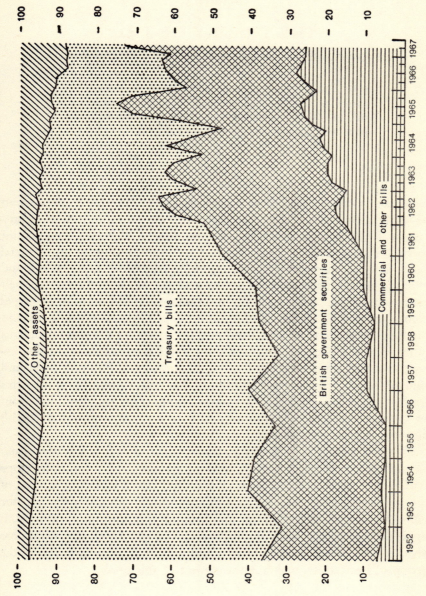

Reproduced by courtesy of the Bank of England.

Chapter 3

THE THEORY OF THE
CENTRALISED BANKING SYSTEM

'In Britain the argument about the usefulness of operating
directly on the money and credit supply has swayed back and
forth for a Keynesian generation. . . . It is decidedly awkward
that no one agrees on exactly how the mechanism works.'

Economist

I

IF THE DEVELOPMENT and present function of the discount market are to
be understood it must be seen in relation to the whole British monetary
system of which it forms an integral part. Indeed, although the discount
market is a very clearly discernible and homogeneous group of financial
institutions its widest interest, save to those who work in or with it and
who are concerned in its everyday procedures, lies not so much in itself
but in the complex relations which exist between it and the other principal
components of the British banking system; in the part which it plays in
the functioning of that system and its significance for the main problems
of monetary policy. For this reason any detailed examination of the discount market must be preceded by some account, however brief and
rudimentary, of the typical centralised banking system. It is into this
framework that a market in short-term paper must be fitted, and from
an understanding of this framework that we may judge the British
discount market's usefulness.

Our first task in this chapter is, therefore, to sketch briefly the *modus
operandi* of a modern centralised banking system and to define the scope
within it of the discount market. The second task is to examine some of
the peculiarities of the British banking system which, although the
pioneer and archetype of centralised banking systems the world over, is
none the less unique in its applications of the general theory which has
been evolved from it—not least in the existence and character of the
group of institutions which is the subject of this book.

II

The management of money is a new and somewhat self-conscious art,
a product and necessity of the modern mature economies. Barely a

hundred years have passed since the British banking system became discernible as a system and its functional relationships were scrutinised by the shrewdest economic intelligences of a perceptive generation. Since then we have submitted it to searching analysis. The centralised system with its sun, attendant planets and lesser satellites has become familiar enough but to some degree the subtleties and nuances of their relationships still elude us and our control is still partial. As new countries have acquired monetary systems of their own the sharper outlines and clearer paths of these new solar systems have taught us much. The old original system which was the prototype is nebulous. The first task is to sketch in barest outline the blueprint according to which all these systems function. The first part of this chapter is, therefore, a mere circuit diagram; the second is an application of that circuit in a complex apparatus. But we must be cautious. All descriptions of banking systems are misleading for they imply a precision in the mechanism and its operation which is rare, if indeed it exists at all. Monetary systems are not constructed, they mostly grow; certainly the British one did. They are not mechanisms, but we read system into them. In the end we see they are hardly systems but groups of institutions whose ordering and co-ordination is more an art than a science.

The main purposes of a centralised banking system are four in number. Firstly, such a system must be able to control, or at least partially control, the level of effective demand for goods and services in the economy. This function, so far as the system performs it effectively, places it as an instrument of the main economic policy of the country. Secondly, the central bank must control the note issue and the issue of token coinage. This task, for long the subject of so much debate and controversy, has, in modern banking systems, been subjected to routine procedures based on the criterion of convenience and will not be our concern in this book. Thirdly, in controlling the total volume of credit created by a banking system some attention must also be paid to how this credit is distributed. Our concern should be qualitative as well as quantitative. For example, it is important whether new credit goes to the public or to the private sector, whether it is creating consumer demand or investment demand, demand for travel or demand for houses. Finally, a centralised banking system must give unity and cohesion to the banking, financial and credit institutions. They must have a sense of belonging to a group which has responsibilities for the carrying out of national policies. There must be no question of their being or becoming a disparate congeries of self-interested entities pursuing unilateral policies for their own ends.

The most significant economic function of the modern monetary system is that it influences and, in part,[1] controls the main pressure of effective demand in the economy, thus, in turn, conditioning the levels of income and employment, the level of prices and the condition of the balance of payments. Until comparatively recently this function was seen in terms of the banking system's control over the total supply of money,[2] money being defined as consisting of notes, coins and immediately usable bank deposits. The problems of monetary policy lay in regulating the quantities of these and varying them in accordance with the aims of a general economic policy which was theoretically conditioned by the Quantity Theory of Money. Even in this simplified picture the importance of the banks and their associated financial institutions was apparent. In most industrialised countries bank deposits account for 60–75 per cent of the total monetary supply and it is through the banking system that the State exercises its control of the issue of notes and token coinage. But in the picture which results from more recent thought, in particular from that body of ideas which we insist rightly or wrongly on calling 'the Keynesian revolution', the interest in the functions of the banking and allied institutions is greatly enhanced and a far wider and more searching scrutiny of their scope and operations is called for. The view is now that, while the total quantity of money is certainly an important element in determining the level of total effective demand, it is not the sole element. To it must be added those other sources of available funds from which people and institutions may implement spending decisions. These other sources are broadly twofold: they depend primarily upon the assets held by would-be spenders and upon how quickly these may be mobilised and converted to a form to make their demand effective; and secondarily, on the mood and resources of financial institutions and others whose function it may be to create credit and finance spending. Thus, if we are to understand the monetary aspect of total effective demand, we must now think not only of the total supply of money but of 'the whole liquidity position that is relevant to spending decisions'.[3]

It is not our purpose to enter into the theoretical controversy between the old and the new. This is not a book on monetary theory—a sector of economics on which the dust seldom settles. This controversy will persist

[1] Only 'in part' since several other weapons, notably fiscal policy, are brought to bear in this connection.

[2] Until, to be precise, the publication in August 1959 of the Radcliffe Report. This was the first recognition by an official body, including a number of distinguished economists, of the general liquidity approach to monetary policy.

[3] Cf. Committee on the Working of the Monetary System. Cmd. 827 of 1959. Throughout the remainder of this book this document will, for the sake of brevity, be referred to as 'the Radcliffe Report'.

for some time. Fierce rearguard actions are being fought, the nuances of emphasis and definition are being argued but these excitements are not for us. We must take rather the view which is now widely accepted,[1] which forms the basis of most analyses of banking problems and which the Radcliffe Committee took as the basis of their examination of the monetary system. We proceed on that basis.

For us, perhaps, the most important implication of that view is the directive it gives to examine not only the central core of the banking system, the central bank and its satellite commercial banks, but also the operations of a whole host of ancillary institutions whose influence on the general liquidity situation now becomes important. As long as the quantity of money was regarded as the strategic variable, interest necessarily centred on the note-issue and upon the central bank's ability to control the total deposits of the banking system by varying its own liabilities to the banks. Now that it is the general liquidity situation which concerns us the focus broadens until it includes not only this important relationship but a whole series of related markets for monetary assets of varying liquidity.

To summarise the argument so far: we are concerned in a modern monetary system with the ways in which changes in the general state of liquidity bear upon total spending power. This involves, in turn, an examination of the determinants of (a) the total supply of money, i.e., coin, notes and bank deposits, and (b) the ability of would-be spenders to acquire spending power (i.e. liquidity) either by a switch of their own assets or by the giving of credit by specialised firms existing for that purpose. In moving forward from here we shall find ourselves concerned progressively with a number of main institutional groups the nature of which should now be defined.

First of these (not a group but an entity) is the central bank, now usually a department of government or at least a non-profit-seeking agency deriving its power from and accountable to the State but perhaps possessing also vestigial attributes of an ordinary banking business, which betrays its origins and certainly widens its expertise. This central bank will exercise certain important functions. It will control, in matters of major policy, the activities of all other banks. It will itself act as banker to the government and as administrator of the national debt, forming thereby a bridge between the public and private sectors of the economy. It will have complete control of whatever mechanisms exist for the issue of notes and coin. It will perform for its country certain important tasks in the field of international finance such as administering the exchange reserves, overseeing exchange rate policy and the like. Finally, bearing

[1] What I have called in Chapter 1 the 'current orthodoxy', cf. p. 16.

as it does the responsibility for all these important matters it feels itself competent and entitled to share with the government in formulating general economic policy and in the taking of all those varied and diverse decisions which, collectively, we call monetary policy.

The second group of institutions is that of the commercial banks.[1] These may be few or many; few in the United Kingdom, Canada and Germany where large, powerful, nationwide branch networks carry on a banking service; many in the United States, where factors peculiar to economic development and the political beliefs of that country have produced a predominantly unitary banking system. The distinguishing characteristic of these banks, whatever their organisation, is that, in contrast to the central bank, they are profit-seeking firms subject to all the normal motivation born of carrying on business in competition with their fellows. They exist to maximise profits by carrying on ordinary banking business, that is by accepting deposits and transferring them via the cheque system, by dealing in certain types of assets, and by providing numerous services of a financial and quasi-legal nature for their customers. The commercial banks operating as they do, first as profit-making firms with responsibilities to their shareholders and second as the media through which the central bank operates in the interests of monetary policy, thus stand in the monetary field between the public and private sectors of the economy. They must, while seeking profit, be conscious of certain public responsibilities. Their actions have public significance and are not solely their own business.

The third group of financial institutions lies wholly within the private sector and consists of what may be called 'the ancillary financial institutions'. These form a heterogeneous group, differing from country to country. Their activities are extremely diversified and impossible to describe as long as this description is kept in general terms. In the main it is possible, however, to distinguish two sub-groups: those institutions which carry on activities close to or within the banking system itself, as for example, the overseas and foreign banks and, in the United Kingdom, the merchant banks, acceptance houses, and discount houses; and those institutions which lie outside the banking system but whose operations in the financial field, either in making credit available to the public or by their being leading operators in financial markets, make them of great importance in the carrying out of general monetary policy. Into this category fall such organisations as insurance companies, the hire-

---

[1] The nomenclature here provides us with the alternatives of 'commercial banks', 'member banks', or 'clearing banks'. Since the second has American and the third British overtones while the first implies in the title only that these are profit-seeking firms, the writer prefers the first title.

purchase and finance houses, the building societies, unit trusts and super-annuation and pension funds.

The essence of a centralised banking system is that it is a mechanism for the controlled creation of money and credit. It is necessary to consider briefly how this creation takes place, how the control upon it operates and what are the relationships between the various groups of institutions which we have already described. This enquiry had best start with the commercial banks which are the main vehicles for the creation of money and credit.

Banks of this type carry on business by taking in assets of various types, giving in return their own deposit liabilities. The total of these assets then equals at all times the banks' total external liability[1] while the interest earned on the assets is to the banks a main source of revenue. The assets may consist of cash, in which case the balance sheet position of an imaginary bank newly opened which takes in £1,000 in cash will be as follows:

Liabilities		Assets	
	£		£
Deposits	1,000	Cash	1,000

To this cash asset the bank may add a Treasury bill for £3,000 purchasing it from a customer or from a discount house. This causes the balance sheet position to change as follows:

Liabilities		Assets	
	£		£
Deposits	4,000	Cash	1,000
		Bills	3,000

In both these cases the assets acquired by the banks are tangible paper titles—cash notes, a Treasury bill—but less tangible assets are also accepted, notably the promises to pay of trusted customers. Let us suppose the bank advances £1,000 to a farmer for the purchase of seed and fertiliser then the process is, in principle, the same as before. The bank acquires the asset which is constituted by the farmer's promise to pay £1,000 to it at some stated future time and gives in return its own immediate deposit liability of £1,000. The balance sheet now looks like this:

Liabilities		Assets	
	£		£
Deposits	5,000	Cash	1,000
		Bills	3,000
		Loans	1,000

[1] We exclude for simplicity such balance sheet liabilities as 'capital' or assets such as 'premises', etc. which of course exist for banks as for all firms but which are irrelevant to the above argument.

Finally, the bank may acquire assets in the form of government bonds. This it does, paying for the bonds by a cheque against itself. If we suppose that it buys £1,000 worth of bonds this makes the balance sheet look like this:

Liabilities		Assets	
	£		£
Deposits	6,000	Cash	1,000
		Bills	3,000
		Loans	1,000
		Investments	1,000

If we regard this process from the point of view of the banks we see that they are acquiring assets of various kinds and paying for them by the creation of deposit liabilities, i.e., by becoming indebted to the sellers of the assets. These deposit liabilities constitute an addition to total purchasing power, i.e., to the money stock. As for the banks, from the interest on assets acquired they derive an income which they will wish to maximise by so distributing their assets as to hold the bulk of these assets in the form which yields the highest interest. Moreover, in the absence of any check on their acquisition of assets they may go on increasing their income by acquiring more assets and thus creating more deposits. The check is, of course, provided by their own desire to distribute their assets in such a way as to meet any calls which may be made upon them by depositors for actual cash, i.e., notes and coin. The ideal distribution is, therefore, one in which a certain minimum cash holding is backed by a second reserve of liquid assets such as bills, the whole to buttress the banks' holding of relatively illiquid income-earning assets. Only when the liquid-assets-backing for deposits has been provided can the banks think of expanding their earning assets. Moreover, even then they can only do this if further liquid assets are available to add to the liquid reserve as total deposits rise. Availability of liquid assets is therefore a prime consideration to the banks in the process of deposit creation. In the example given, the bank concerned is holding £4,000 in liquid assets against deposits of £6,000, an unnecessarily high liquid reserve ratio. It is, therefore, to its advantage to expand its income earning assets (Loans and/or Investments) to such an extent as to reduce its liquidity to an appropriate reserve level. This it may do by making further loans of £3,000 and buying additional bonds of £3,000, making its balance sheet as follows:

Liabilities		Assets	
	£		£
Deposits	12,000	Cash	1,000
		Bills	3,000
		Loans	4,000
		Investments	4,000

In this position with a ratio of cash to deposits of $1:12$ and a ratio of liquid assets to deposits of $4:12$[1] the cash and liquid reserves set a limit to further asset expansion.[2]

It is clear then that, if the banks are preserving, in the interests of liquidity, a certain minimum relationship between their liquid assets and their total deposits, two things must control the total of their deposits: the size of the liquid reserve ratio itself, i.e., the proportion of their total assets which the banks hold as liquid or near liquid reserves against deposits; and the nature and availability of the assets which the banks class as liquid and include in their reserve. Both of these conditions are satisfied in practice. So far as the liquid reserve ratio is concerned either the banks maintain voluntarily a conventional reserve ratio prescribed by the central bank or they honour a defined reserve ratio statutorily imposed by the State. So far as the constitution of the liquid assets is concerned it may be decided to preserve within the liquid assets a simple cash ratio under which a minimum ratio of cash to deposits is preserved by the banks. In addition, however, it is now usual practice in most banking systems to work through a liquid assets ratio in which certain defined groups of assets (including cash) must in total satisfy the defined liquidity reserve ratio. What these liquid assets have in common is that they are themselves liabilities of the State, whether they are cash in the form of notes and coin, or short bills issued by the State for its own borrowing purposes. Thus these assets, which are themselves liabilities of the central bank (as State banker), determine, by their magnitude, given the preservation by the banks of the necessary reserve ratio, the limit of deposit creation by the commercial banks. Two examples may clarify the point. If the country concerned is operating a simple cash ratio system

[1] Both of which are typical working reserve ratios.

[2] It is implicit in this example that in the process of credit creation individual banks do not create new money to a multiple of their deposits; it is the banking system as a whole which does so. This point must be clearly understood. An individual bank can only create credit to $\frac{9}{10}$ of its deposits if it is working to a $1:10$ cash ratio, $\frac{4}{5}$ of its deposits if it is working to a $1:5$ ratio and so on. Each time it receives a deposit it must keep the stipulated proportion as reserve, distributing the rest as income earning assets. But the payments, which it makes for the income earning assets it acquires, return to other banks in the banking system as deposits, on the basis of which further new income earning assets may be acquired, by the system as a whole. Thus, an initial new deposit (or cash creation) of £1,000 with a reserve ratio of $1:10$ creates new money as a geometric progression in the form $1,000 \times [1 + \frac{9}{10} + (\frac{9}{10})^2 + (\frac{9}{10})^3 + \ldots (\frac{9}{10})^n]$. The sum of this geometric progression to n terms is £10,000. The whole banking system has created new money of ten times the original cash increment. Readers who wish to explore the interesting process of deposit creation further should consult any of the many excellent textbooks on monetary economics. See for example, *Economics*, Paul Samuelson, 7th edition, pp. 285-294.

under which banks hold a cash reserve ratio of 10 per cent then the total of bank deposits cannot exceed ten times the total cash created by the central bank. Alternatively if the reserve ratio is one under which a stipulated group of liquid assets (which will of course include cash) must be at least 33 per cent of total deposits, then the total of bank deposits cannot exceed three times the total of these assets held by the banks. Thus a general principle emerges. It is that the rate of deposit expansion is equal to the liquid assets held by the banks multiplied by what we may call 'the deposit expansion multiplier', i.e., the reciprocal of the reserve ratio. This principle is summarised in the expression:

$$\text{Expansion of total deposits} = \text{Liquid assets included in reserve} \times \frac{1}{\text{Reserve Ratio}} \tag{1}$$

This in turn approximates to the expression:

$$\text{Expansion of total deposits} = \text{Liquid assets created by the monetary authorities} \times \frac{1}{\text{Reserve Ratio}} \tag{2}$$

To the extent that this latter expression is true there is then a direct means of control of total bank deposits open to the monetary authorities, for these depend upon (a) the liquid assets they create, and (b) the reserve ratio preserved by the banks. There is, however, a difference between the two expressions—a difference which makes the first precise and the second approximate. This lies in the fact that the liquid assets included by the banks in their reserve (expression 1) may not be the same as the liquid assets created by the monetary authorities (expression 2). The two will only be the same if all liquid assets are created by the monetary authorities and are taken up directly by the commercial banks, an assumption which may not be true in practice. To the extent that it is not true, we must interpret the second equation as being subject to a leakage; a leakage which is the greater the greater is the amount of central bank short-term liabilities, held outside the commercial banks.[1] It should be noted, however, that this leakage serves only to reduce the force of the deposit-expansion multiplier so that the multiplier in fact sets an upper limit to the process of money creation. In practical terms the power of the monetary authority to create liquid assets to be held as reserves by the

[1] During a progressive expansion of bank deposits this leakage will tend to increase for two main reasons: firstly, because the increase in bank deposits will set off an increase in income which will give rise to an increase in the holding of cash outside the banking system; and secondly, because with the rise in income the assets distribution of firms may tend to change in such a way as to cause them to hold Treasury bills, thus reducing the amount of these held by the banks.

commercial banks limits in greater or lesser degree the creation of deposits by the banks as long as a minimum reserve ratio of these liquid assets is held by the banks.

This brings us to the point at which we must ask what forces condition the creation and distribution of the quick liabilities of the monetary authorities—these quick liabilities of the central bank which are in turn the liquid assets of the commercial banks. Such liquid assets are of two classes: cash, which includes notes and token coinage; and short-term government bills, which are usually the main medium of short-term government borrowing and which therefore must be regarded by the authorities not only as the basis of bank deposit creation but also in the light of national debt policy and exchequer needs for borrowing.

So far as cash is concerned it is first necessary to look more closely at just what the commercial banks include under this item. In fact the banks order their holding and demand for cash very much as does a private individual. Each bank holds a supply of notes and coins in its vaults for everyday use in meeting the demands of the public. This 'till money'[1] they adjust daily by varying the deposits which they each hold at the central bank. In effect notes and coin serve as the small change of the economy and are adjusted by variation of the commercial banks' deposits at the central bank in just the same way as a private person holds only in notes and coin in his pocket what is convenient and safe, regarding his bank current account as the strategic variable of his liquid needs. From the central bank's point of view then cash consists of its own 'deposits of bankers', its note issue and its coin issue. The last two of these can be quickly disposed of. The central bank regards it as necessary to regulate the notes and coin in circulation merely to meet public and bank convenience and in accordance with the demand of the economy for loose change. It regards as relatively unimportant what proportion of its total cash liability the banks wish to hold in notes and coin. It does, however, regard as important the figure which is the true cash base, namely bankers' deposits. This importance becomes greatest in the banking system of countries which rely on a simple cash ratio[2] as the means of adjusting the total of bank money. In this case the commercial banks will each be preserving a fixed relation between their deposit liabilities and their deposits with the central bank. Control by the central bank depends, therefore, on its own ability to vary the total of bankers' deposits, i.e., its own liability to the banking system. Even in banking systems governed by a liquid reserve ratio, however, it must be remembered that cash forms part of the reserve and its variations thus have some effect on the central bank's control. Nevertheless, it is true to say that generally where

---

[1] 'Vault money' in the United States.   [2] That is a ratio of cash to deposits.

the central bank operates in such systems it does so to influence the level of total liquid assets through bills rather than cash. In such systems cash and the cash reserve ratio have been relegated to a minor rôle and the aim is to 'neutralise' cash by keeping a fixed ratio of cash to deposits.

From the commercial banks' point of view the central bank's control of their cash has one very important aspect. They themselves are unable to create cash yet they are in the awkward position where they must meet demands for it from their customers and where failure to meet these demands provokes a crisis. Unsupported by any supply of cash from elsewhere they would adopt a critical view of their cash reserve holding, increasing its ratio to deposits in response to any sign of an increase in cash demand, of economic or financial danger and perhaps reducing it to a low level in times of boom and confidence. Since the central bank requires for its own purposes of control a cash reserve ratio which is held tautly at a chosen level, and it has the more general reason that it wants a stable and solvent banking system, it does not leave the commercial banks unsupported in the matter of cash. Rather, it stands ready at any time to supply cash either by lending directly to the commercial banks or by some other and more devious means. It accepts in short the rôle of 'lender of last resort' which is so fundamental to its position and to a centralised banking system. It should be noted also that when the central bank thus lends to aid the commercial banks it may do so on any terms, that is at any rate of interest. In this position it becomes not only the monopolist of cash but a discriminating monopolist. It has in its power the means to make any given rate of interest effective.

The second form of State liability which is held as liquid asset by the banking system is that of short-term government-issued bills. These are issued at regular intervals and in varying amounts, the amounts reflecting the ebb and flow of exchequer receipts and expenditure. They are taken up by the banking system and by financial institutions; are dealt in in the market which prevails for such short-term paper; but find their way more or less quickly to the commercial banks who hold them as liquid assets to maturity. The considerations which govern operations in this market, the implications of government and bank action in issuing and taking up bills and the actions of other operators in the short-term market may be many and complex. They are important and form much of the later subject matter of this book. We are concerned at this stage, however, only with first principles and two features only claim our attention.

Firstly, from the banks' point of view these bills form the ideal liquid asset. Given that cash, being a sterile (that is non-interest-earning) asset, will be held by the banks only up to that minimum directed by the cash ratio, bills may then be held as a reserve asset. They can be graded as to maturity and the holding may be suitably distributed as between short and long dated bills to suit the banks' judgement of their needs. A well tapered portfolio constantly augments the cash reserve with cash from maturing bills. At the same time the bills constitute an earning asset.

The second aspect of such bills is that they are one of the vehicles through which the central bank operates to control its own liability to the commercial banks, that is bank cash and ultimately bank deposits. This function, however, brings us face to face with the broad question of central bank control and it is to some of the general aspects of this that we now turn.

Central bank control of commercial bank liquidity varies in method and emphasis from country to country and new methods and refinements of the old are being introduced continually. It is, however, on two features, the process of open-market operations and control of the structure of interest rates, that control ultimately rests.

There is a danger that any short description of the rôle of the central bank will give an impression of a mechanism which is precise, simple and proceeds with smooth efficiency. This is far from the truth. The central bank works with a multiplicity of aims in view not all of which are compatible. Only if the control of credit were the sole aim of central banking policy would the facts approximate to this mechanistic picture. In fact the central bank will at any time be conscious of the following considerations motivating its actions:

(a) It must satisfy the needs of the banking system for cash;
(b) It must influence the liquidity of the commercial banks bearing in mind its own and the government's wishes with regard to the desirable level of bank lending to industry and the public;
(c) It must operate in the short-term market to establish a chosen pattern of interest rates;
(d) It must administer the national debt, arranging maturities, redemptions and fundings and minimising the debt burden;
(e) It must endeavour to reconcile the patterns of long- and short-term interest rates suitable to domestic policies with the interest rates which it may wish to establish for balance of payments reasons.

We have already said something of (a). We are now interested predominantly in (b) and we shall glance briefly at (c). The complicating influence of the other factors must not, however, be forgotten. Reconciliation of these varying and sometimes conflicting aims is the art of central banking.

To control the liquidity of the commercial banks the central bank resorts to open-market operations, that is, it buys and sells financial assets in the ordinary markets appropriate to those assets. Such assets are of two types: the short-term government bills already discussed and longer-dated State bonds and securities.[1] It is clear that operations by the central bank in the markets for either of these assets have immediate significance for almost all other aims of central bank activity, for example, for short- and long-term interest rate policy and for national debt management. These complications we must, however, set aside in the interest of simplicity. This done, it matters little for the purposes of controlling commercial bank liquidity which asset is used for such operations.[2] Let us suppose that the operation is in long-term securities. When the central bank buys these in the open market it pays for them by cheques drawn against itself and in favour of the sellers. These cheques when paid into the commercial banks by the sellers and passed through the clearing banks have the effect of raising the commercial banks' deposits and raising their cash (i.e., bankers' deposits at the central bank) by the same absolute amount. The cash ratio rises and is now unnecessarily high and the banks cast around for means of lowering it again by the purchase of income-earning assets. These are speedily forthcoming for the central bank has been forced to issue additional short bills to cover the cost to the Exchequer of buying the long-term securities. These the commercial banks acquire and the result is a rise in their liquid assets ratio.[3] If we assume that, in the original position before the process began, this was at the required level, the banks are, in the final position, overliquid and are able to switch the surplus liquid assets into more lucrative earning assets, probably to *Loans and Advances*. In this way a process of open-market buying by the central bank will have the effect of increasing commercial bank liquidity, increasing bank lending and easing credit generally. Sales of securities by the central bank will by the reverse process have the opposite effect.

The description of this process, by ignoring the effects of open-market operations upon other central bank activities, gives the impression that the central bank's power to vary commercial bank liquidity is precise

---

[1] The nature of the assets dealt in by the central bank is not important for the process of central bank control. As will be seen the mechanism for the control of commercial bank liquidity would be exercised even if the central bank bought and sold potatoes. These would scarcely be a suitable or durable asset, however, and the central bank has other good reasons for sticking to the types of assets mentioned in the text.

[2] In fact dealings in bills are used to ease cash shortages and make day-to-day market adjustments: dealings in bonds are used to control commercial bank liquidity.

[3] We are here assuming that there is no acquisition of the new bills by outside (i.e. non-banking) operators when they are issued. This is an unlikely assumption. A large leakage of bills of this kind has the effect of weakening the influence of open-market operations.

and absolute. It is not: other factors intrude. What for example is the situation in the bond market? Are prices such that large scale central bank operations will create rates of interest which are not acceptable to the government's national debt or balance of payments policies? Alternatively the central bank may require, for the purposes of interest rate policy, to undertake operations in the bond market which in their turn will have unwanted effects on commercial bank liquidity.

Central bank control of interest rates, like open-market operations, has widespread implications outside the purely banking field, in particular for national debt administration. Then there are wider theoretical issues. We are here concerned, however, with the banking processes by which changes in interest rates may be initiated and how they may be made discriminatory in effect. We are not here concerned with the broader and general economic issue of the effects which changes in interest rates have upon total demand, upon saving investment decisions and upon movements of funds to and from a country. That the level of interest rates has some considerable influence upon these variables is surely demonstrated by the banking developments and theory of two centuries. We must leave to others the discussion of the rôle of interest rates in the general economic system.

In general the monetary authority aims to influence the investment/saving pattern of the economy by influencing the general assessment of the profitability of investment and 'the cost and difficulty of raising money'.[1] By the processes we have already discussed the central monetary authority controls the quantity of money and credit: by the processes of interest rate control it influences the price, or prices, at which money and credit is made available.

It is necessary to think of interest rate control in terms of a spectrum of interest rates which shades from the ultra short rate at one extreme (e.g. the rate for day-to-day loans to financial houses by banks) through short rates (e.g. bill rates) to long rates (e.g. bond rates); ultra long rates (e.g. housing mortgage loans) and irredeemable securities such as Consols. An effective influence by the central bank over the interest rate structure will extend as widely over this spectrum as possible and will operate by the intervention of the authorities in the markets for various financial assets. In some markets the intervention may be direct and almost monopolistic. In others (e.g. the bond market) it may be indirect and somewhat tentative. In a few markets (e.g. that for housing loans) the government may not interfere at all, contenting itself with that mixture of economic homily and official cajoling which the monetary mechanists have come to

[1] Committee on the Working of the Monetary System. Principal Memoranda of Evidence. Vol. i, p. 35.

E

call 'moral suasion'. The authority's influence is greatest at the short end where the central bank's influence is direct. Here, as we have seen, the central bank has power to control the cash and liquid assets base of the commercial banks, while the commercial banks have the right to resort, if need be, to the central bank for replenishment of these assets. This connection gives to the central bank the means to make a given interest rate effective. After initiating conditions which drive the banks to seek assistance from it, it may exercise its right to provide this assistance at its own price—that is, it may make loans to the commercial banks at its own chosen rate or make assets (e.g. bills) available to them on certain terms. In any event it is making a chosen interest rate effective in a market in which it has created for itself a monopoly of supply. By so doing it forces the banks to consider revising their own rates in respect of the other assets in which they deal with the public and the economy in general.

It is through this process of 'interest rate spread' that the strategic rate charged by the central bank for assistance becomes important. Moreover, the variations of the central bank's discount rate are widely recognised, at home and abroad, as an indicator of the developing state of the economy and of the monetary authority's policy. As a result they have widespread psychological effects and economic influence apart from their more direct effects in the credit market. To this rate (which we shall call bank rate) a number of other important short-term rates are directly linked. These vary with bank rate. Others are influenced indirectly through the processes of the market. The change in interest rate effected by the central bank thus fans outwards to affect all short-term rates. In time long-term bond rates will be altered and ultimately all long-term interest rates.

When short-term rates rise as a result of central bank action, holders of long-term assets, reassessing the relative profitability of long- and short-term asset holdings, switch from long to short assets. Their sale of the former in the organised markets for such assets causes their prices to fall and, for fixed interest assets, their yield to rise. Thus the initial rise in the short-term interest rate spreads to long-term bonds and after a lapse of time, since new long-term loans can only be raised at a price comparable to existing yields in the market, the rise in interest rates becomes general. This process of interest rate spread is slow and uncertain, however, and the central authority is unlikely to rely on it to any great extent. Left to itself the 'seepage' of interest rate changes from short-term assets to long must depend on the degree of intervention of the monetary authority in the market for assets and on the willingness of asset holders to switch from one form of asset to another.

This process is too hedged about with impedances and qualifications to prove an efficient means of controlling interest rates in general. Because of this slowness the authorities may intervene in long-term assets markets as well as short, extending their control to a wider range of key interest rates if they wish to initiate a general upward or downward movement of rates. A further advantage of this deliberate intervention is not only that it becomes possible to influence particular rates, whose variation may temporarily be demanded for particular policies, but that it becomes possible to raise short-term rates if necessary while keeping long-term rates unchanged. Such refinements of interest rate control imply, however, a degree of interference in the financial markets which some countries regard as unjustified. Others are prepared to accept this as the price which must be paid for a tighter and more efficient control.

It is time to draw the threads together. The model of the centralised banking system which has been presented in this chapter is a highly simplified one aimed at showing the outline of the system—the main elements and the significant relations between the components. This model provides only the theme upon which the centralised banking systems of the world devise many interesting variations. In the succeeding section we examine how the British banking system interprets the theme and where its individuality lies. Before proceeding to this, however, it may be useful to summarise very briefly the model which we have evolved in this section.

(a) The main purpose of monetary policy, that is of purposive manipulation of the centralised banking system, is to influence the general climate of liquidity in the economy and thereby also the total level of effective demand. A subsidiary aim, varying in dominance from economy to economy, is to influence the balance of payments.

(b) Central bank, commercial banks, financial intermediaries and the State itself make up the quartet of significant institutions involved in making monetary policy effective.

(c) The importance within this quartet of the commercial banks lies in their ability to create bank deposits, to vary and distribute credit under central bank limitation.

(d) The essence of this limitation lies in: (i) certain variable liabilities of the central bank which form reserve liquid assets of the commercial banks, and (ii) the ratio between these commercial bank reserves and their deposits. Changes in total bank deposits then approximate to the expression:

$$\text{Expansion of total deposits} = \text{Liquid assets created by monetary authorities} \times \frac{1}{\text{Reserve Ratio}}$$

(e) The reserve assets of the commercial banks consist of cash, that is

notes, coin and deposits at the central bank, and short-term government bills. The central bank may vary the commercial banks'
cash by open market operations but it is also obliged to act as
'lender of last resort' to guarantee replenishment of the banks' cash
if need be. If, as is often the case, a fixed ratio of cash to deposits
is preserved it is the variation of the other reserve asset, namely
short-term government bills, which is strategic in determining the
total of bank deposits.

(f) The central bank is not only able by its operations to vary the
amount of bank credit but also to influence interest rates—that is
the price at which credit is available. This it does by operating in
various markets for financial assets. In one of these it operates under
its own conditions as a virtual monopolist and may settle the
interest rate at will. In others its influence and the extent of its
operations varies in strength.

With these general principles in mind we turn to consider their application
in the British banking system.

III

The British banking system has been the model and archetype of other
central banking systems, not only because it was the first system to evolve
but also because it was submitted from the beginning of the twentieth
century to minute analysis[1] and from it the essence of central banking
theory has been distilled. Yet the system itself is untidy and in many
respects the result of an irrational and haphazard process of development.
Its most experienced practitioners look upon its working as an art rather
than a science—a view which appears incongruous and out-of-keeping
with the precise approach of the monetary analyst.

Our task in this section is twofold: to examine the structure of the
British system in relation to the model set out in the previous section;

[1] It is difficult to be specific about the precise origins of banking theory. On the
broadest view discussion of banking problems began in the 'currency and banking'
controversies in the early nineteenth century but conscious analysis of the centralised
banking system as such had to wait until such a system had evolved and its elements
were recognisable. Bagehot's *Lombard Street* in 1873 did much to lay the foundations
for the academic probings which were to follow. Central banking theory did not,
however, develop until the interwar period when it did so under the stimulus of Keynes,
Hawtrey, Sayers and others, and with the publication of the Macmillan Report. Cf.
R. G. Hawtrey, *A Century of Bank Rate*, London, 1938; J. M. Keynes, *The Treatise on
Money*, 1930; R. S. Sayers, *Central Banking Since Bagehot*, Oxford, 1957; and *Modern
Banking*, seven editions, latest, 1967.

and to examine the rôle within the British system of the discount houses and the markets for short money which centre around its operations.

First, to identify the main characters. The Bank of England, as central bank, controls the commercial banks which are eleven in number and which, as members of the Bankers' Clearing House, we shall from now on call 'clearing banks'. Peripheral to the clearing banks stand the Scottish and Northern Irish banks which are subject to Bank of England control, but which, for certain important purposes such as money market operations, operate independently of the clearing banks.[1] To complete the purely banking group: there are in London some ninety-five overseas banks which are branches of foreign banks or, in some cases, the head offices of British companies whose chain of branches is overseas. Finally, there is the small but important group of merchant banks. Both of these latter groups compete with the clearing banks for deposit business.[2]

Linked with the banking group is the group of firms which operate with it in the London discount market—the twelve discount houses. These derive their operating capital from short loans from the clearing banks and act as dealers in commercial bills, Treasury bills and short-term bonds. They discount trade bills for commercial clients and pass these on at later stages in their maturity to the clearing banks who hold them as liquid assets. By far the greatest part of their bill turnover is, however, in Treasury bills for which they tender as a group, passing on the bills to the clearing banks and the Bank of England. Finally there exists a significant non-banking group of financial intermediaries, claims upon which represent an important part of the total liquidity of the country and have great influence upon total demand—savings banks, hire-purchase finance companies, building societies, and insurance companies.

When we turn to examine the ways in which these groups combine in the British system, variation from the general model of the previous section quickly becomes apparent. The first point of variance lies in the existence and operations of the discount market, which produce important complications in the relations between the central bank and the clearing banks. These must be briefly examined.

The first complication lies in the fact that, since the discount houses operate with the aid of funds borrowed from the clearing banks on a

---

[1] These banks still possess the right of note-issue but, as their notes have to be backed pound for pound by Bank of England notes, this is an archaic practice maintained only for reasons of prestige.

[2] They compete very successfully. Between 1960 and 1965 the share of the clearing banks' net deposits to GNP fell by 3 per cent to 30·2 per cent, largely as a result of the aggressive competition of the merchant banks and overseas banks for this business.

very short-call basis, these loans constitute in themselves a highly liquid asset to the clearing banks and a first line reserve for the replenishment of cash. Through the existence of this asset the impact of changing public demand for cash upon the liquid assets structure of the clearing banks is cushioned, any sudden increase in bank depositors' demand for cash being met by the clearing banks calling in their short loans to the discount market, and any surplus cash in the banks being quickly lent to the houses. The liquid assets of the British clearing banks are then three in number: *Cash*, which consists of till-money held in the banks themselves plus deposits at the Bank of England; *Money at Call and Short Notice*, consisting of loans made to the discount houses and renewable from day to day, and *Bills* made up of British Government Treasury bills, commercial bills and a small amount of government guaranteed loans for export business. Within this liquid assets structure certain conventions govern the orders of magnitude. A simplified balance sheet of the clearing banks reflects the relationships:

Deposits	Cash Ratio 8%	Cash: Till money Deposits at Bank of England Money at Call and short Notice Bills Advances Investments	Liquid Assets Ratio 28%

The total of these liquid assets should not fall below 28 per cent of total deposits, while a fixed ratio of 8 per cent as between cash and total deposits is also required. While these reserve ratios, referred to respectively as the 'liquidity ratio' and the 'cash ratio' have no legal sanction they are requirements of the Bank of England to the clearing banks.[1] Both liquidity rules are regarded by the banking fraternity and by the informed outside observer as *de facto* regulations for the restraint of bank deposit creation. Of these two reserve ratios the liquidity ratio is of greater importance. If, in the British system, the Bank of England wished to control total deposits via the cash ratio it would come across the complication that open-market operations which reduced clearing bank cash could be countered by the clearing banks who might call in short loans from the discount houses,

[1] A significant move away from the old view of the liquidity ratio as a clearing bank convention took place in July 1963 when the Bank of England informed the clearing banks that the then ratio of 30 per cent should be reduced to 28 per cent. By this the principle was established that the ratio was fixed by, and variable on the request of, the Bank of England.

that is, execute a switch from *money at call* to *cash* which would serve to nullify the controlling power of the cash ratio. As long, however, as the clearing banks are obliged to preserve the 28 per cent liquidity ratio, the ratio cannot be raised (or lowered) by switches between the liquid assets themselves and any fall of the ratio below 28 per cent must be adjusted by immediate curtailment of *Advances* and/or the sale of *Investments*—either action having deflationary effects.

For purposes of deposit control the fixed cash ratio of 8 per cent is therefore neutral and the Bank of England's actions aim only at holding bank cash at the level appropriate to the needs of the economy.[1] In this, however, the discount houses play an important part which is unique to the British system. Traditionally they stand between the clearing banks and the Bank of England. When, as a result of increased public demand for cash, the clearing banks require to replenish their cash holding, they do so by calling in their short loans from the discount houses. So long as the calling-in is limited to a few banks the discount houses may get funds from another bank, but if the calling-in is general they then have the traditional right to borrow from the Bank of England, which may in its turn make the loans at whatever rates of interest it wishes to make effective. Thus, in the British system, the central bank's rôle of lender of last resort is exercised predominantly through the discount houses, which act as a reservoir of liquidity between the Bank of England and the clearing banks. Indeed, from the beginning of the nineteenth century,[2] British clearing banks have regarded as anathema the practice of direct assistance by the central bank to the commercial banks, which logical tidiness might dictate. Only in very recent years has this principle of 'no direct assistance' by the central bank been infringed by the working of an alternative procedure known as 'the open back door'. Since the Second World War the practice has grown whereby cash shortages, particularly those due to variations in the Exchequer balance at the Bank of England, are relieved by the Bank of England purchasing (through its own special buyer) from the clearing banks Treasury bills of convenient maturities. This results in a fall in clearing bank *Bills* and a rise in *Cash*—a direct solution to the problem. Such a direct approach to the clearing banks arises partly from the necessity to relieve temporary cash shortage but also from the Bank of England's debt management activities. For these the Bank may often wish to hold bills of particular maturities. Should the bills with suitable maturities be held by the clearing banks then the buyer purchases them from the clearing

[1] There is more to the operation of the cash ratio than can be discussed here. Cf. *The Theory of Money*, W. T. Newlyn, pp. 13-23.

[2] To be precise, since the crisis of 1825.

banks and the credit easement is direct; if they are held by the discount
market he purchases them from the discount houses and the help given
is indirect. This means in effect that there is operating, in addition to the
normal front door method, a method whereby help is given through the
'open back door' on many days in the year. The choice of method
depends on circumstances and conditions. The buyer[1] is familiar with
conditions in the money market and also with the establishments where
the Bank can obtain given maturities. If cash is short a word by him to
a discount house or clearing bank that the Bank of England would take
such maturities is sufficient. There is a useful informality and flexibility
in such a system which seems to justify it in all eyes even though it has
violated a tradition of a century's standing. There are, it seems, few
generalisations which the British are not prepared eventually to disregard in the interests of convenience.

There is a further complication in the British system which had best
be dealt with at this stage. In the preceding section[2] it emerged as the
strategic principle of central bank control of deposit creation by the
commercial banks that certain of the liabilities of the central bank were
the asset reserves of the commercial banks and the basis for their deposit
creation. All hinged then on the purposive variation of such central bank
liabilities. The trouble is, however, that, in the British system, the Bank
of England has deposit liabilities other than those which it has to the clearing banks. Of these there are two: *Public Deposits*, the balance of the
Government's account at the Bank, and *Other Deposits*, the total of the
deposits of the Bank's remaining private customers. Variations in either
of these items may upset the clean mechanistic relationship between
Bankers' Deposits at the Bank of England and the deposits of the clearing
banks. If we take the case of *Public Deposits* an increase in government
payments to the public lowers this balance and when the public places
the amounts of the government payments it receives in the clearing
banks, and when the cheques are cleared, the deposits of the clearing
banks have risen. There has, in short, been a switch of Bank of England
liabilities from *Public Deposits* to *Bankers' Deposits*, this in its turn causing
an increase in the liquidity of the clearing banks through an expansion
of the cash base. The very large seasonal variations which take place in
Public Deposits would, in the absence of counteraction by the Bank of
England, result in wide involuntary variations in the clearing banks'
cash and in their liquidity ratios. Similarly, but on a much smaller scale,
an excess of payments over receipts by persons holding accounts at the

[1] The smallest of the discount houses, Seccombe, Marshall & Campion, acts as 'special
buyer' for the Bank of England.
[2] Cf. p. 52.

Bank of England causes a switch from *Other Deposits* to *Bankers' Deposits* with similar effects. The result of these switches in Bank of England liabilities is that a good deal of the Bank of England's attention has to be given to adjusting the involuntary variations in bank cash to which these switches give rise. If large payments have been made by the private sector to the government, thus reducing clearing bank cash and causing the banks to call in loans from the discount houses, then help will be given by the Bank of England in one of two ways: either by allowing the discount market to be forced into the Bank, that is, to come to the Bank (by the front door) to obtain funds either by discounting bills at bank rate or by borrowing on the security of approved bills at some rate in excess of bank rate,[1] or to give help at 'the open back door' by taking Treasury bills either from the discount houses or the clearing banks at prices which reflect the market rate for such bills. The deciding factor in the official choice between the two methods of giving help lies in whether the authorities wish to alter short-term interest rates or leave them unchanged. By using the first method and forcing the market into the Bank they give an upward thrust to short-term rates since discount houses, by having to pay more for accommodation, will themselves charge higher rates for their discounts and will, if the market remains long in the Bank, adjust their tender rate for Treasury bills. By using the second method the authorities may give help at the market rate thus leaving other short-term interest rates unchanged. Indeed, since the open-market operations of the Bank are many and frequent and since it is essential that adjustments can be made to allow for day-to-day variations in the cash supply without the necessity of altering the interest rate structure, some method such as that of the open back door is called for.

The most important item in the liquid assets of the clearing banks is the Treasury bill which accounts for 53 per cent of the Bills item in their balance sheets.[2] With a fixed cash ratio of 8 per cent the control of the volume of bills in the market and reaching the clearing banks is a first necessity in influencing the banks' power to create deposits. Indeed one can go further and regard the bills held by the discount houses as being indirectly held by the banks, inasmuch as the discount houses hold these bills on the strength of the *Money at Call* lent to them by the banks. The amount of liquid assets available to the banks therefore depends upon (a) the total available commercial bills, (b) the total available Treasury bills, and (c) such other short assets, viz., guaranteed export credits and short bonds, as the discount houses and clearing banks may hold and

---

[1] The latter method is now the usual one whereby Bank of England 'front door' help is given.
[2] In May 1967.

which are classed in with the bill item on their balance sheets. Since (c) is not large in amount and does not vary significantly in the short run we may disregard it; but (a) has grown in importance in recent years and now demands separate methods of Bank of England control. We cannot as formerly regard Treasury bills as the main liquid item with commercial bills as peripheral. Nevertheless, the Treasury bill item is important and likely to remain so.

The Treasury bill is the means by which the Exchequer finances week by week that part of its financial requirements which cannot be met out of current receipts. It is therefore a liability of government created by the government at will. The rule embodied in our model is that the observance of a minimum ratio of defined central bank or State liabilities to bank deposits gives the creator of the liabilities power to control the creation of bank deposits. In the British banking system the State liability basic to bank deposit creation is that of Treasury bills, in contrast to the practice in many other countries where the strategic State liability is the deposit liability of the central bank to the commercial banks, i.e., cash. It is apparent therefore that not only is the British system different in principle by basing the process of credit creation on Treasury bills rather than cash, but that other differences of substance may emerge if we examine the nature of the Treasury bill more closely.

It will be observed that for the Treasury bill to be a precise determinant of total clearing bank deposits it would be necessary for all Treasury bills on issue to be taken and held by the clearing banks. This does not happen. The bills are not issued by the central bank, which although a State agency in Britain is not part of the Treasury, whose duty it is to issue the bills weekly in accordance with Exchequer needs. Moreover, the bills, when issued, are issued by tender and a substantial proportion of the weekly issue may be taken up by non-banking groups, by industrial and commercial companies, insurance companies and building societies and by foreigners with balances to invest in London. It is not possible to control the amount of weekly leakage of Treasury bills to non-banking holders, and this leakage, due to the holding of Treasury bills outside the banking system, reduces the precision of the control of the authorities over bank deposits. Treasury bills are issued primarily as a means of Exchequer short-term borrowing. It is incidental that they act also as a supply of bank liquid assets. It may well be that at certain periods the authorities will welcome a large non-banking demand for the bills,[1] but to the extent

---

[1] For example, after a rise in Bank rate which has been made to strengthen the balance of payments. A rise in non-banking holdings of Treasury bills in such circumstances will almost certainly reflect a flow of short-term funds to sterling and a demand by foreigners to hold these funds in the form of Treasury bills.

that this occurs Bank of England control over total clearing bank deposits is weakened.

This flaw in the system is less serious than at first appears since the Bank of England has another string to its bow in the use of open-market operations, that is, dealing in long-term bonds in order to vary the clearing banks' holding of Treasury bills.[1] In effect what happens is that for purposes of cash control the Bank of England works by dealing in Treasury bills, selling these to mop up cash, buying them, at front or back door, when it wishes to create cash. Thus it neutralises the cash ratio, establishes its own control over interest rates and throws the real control of total bank liquidity on to the 20 per cent (that is, the non-cash section) of the clearing banks' liquid assets. Then, for purposes of controlling clearing bank liquidity it resorts to open market operations.

How effective in the final issue is the Bank of England's control of banking liquidity? Neat and ingenious as appears the system which we have described, there have been a good many qualifications in our exposition of the lines of control. Moreover, in recent years tentative attempts at improvement by innovations such as Special Deposits and by the use of moral suasion on the banks to order their liquidity in accordance with national policies, together with mutterings among critics of the improvement which would be achieved by the use of a statutorily variable reserve ratio, all indicate a certain degree of dissatisfaction and uncertainty about the efficiency of the present system. It is not our purpose to examine the effectiveness of central bank control of liquidity. This is not a work on monetary and banking theory. It might be useful, however, if we set down very briefly the main qualifications (some might say they are denials) of central bank control of liquidity. They are:

(a) The working of a system in which changes in bank liquidity are a multiple of changes in bank holdings of reserve assets is weakened by leaks of the reserve assets into non-banking sectors of the economy.

(b) There is a potential confusion of aims on the part of the Bank of England between credit control, interest rate policy and national debt administration. For example,

(i) If the authorities wish to expand the Treasury bill supply to cover high Exchequer spending it may result, at the worst, in the banks becoming over-liquid as they receive the newly-created Treasury bills and, with liquidity ratios far in excess

[1] Cf. p. 63 above.

of the stipulated level, subsequent restriction of bank deposits
by the methods we have described becomes impossible;[1]

(ii) Open market operations in the bond market to secure a
change in bank deposits may, for the time being, be in-
consistent with the rate of interest required in that and other
markets for other purposes.

IV

Our final task in this brief survey of the principles of a centralised banking
system is to set down concisely the conditions required for the development within the system of an organised money market. This is the more
necessary in that not all of the great centralised systems have developed
such markets and where they have developed they have done so at varying
speeds and with their own individual traits. In the historical account which
is to follow of the rise of the British discount market it is as well to have
these pre-conditions in mind and to observe the way in which they
influenced that development. Since some of these pre-conditions have
already been discussed in other contexts it is only necessary to set them
down *seriatim* and to comment upon them briefly.

Firstly, the operation of a money market requires a group of institutions, financial and quasi-financial, which hold assets of graded liquidity
which they may wish to switch and interchange according to their own
criteria of reserve stability and income-earning potential. These institutions will consist predominantly of banks and financial houses but the
central bank will also wish, for a variety of reasons, to operate in the
market. Only in main national financial centres are such institutional
groupings to be found and only there are money markets likely to be
developed. In banking systems which are highly centralised such as the
British, where the central bank, the head offices of great banking chains
and the head offices of other financial institutions such as insurance
companies, trust companies and merchant banks co-exist in a single city,
the conditions are favourable. In less centralised systems such as the American where the central bank is a twelve-headed hydra and where unitary
rather than branch banking is the order of the day, money markets
develop less readily and are dispersed, smaller and of less significance.

Secondly, there must exist among the institutions forming the market

---

[1] This over-liquidity of the banking system has placed severe limitations on British
monetary control during several periods since World War II. With the renewed use
of monetary policy in 1951 the Treasury had to mop up excess liquidity in the banking
system by a funding operation before central bank control could be made effective.

a desire to switch their assets and redistribute them frequently in accordance both with changes in the supply of cash and changes in the public's desire to hold cash—in particular a desire to avoid the holding of idle balances.

Thirdly, in order that there should be in the market an active and continuing demand for liquid funds there must exist a considerable group of institutions dealing in particular assets of known quality and tenor. The presence of such a group is not a *sine qua non* of the market but without it the market must necessarily be smaller and limited in scope. This is so because any such group deriving as it does its profits from a large turnover in the assets traded will seek to expand the use of such assets in order to maintain turnover.

Fourthly, the number of operators in the market must be sufficient to ensure an effective market and also ensure at any time the liquidity of asset holders.

Fifthly, there must exist within the market a suitably spaced series of interest rates for money or near-money among which there is one key interest rate which the central bank controls and can make effective.

Finally, there must be some way in which the assets dealt in are vetted and classified.

These six conditions where they exist do not in themselves ensure the development of a money market on the London pattern. Money markets exist in many countries of the world, e.g. the U.S.A., Canada and Australia, which fulfil these conditions, but they are either more limited in scope or less interesting in their functions in the chain of monetary policy than that in London. Other conditions apart from those cited above may cause a money market to assume a greater importance than would these six conditions alone. For example, in the case of London, it is undoubtedly a fact that for a century two and latterly three other features have expanded the money market to its unique size and importance: the position of London as an international centre, the great growth of the Treasury bill as a vehicle of State borrowing and thus as an asset in which to deal, and since 1960 the growth of the market in short-term loans to the local authorities and the establishment of the inter-bank loan market. These have increased enormously the scope, importance, and ramifications of the London money market.

It is hoped that what has been said in this chapter will enable the reader to form a general picture of the centralised banking system within which, in Great Britain, the discount market functions. It is, he will have gathered, in its relations to other sections of the banking system that the discount market has its main importance. Much time will be spent in this book in examining these relations, their evolution, and their present and potential significance. It remains now to give an introductory account of the discount market itself and of its internal activities. In subsequent chapters this will of course be refined and embellished and we shall become engrossed in the market's minutiae and the nuances of its activities. It would be all too easy however to write about the discount market and become preoccupied with its subtleties while omitting an account of the market as it now is. To avoid that omission and to ensure that the reader carries into the historical chapters which follow some knowledge of the end-product of that history we proceed in the next chapter to that general account.

Chapter 4

THE DAY-TO-DAY WORKING
OF THE DISCOUNT MARKET

'Who has not seen the outward manifestation of the discount
market at work . . . a noble body of gentlemen who, armed only
with umbrellas and wearing the protective clothing of their
profession (a topper and stout shoes) daily brave the vagaries of
English weather, the hazards of the City traffic and the terrors of
the banking parlours.'

C. W. Linton

I

LOMBARD STREET, long taken as symbolic of London bill business, is, by
London standards, a quiet street, too narrow for heavy traffic or public
transport. It has changed a good deal since Bagehot's time and in fact
only two discount houses[1] now have their offices there, much of the
street being taken up by merchant and overseas banks and by new office
buildings. But for pedestrians it is a main artery and a short cut from
the banks clustering around Threadneedle Street and Lothbury to the
merchanting area in the streets around the Monument, London Bridge
and the river. There is something symbolic in this, for, if Lombard
Street symbolises the discount market, this is the way in which discount
house directors like to see themselves—as connecting finance and the
City with trade, commodities and the ends of the earth. It is not quite like
that now but it is a pleasant illusion to live by.

There are twelve discount houses operating in London (cf. Table VI)
and forming the most important group in the short-term money market,
which they share with the Bank of England, the clearing banks, the foreign
and overseas banks and the Accepting Houses. The market itself has no single
physical location or daily meeting place but its participants are all situated
within the compact area of the City of London and maintain constant
contact either directly or by telephone.

The firms are, by financial standards, small. The organisation is unitary:
they do not have branches. Apart from the twelve discount houses there
is a handful of small firms who share with them the market in Treasury

[1] Alexander's and Cater Ryder & Company.

bills, short bonds and call money. These are not discount houses in the sense in which we shall use this term but are specialists in other fields. Some are intermediaries between stock jobbers and the banks; some are foreign exchange and bullion dealers. Their interest in the discount market is marginal; they do not have last resort facilities at the Bank of England

TABLE VI

LONDON DISCOUNT HOUSES, JUNE 1966

	Year of Foundation*	Capital Authorised	Capital Issued	Dividend 1965‡
		£m.		%
Alexanders	1891	3·5	3·2	5·4
Allen Harvey Ross	1946	1·75	1·55	15·0
Cater Ryder	1960†	5·5	4·985	13·0
Clive Discount	1959	2·0	1·82	12·0
Gerrard & Reid	1962	1·175	1·175	17·85
Gillett Bros.	1946	2·5	1·75	15·0
Jessel Toynbee	1943	2·0	1·5	12·5
National Discount	1856	5·0	4·470	5·9
Smith St. Aubyn	1943	2·0	1·62	30·0
Union Discount Co.	1885	10·0	7·5	12·5
King & Shaxson	1946	2·3	1·9	12·5
Seccombe Marshall & Campion	1956	·8	·8	15

* In all cases this is the year in which the discount house became a public company. For the majority this was during the consolidation period in the 1940's or later.

† A merger in that year of Cater Brightwen and Company Ltd. and Ryders Discount Company Ltd.

‡ In almost all cases this is the percentage on the ordinary shares less tax.

TABLE VII

ASSETS AND BORROWED FUNDS OF DISCOUNT HOUSES
31st DECEMBER 1966

Borrowed Funds*	£m.	Assets	£m.
London Clearing Banks	978	British government stocks	542
Scottish Banks	94	British Treasury bills	424
Other domestic banks	11	Other bills	404
Accepting Houses and Overseas Banks	201	Other	195
Other Sources	119		
Bank of England	82		
Total	1,485	Total	1,565

* Excludes capital and reserves.

Source: Adapted from Table 7, Bank of England Quarterly Bulletin.

nor are they involved in the joint Treasury bill tender although they may join the outside tender for bills and thus form part of the outside bid. They are, in the main, small firms operating in highly specialised fields that are too small for larger institutions and groups.

Within the discount market the twelve discount houses act as dealers in short liquid assets—Treasury bills, commercial bills, and short-dated government bonds—using for the purpose money borrowed from the clearing banks and the merchant and overseas banks, together with their own capital resources. They acquire these assets at an early stage of their short lives and resell the bulk of them at a later stage to other groups in the market—usually the clearing banks—at a profit. One may, therefore, say that two of the discount houses' leading functions are: making a market and helping to establish prices for these assets; and holding them during periods when they are least liquid and least attractive to other financial institutions. Table VII sets out the sources of borrowed funds and the main assets dealt in during 1966.

TABLE VIII
RECENT DIVIDEND RECORD OF LEADING DISCOUNT COMPANIES

	1953	1954	1955	1956	1957	1958	1959
Alexanders	20	16¼	7½	7½	5	7½	10
National*	10	10	10	10	10	10	10
Union	10	12½	12½	12½	12½	12½	12½

	1960	1961	1962	1963	1964	1965
Alexanders	10	10	12½	12½	12½	12½
National*	10	10	10	10	10	10
Union	12½	12½	12½	12½	12½	12½

* National has A and B stock. Dividends during the period were constant on the A stock. Those on the B stock were slightly higher, 12½ being a modal rate.

Because the period for which the discount houses lend (on average 2–3 months) is longer than the period for which they borrow (day-to-day) and because their borrowing rates are subject to sudden and frequent variation their profits are variable. This practice of lending short funds which are borrowed even 'shorter' necessitates a strong capital position and the Bank of England keeps a 'motherly' eye on their capital structure both in its rôle as lender of last resort and as part of the general surveillance of the market which it regards as its prerogative.

The profits of the discount houses come from two sources: first, the

F

margin between the rate of interest which they pay to the clearing banks and others for their operating money and the rates at which they themselves lend on bills and short-term government bonds; and second, jobbing profits on the assets themselves. Since both these margins are small it is the very large turnover of the assets that enables the houses to earn their living. For example, it is normal for the market to sell Treasury bills to the clearing banks at a profit of $\frac{1}{16}$ per cent per annum, i.e., $\frac{1}{64}$ per cent on a 91 day bill or $3\frac{3}{4}$d. per cent. The jobbing profits on short bonds may be only $\frac{1}{64}$ or $\frac{1}{32}$ per cent. These are fine margins. So far as turnover is concerned it is thought that the average turnover in money is about £250m. a day for the market and, in bills alone, about £70 to £80m. a day. Bonds are more erratic and might vary from zero to £60m. a day.[1]

The discount houses as they exist today constitute a group which is the result of nearly two centuries' development. There has, however, been little continuity among the firms themselves. The oldest of these dates from the third quarter of the nineteenth century, a period when the modern discount houses began to appear after the Overend, Gurney crisis of 1866. Three of the new firms were public companies from the start but mostly they were partnerships or private companies. Amalgamations and retirements during the thirties and the Second World War winnowed the field to twelve—now all public companies. Among these, however, there is great disparity of size (the three original public companies, Alexanders, the Union and the National, are much larger than the rest) and some specialisation in the type of bill business carried on. The organisation of the houses is simple and for the volume of business handled staffs are small. Radcliffe, in 1959, estimated the total employees of the houses at 400.

The interests of the discount houses as a group are guarded by the London Discount Market Association to which all of the twelve firms belong. This Association has a chairman and a deputy chairman, one of whom, by tradition, is drawn from one of the three large companies. The most important task of these functionaries is to meet the Governor of the Bank of England on Thursday afternoons to discuss matters of common interest, in particular, to hear his views on the coming Treasury bill tender. The full Association meets on Fridays when it hears a report of the meeting with the Governor and fixes the offer price for the current tender. The Association has no separate offices, using the Union Discount Company's office as its meeting place. The secretarial work of the associa-

[1] No published figures are available. These figures were given by H. F. Goodson in his lecture: *Functioning of the London Discount Houses*. Institute of Bankers, London, 1962.

tion is done by a few of the staff of one of the discount houses, as an addition to their own work.

The original purpose of the houses was to trade in commercial bills of exchange, discounting them for commercial clients, grading them as to quality and tenor and reselling them in parcels to the clearing banks who held them as liquid assets to maturity.[1] This service still remains a part of their activities and large numbers of bills from a wide variety of trades are discounted across the counter each day. Such bills are acceptable to the clearing banks since they carry the discount houses' endorsement which, with the name of a good acceptor, makes them eligible bills and because parcels[2] of bills can be supplied by the houses with graded maturities to satisfy the banks' bill portfolios. Typically there are £300m. to £400m. of such bills circulating at any given time in the London market. In this activity the discount houses have great expertise and in their absence 'some kind of market machinery would be required to bring together those who had commercial bills to sell and those who wished to invest in them, if London were to continue to play its traditional rôle in the finance of commerce both in this country and overseas.'[3] The discount houses' importance in the commercial bill market is shared by the Accepting Houses, a group of seventeen within the much larger group of merchant banks—the list including some of the most distinguished names in the world of finance. These grant acceptance credits to approved clients on whose behalf they accept bills of exchange in return for a commission and reimbursement when the bill falls due for payment. Since the purpose of this practice is to give to the bill which is so accepted an unimpeachable quality by the name of the acceptor, thus facilitating its rediscount, Accepting Houses must maintain a very high degree of liquidity and financial probity. This is the more necessary in that the Bank of England gives special privileges on rediscount to bills bearing the name of an Accepting House and so takes a shrewd interest in the financial stability of the houses. Although most of the leading Accepting Houses are private companies and so do not require to publish balance sheets, they submit their financial position to the Bank of England each year and advise the Bank of any major projects into which they enter. Their financial viability is a matter of keen interest to the Bank.

Although the discount houses give, at first sight, an appearance of conservatism and of association with the establishment, they have throughout the last thirty years displayed adaptability and readiness for

[1] Banks do not rediscount bills.

[2] A 'parcel' of bills is usually a sheaf of bills, perhaps a mere dozen, perhaps many, held together by a paper clip.

[3] Cf. Radcliffe. Minutes of Evidence, Vol. i, p. 11.

change. To this they owe their survival. Like the merchant banks they have a keen nose for business and, although there have been times when some of the houses have needed support to carry on, their acceptance of changing conditions has enabled them to exploit, rather than suffer from, changes in the financial scene. Their adaptation from commercial bill operators to Treasury bill dealers, their skilful yet guarded move into the short bond market, their quick response to the return of the domestic bill in the sixties and their interest, as this is being written, in new fields bordering on foreign exchange[1]—all these show a capacity for survival which is a phenomenon in itself. In part their survival through difficult years has been the result, however, of the aid and influence of the Bank of England, which seems to have decided at some time in the thirties that they were an important integral part of the monetary system and were not to perish.

II

Although the discount market is traditionally associated with commercial bill business, with the Accepting Houses, and with all the pomp and panoply of the 'bill on London' and the rôle of sterling as an international currency, this belongs largely to history. Commercial bill business, particularly with overseas, has, since the thirties, formed a secondary and fluctuating yet important part of the activities of the discount houses. Recently the volume of commercial bills has increased and in 1967 account for about 25 per cent of the assets dealt in.[2] The largest group (nearly 50 per cent in mid-1967) of assets traded by the discount houses now consists of short bonds. The dealings of the discount houses in the short bond market are of later date than its bill business. Such dealings began in earnest in the thirties and since then have been pursued with varying intensity and success. Finally, Treasury bills, which were for so long the discount market's staple, have shrunk (1967) to the lowest level since 1950, accounting for less than a fifth of total assets. Although the market's dealings in these three assets[3] will form recurring themes in this

[1] Such interest is being shown by discount houses acquiring interests in firms operating in other fields. For example, in 1965 Clive Discount Company Ltd. acquired a controlling interest in Guy Butler & Company Ltd., brokers in the inter-bank loan market and the local authority loan market. In 1966 Gerrard & Reid acquired interests in Long, Till & Colvin Ltd., and later in P. Murray-Jones Ltd., both brokers in the local authority market. In February 1967 Cater Ryder & Company Ltd. acquired interests in a firm of foreign exchange brokers, M. W. Marshall & Company.

[2] In 1965 commercial bills were 23·3 per cent of total discount market assets.

[3] There is some dealing, particularly since 1963, in other assets: in local authority bonds, in the Euro-dollar market and in 3 months local authority bills. Such dealings are small and not done by all the houses.

book we must here deal briefly with the day-to-day activities in connection with each of them.

The bills dealt in by the London discount houses have already been described in Chapter 2. It is unnecessary in this context to do more than recall them to mind. Overseas bills are deeply entrenched in the overseas trade in primary commodities. Inland trade bills remain only in a vestigial sense, lingering on in a few trades connected with importing. The new bill business of recent years (since about 1960) has been of another order but is a late reflowering of the inland bill, now appearing as a finance bill, a vehicle of short-term credit in competition with the bank advance and bringing the houses into contact with sectors of industry and trade whose business is new to them.[1]

In their task of discounting commercial bills the discount houses have two main considerations. First, and to the whole group, there is the question of the total amount of the bills which the market can absorb in the light of both available funds and the amount of bills which it can resell to the banks. Second, and for each individual house, is the sifting and vetting of bills offered and their discount at rates reflecting their credit-worthiness. So far as the first of these considerations is concerned the ability of the houses as a group to absorb bills depends upon two things: the price and volume of call money available and the extent to which banks will buy bills for their portfolios. Any check coming from these sources will result in discount houses looking critically at the size of their bill portfolios and, if necessary, advancing their discount rates to reduce the flow of offered bills. All this must also be done in the light of other assets to be dealt in with the funds available, namely, the current offering of Treasury bills by the government and the discount houses' obligation to cover the Treasury bill tender. Discount houses do not ever wish to refuse eligible bills for discount. The loss of goodwill involved may jeopardise future business, while any action which reduces turnover thereby reduces profits in a none too profitable business.

So far as the discounting of commercial bills is concerned such bills must be divided into two groups: bank bills and trade bills. The former, as acceptances of clearing banks, overseas banks or acceptance houses, carry little risk and are therefore discounted, according to tenor, at lower rates than trade bills. They are, moreover, welcomed by the clearing banks in parcels from the houses to swell their bill portfolios as liquid assets. As can be seen from Table IX a gap of $1\frac{1}{16}$ to $1\frac{1}{2}$ existed in August 1966 in favour of trade bills. This gap, together with a brisk turnover,

---

[1] The big growth in accommodation bills has, in great part, been in the bills of large public companies having capital in the £10–£100m. bracket. Contact between industry (as distinct from trade) and the discount houses is new.

TABLE IX

MONEY MARKET RATES—SOME EXAMPLES

	October 1945	9th November 1951	23rd October 1953	30th November 1957	6th August 1960	31st August 1966	1st December 1967
							Per cent
Bank of England rates:							
Bank Rate*	2	$2\frac{1}{2}$	$3\frac{1}{2}$	7	6	7	8
Treasury bill rates:							
Tender rate	10s. 1·6d.	17s. 3d.	£2 2s. 0d.	£6 9s. 2d.	£5 10s. 11d.	£6 14s. 6d.	£7 11s. 4d.
Discount houses' rates:							
Bank bills†—3 months	$\frac{17}{32}$	$1\frac{1}{8}$	$2\frac{3}{16}$	$6\frac{5}{8}$-$6\frac{3}{4}$	$5\frac{23}{32}$-$5\frac{25}{32}$	$6\frac{15}{16}$-7	$7\frac{3}{16}$-$7\frac{7}{16}$
" —4 months	$\frac{9}{16}$	$1\frac{5}{8}$	$2\frac{1}{4}$-$2\frac{5}{16}$	$6\frac{5}{8}$-$6\frac{3}{4}$	$5\frac{23}{32}$-$5\frac{25}{32}$	7-$7\frac{1}{16}$	$7\frac{3}{16}$-$7\frac{7}{16}$
" —6 months	$\frac{9}{16}$ $\frac{5}{8}$	$1\frac{1}{4}$	$2\frac{3}{8}$-$2\frac{1}{2}$	$6\frac{11}{16}$-$6\frac{7}{8}$	$5\frac{23}{32}$-$5\frac{27}{32}$	$7\frac{1}{16}$-$7\frac{7}{8}$	$7\frac{3}{16}$-$7\frac{7}{8}$
Trade bills—3 months	1-$1\frac{1}{8}$	$2\frac{1}{4}$-3	$3\frac{1}{8}$-$4\frac{1}{2}$	$7\frac{1}{2}$-8	$6\frac{1}{2}$-7	8-$8\frac{1}{2}$	9-$9\frac{1}{2}$
" —4 months	$1\frac{1}{4}$-$1\frac{1}{2}$	$2\frac{1}{2}$-3	$3\frac{3}{4}$-$4\frac{1}{2}$	$7\frac{1}{2}$-8	$6\frac{1}{2}$-7	8-$8\frac{1}{2}$	9-$9\frac{3}{4}$
" —6 months	$1\frac{1}{2}$-$2\frac{1}{2}$	3-4	4-$4\frac{1}{2}$	8-9	$6\frac{3}{4}$-$7\frac{1}{4}$	$8\frac{1}{4}$-9	$9\frac{1}{4}$-10
Clearing banks' lending rates to market (call money):							
Against bank bills	$\frac{1}{2}$	$1\frac{1}{4}$	2	5-$6\frac{1}{4}$‡	$4\frac{1}{2}$-$5\frac{1}{4}$	$6\frac{3}{8}$-$6\frac{3}{4}$	$6\frac{1}{4}$
" Treasury bills	$\frac{1}{2}$	$\frac{3}{4}$	$1\frac{3}{4}$				
" bonds	$\frac{3}{4}$	$1\frac{1}{8}$	$2\frac{7}{8}$				

* Apart from a brief period of two months at the outbreak of war in 1939, the Bank Rate remained unchanged at 2 per cent for the whole period between 30th June 1932 and 7th November 1951. On 8th November 1951 it was raised to $2\frac{1}{2}$ per cent. Since then, it has been altered on numerous occasions in accordance with changes in the level of economic activity. The highest level it has reached is 8 per cent from 18th November 1967 to the date of going to press; and the lowest 3 per cent from 13th May 1954 to 27th January 1955.

† i.e., bills bearing the acceptance of United Kingdom banks (mainly accepting houses).

‡ In January 1955 the clearing banks agreed in future to charge the same rate for money lent against any security (bills or bonds).

brought a good dealing profit on such bills at that time. Small trade bills are perhaps the most expensive asset in which the houses can deal since checking the credit-worthiness of a multitude of small traders is a costly business.[1] For this reason only a few of the larger houses deal with small trade bills in any quantity. Large trade bills, of which there has been a considerable growth in recent years, are much less difficult to assess, the standing of the parties being more widely known. Mostly, they are accepted by accredited acceptors for commission and thus rank as bank bills.

The buying rates of the houses for commercial bills fall into two brackets: the spread for bank bills ($7\frac{3}{4}$–$7\frac{13}{16}$ for the latest date in Table IX) and the spread for trade bills (9–$9\frac{1}{2}$ in Table IX), each of these spreads rising as the tenor of the bill lengthens. The rates for bank bills vary narrowly—from the finest rate applicable to bills accepted by first-class banks and acceptance houses, to slightly higher rates for acceptances of London offices of overseas banks where some slight risk of a political nature is involved. The range of rates for trade bills is wider, for the inherent risk on such bills is greater. Indeed, every trade bill is assessed for discount on its individual merits and the published rates are only an approximate indication of charges.

A major consideration to a discount house in its bill buying is the later acceptability of the bill, either as collateral for call money or for resale. The Bank of England's criterion of acceptability, that the bill should bear two good British names, one of them the acceptor's, must be applied widely by a discount house, for the house must have bills to offer as collateral for loans should the market be forced into the Bank. The wishes and criteria of the clearing banks must also be respected. The Bank of England, by its policy of testing, through its agents, the quality of the bills in the market, does much to maintain the quality of such bills. In the last two or three years the Bank has relaxed its eligibility rules somewhat and has been prepared to accept good trade bills as collateral for loans to discount houses. This in turn has made clearing banks more ready to buy eligible trade bills from the houses. It might appear from this gesture by the Bank that its view of the new growth of the trade bill goes beyond mere tolerance and extends to a genuine desire for resuscitation.

The Treasury bill, until recently the staple bill diet of the market, is a British government promissory note.[2] Its history and use has already

---

[1] The total value of such bills in the market may not be large but, since individual bills are often for small amounts, the number of bills is large.

[2] An article in the Quarterly Bulletin of the Bank of England (Vol. 4, No. 3) describes the Treasury Bill as 'a bearer security of great simplicity'. In law a Treasury bill is neither

been described and we shall include in this chapter only such aspects of it as are appropriate for the present purpose. These bills are issued as required by the Treasury to finance such part of the overall cash deficit of the Exchequer as cannot be financed by long-term borrowing or other means. They are issued weekly, partly by 'tender' and partly 'through the tap', the tap issue being available only to government departments with surplus funds to invest and to overseas monetary authorities. The tap issue is at a rate of discount fixed by the Treasury. It has no further relevance to this discussion.[1]

The tender issue is made each week to banks, discount houses and brokers, but through these anyone wishing to tender may apply.[2] Application for the tender is made by those wishing to take up bills. These offer a price to be paid for the bill at issue for every £100 to be repaid by the Treasury thirteen weeks hence. Thus an overseas bank tendering for an amount of bills at £98 18s. od. is in effect offering to lend to the Treasury, up to the amount for which it tenders, at £4 8s. od. per cent per annum. If its tender were accepted at this rate for a £100,000 bill it would pay into the Bank of England on acceptance of its offer the sum of £98,900. Thirteen weeks later it would receive £100,000 from the Treasury on surrender of the bill.

On the government side the amount of the weekly tender issue is determined by the continual variations in government receipts and expenditure. The usual amount is £100–£300m. per week but this is subject to a seasonal variation which reflects the ebb and flow of the Exchequer year.[3] During the buoyant spending period from April to December there is a tendency for borrowing each week to exceed maturities; during the period January to March when revenue reaches its maximum, bills may be allowed by the Treasury to run off allowing maturities to exceed new issues. This seasonal pattern may, however, be upset at any time by bond maturities or extraordinary government

a bill of exchange nor a promissory note. Because it is a charge on a particular fund—the Consolidated Fund of the United Kingdom—it is not an *unconditional* order, or promise, to pay, in the terms of the Bills of Exchange Act. However, in general rather than legalistic terms it is describable as a promissory note.

[1] It may, however, be of interest to note typical orders of magnitude in the distribution of outstanding Treasury bills. At 31st March 1964, total Treasury bills outstanding were £4,418m. Of this £1,823m. was in the hands of government departments (Bank of England, Exchange Equalisation Account, National Debt Commissioners) leaving £2,595m. in the hands of the market.

[2] The minimum tender is £50,000. Bills are in large units, i.e., £5,000, £10,000, £25,000, £50,000 and £100,000. This limits Treasury bill holding to large institutional operators.

[3] Which runs 6th April 1963 to 5th April 1964.

expenditure. From 1955 to 1962 it was the practice to issue nine-week bills during the months of November and December. These would fall due for repayment in the heavy revenue season (January to end of February) and thus induce larger Treasury bill issues in those months, in this way evening out the flow of issues over the year. Since 1963 this tactic has not been adopted, partly because large Exchequer payments have been rephased and partly because 63-day bills were not popular in the market and proved to be an expensive form of borrowing.

The part played by the discount houses in the weekly tender is important and they are one of the leading groups in a procedure which is now highly formalised and 'the subject of close understanding between the banks, the discount houses and the authorities.'[1] Once the amount of bills on offer is announced tenders are made by several distinct groups. The discount houses tender together as a syndicate, their tender price being based on their expectation of market conditions, in particular on their expectation of the rates of interest at which they must themselves borrow money (that is the banks' call rate and bank rate) during the next three months. One other factor conditions their offer: the fact that they agree to take up as much of the total issue as is allotted to them by the Treasury, up to the limit of covering the whole tender.

Second, among the tender applicants for Treasury bills may be the overseas banks, tendering for themselves or on behalf of clients who, holding sterling, look for a highly liquid interest-earning asset. Finally, a number of industrial, commercial or financial concerns, with balances which they may wish to hold in liquid form, may tender through the clearing banks.[2] Allocation of the bills to be issued is made according to the tender prices. In order to get bills the outside tender prices must be as high as or higher (i.e., the rate of interest lower) than that of the discount house syndicate. When they are at a price that is favourable to the Treasury the outside tenders are accepted in full and the syndicate gets the rest, their rate being somewhat higher. The allotment as between the individual discount houses which form the syndicate is proportionate to their share of the original tender. Finally, the Treasury announce the *average* price at which the bills have been allotted and the division of the tender between the syndicate and outside borrowers. It should not be imagined that the discount houses almost monopolise the weekly tender with a few peripherals taking the residue. In fact the competition at the

---

[1] Cf. R. S. Sayers, *Modern Banking*, 6th edition, p. 56.

[2] Companies often wish to hold Treasury bills in order to obtain an income on their temporary cash surpluses, e.g., on funds set aside for payment of taxes—a considerable aggregate in the United Kingdom where firms pay income tax on profits nine months after the profits are earned.

tender is often severe and it is not unusual for the syndicate to 'miss the tender', that is, to be allocated only a small proportion of the total bills offered. Nevertheless, the position of the discount houses in the tender is dominant. Their undertaking, if necessary, to cover the tender means for the government that they can always rely on their weekly needs for Treasury bill borrowing being satisfied. Moreover, the rate at which the market tenders normally becomes the guide for Treasury bill rates until the next tender.

Conspicuous in their absence from this account of the tender have been the clearing banks. As the largest holders of Treasury bills it might have been expected that they would obtain these directly through the tender, especially as Treasury bills, unlike trade bills, do not require vetting or grading and there is no advantage to the clearing banks in buying them through the discount houses. The absence of the clearing banks from the tender (save when they tender on behalf of customers) is the result of an agreement made with the discount houses in 1934. The clearing banks then agreed not to tender for bills but to buy them from the discount market after they have been a week in currency. This agreement ensured for the discount houses a main share in the Treasury bill market without which they would almost certainly have failed in the difficult conditions of the thirties. Cheap money and contraction of the volume of commercial bills made them dependent on Treasury bill business for long periods before, during and after World War II.

One feature of the Treasury bill issue in recent years has been its declining size. In mid-1967 the total of market Treasury bills was at its lowest level since 1952. (Cf. Chart I.) Two factors account for this: the behaviour of holders of government debt—the clearing banks, discount houses, overseas banks and others; and Exchequer requirements. In 1962 and 1963 there was a marked fall in the need of the Exchequer for Treasury bill finance and this, together with other and more remunerative outlets for the funds of lending institutions, produced the decline shown in the figures. How far this decline is a temporary phenomenon and how far it marks a permanent decline in the Treasury bill issue, it is much too early to say.

The largest asset now held by the discount houses is that of short-term bonds. Although these have been dealt in by the houses since World War I the volume of dealing in the twenties was small and they became a recognised discount market asset only in 1934–35. During the depression (1929–34) the amount of commercial bills outstanding at any time had fallen to about £100m. while the profit margin on Treasury bills had dwindled and indeed was sometimes negative. It was then that the market was driven for survival to operate extensively in short-term bonds. When, in 1934, the clearing banks agreed to accept bonds as security for call loans they became a recognised and approved asset in which the houses might deal. In the years which followed, short bonds came to be a staple for the houses. During World War II and in the years immediately following, the houses played an important rôle in providing a market for the great volume of short bonds resulting from war finance, supplementing the market provided by Stock Exchange jobbers which was proving inadequate for the greater volume of bonds. From 1951 to the end of 1957 the

TABLE X

CHANGES IN THE SIZE AND DISTRIBUTION OF TREASURY BILL HOLDINGS, 1961–66

	at 31st March				
Holder	1961	1962	1963	1964	1966
			£m.		
Discount houses	365	371	366	363	400
Domestic banks*	808	812	675	678	671
Accepting houses and overseas banks†	102	92	83	108	80
Overseas central monetary institutions and international organisations†	1,048	988	1,061	1,086	964
Other identified overseas holdings }	656	496	66	50	31
Other holders			334	310	165
Total	2,979	2,759	2,585	2,595	2,311

* London clearing, Scottish and Northern Irish banks.
† The coverage of this category is not uniform throughout the table.

Source: Bank of England Quarterly Bulletin, September 1964 and November 1967.

amount of short bonds handled shrank but from 1958 to the present it has expanded rapidly and remains an important although variable source of revenue to the houses.

Such bonds are of two main types: true short bonds, issued originally as one, two or five year Exchequer bonds; and bonds, originally of longer terms but now come to the last years of their currency. Most of the market's bond holdings are in British government short-dated stocks; but there is a small business in short-dated dominion, colonial and British corporation issues.

Short bonds (particularly if they stand at a premium) are not attractive to the public as new purchases and holders might find them unsaleable. The discount houses offer attractive prices for such of these bonds as come on the market (e.g. through the processes of death, bankruptcy, etc.) and hold them as assets which, if not as liquid as bills, at least are fairly liquid and yield a positive return over the call money by which they are financed. There is, however, a certain element of risk in this asset which does not arise with bills. If the discount houses were forced to sell their bonds in a period of rising interest rates (i.e., falling bond prices) their capital loss might well exceed the gain they had had from interest. If, of course, they could hold them to maturity this would not arise since they would be redeemed at par but at the least a writing down of book values of assets is involved. Moreover, since bonds are lodged with banks as collateral for call loans a fall in book values involves the lodging of additional collateral. This risk element, endemic in bond dealings, was at first frowned upon by the authorities in the thirties but came to be tolerated when it was realised that bond dealing was a necessity to the discount houses if they were to survive but that, moreover, the participation of the discount houses in the short bond market greatly facilitated national debt operations. The Bank of England remained uneasy, however, and felt that only if the capital structure of the market could be strengthened would it be possible for dealing in short bonds to be pursued without risk.[1] For this reason the first stage of a process of amalgamation took place during the later thirties (the second was during World War II) by which a number of the smaller houses merged and there was a general move to increase capital. Bond dealings came to be regarded as a legitimate discount market activity and the Bank of England agreed to accept bonds as collateral when acting as lender of last resort. Qualitative tests remain, however, as a pre-requisite of official approval to a discount house's bond operations. These relate to the total amount of bonds held and to the constitution of the portfolio. This must be weighted at the short end and no bond with a life exceeding five years should be held against borrowed money. Any discount house will normally have about half of its portfolio of bonds of less than two years' maturity, with the rest spread according to the availability of various maturities.

The experience of the houses in their bond dealing has been variable. Between 1946 and 1951, a period of cheap money, good profits were derived from bond business and contributed to the growth and strengthening of the market, but in the period of dearer money in the fifties, when bond prices fell, the high gearing of bond holdings to capital resources produced a situation of strain and anxiety. After 1955 the depression in the gilt-edged market caused bond prices to fall by as much as 10 per

[1] The Bank regarded as desirable a situation in which discount houses should have capital resources of at least £500,000. This figure was later revised to £1m.

cent. For example, Exchequer 3 per cent 1960, stood at 103¼ in January 1955; by September it had fallen to 93. Although losses in capital values are book losses and are not incurred unless the bonds are sold they have two immediate effects: firstly, the ratio of bonds held to published resources, which is the house's yardstick limiting its bond dealing, is lowered;[1] and secondly when bond prices fall the house must immediately provide, out of its own reserves, additional margin on its call money to compensate for the fall in the bond prices of the bonds lodged with the lenders as collateral.[2] It is not difficult to see how easily a discount house with a large bond portfolio might be forced into bankruptcy by a sudden fall in bond prices stemming from a rise in interest rates. This risk element places a very definite limit to the amount of stock which houses, and the market in aggregate, can absorb. Moreover, when interest rates rise, as in 1957, 1961, and 1965, the yield on bond holdings may be less for the houses than the rates for which they borrow at call, involving them in a running loss. They may at such times be faced with the choice of accepting the running loss or of selling the bonds at a heavy realised capital loss. All in all bond dealings and the management of the bond portfolio is a perilous business for the houses, requiring skill, foresight and coolness.

The monetary authorities on their side derive considerable advantage from the participation of the discount houses in the short bond market. Briefly the advantages are threefold. The first is that the houses do provide a market for short bonds which might otherwise prove unsaleable, assisting the gilt-edged jobbers of the stock exchange by handling business which they do not want and which, in certain periods, they have been inadequate to handle. The second is that by providing such a market and thus ensuring liquidity for investors, the government may, if it is on public finance grounds appropriate, borrow short when it wishes to do so thus getting the benefit of lower rates of interest and reducing national debt servicing charges. Thirdly, if the discount houses ceased to operate in the short bond market the Bank of England would itself, as administrator of the national debt, have to operate, taking up short bonds when others were shy of them and unloading when there was a demand for them.

In early 1964 local authorities began the practice of issuing short-term bonds and by the end of 1967 over £200m. of these were outstanding. The discount houses have helped to make a market for such bonds, either by taking them on their issue as placements or by buying them from

[1] If a house holds £100m. in bonds against £10m. in published resources, a bond ratio of 10, then a fall of 10 per cent in the bonds' value due to depreciation will wipe out all resources. This loss is of course a paper loss incurred only on sale of the bonds.
[2] For a description of the arrangements governing collateral for money borrowed against bonds, see p. 95 below.

other financial institutions. Such bonds are not eligible as collateral for advances from the Bank of England.

III

The time has come to look a little more closely at the sources of the funds with which the discount houses carry on their activities. These sources we have been content to describe up to now as 'call loans' from the banks. In fact the discount houses borrow from more than a hundred lenders, including the English clearing banks, the Scottish banks, a large number of foreign and colonial banks and the merchant banks. Of these the London clearing banks and the overseas banks are the most important, providing about 66 per cent and 13 per cent of the total funds respectively at the end of 1966. (Cf. Table VII.)[1] Latterly and for reasons which will be explained the overseas banks have dwindled in relative importance as lenders to the discount market.

The borrowing of call money is on a day-to-day basis and is renegotiated each morning. It is traditional for members of the discount houses to visit each morning the institutions from which they borrow. Later business, including the negotiation of 'night money', is transacted by telephone. For the morning visits a discount house will divide the circuit of its lending institutions into a number of rounds. Since there are about 140 lending banks to be visited and since each bank visited involves a period of waiting, plus an interview which, we are told, is chatty and unhurried as befits business done between gentlemen, the daily round is something of an imposition. The discount houses argue, however, that the personal relations engendered are worth the trouble. One typical large discount house divides the morning calls into six 'rounds' of approximately 20–25 banks each, the 'roundsmen' being reshuffled every 14 days.

For money borrowed short-term the discount houses pay a variety of interest rates (cf. Table IX). Close scrutiny of these shows, however, that all are related to bank rate and vary with it although in some cases the

[1] It is interesting to compare the shares of these sources of lending in December 1965 with those quoted for 31st December 1958 in the Radcliffe Report when the clearing banks provided about half of the borrowed funds and the overseas banks about a quarter. By December 1965 the share of the clearing banks had risen to 61 per cent, while the shares of the overseas banks and accepting houses had fallen to 13 per cent and 5 per cent respectively. In December 1958 they accounted together for 25 per cent. This fall in lending to the discount houses by the overseas banks and accepting houses is explained by the very great increase in their call loans to local authorities over the same period and by their participation in the inter-bank loan market, cf. p. 100 below. The clearing banks appear to have made this shortfall good to the discount houses.

connection is tenuous. Bank rate determines the deposit rate[1] of the clearing banks, which, since February 1955, has been 2 per cent below bank rate. Since the clearing banks must obviously lend at some rate higher than that which they pay on their own deposits, their rate for short loans to the discount market is usually $\frac{3}{8}$ per cent above deposit rate. This is their so-called 'basic rate'. 'Good money' lent at the basic rate seems to account for around 40 per cent of the total. Such money is left with the houses semi-permanently and called only in an emergency. 'Privilege money', which is the small traditional amount to which the houses are entitled from the clearing banks at the close of daily business in order to balance books, is given at $\frac{1}{2}$ per cent over the banks' rate for basic money.[2] 'Night money', that is money granted late in the day to the houses for the nightly balance[3] is lent at rates varying with market conditions and may rise quite steeply when the market is short of funds. In effect then, the discount houses' borrowing consists of 'regular' money which is the core of their borrowing and this (with the thin cushion of 'privilege money') is augmented by variable daily borrowings at higher and varying rates. All borrowing is secured by bills or bonds lodged daily with the lending institutions.[4] From the clearing banks' side the amounts lent to the houses are also decided daily. In the head offices of the banks an estimate is made each morning on the basis of an inflow/outflow estimate of cash for the day of what may be lent at call. From the net result of this estimate plus (a) the closing balance of cash for the previous day plus (b) the

---

[1] That is, the rate paid by the banks on balances held in deposit accounts.

[2] The total amount of 'privilege money' is small, probably not more than £5m. for the whole market. Such money dates from 1925. At that time a large amount of American cotton bills passed through the market. Because New York time is five hours behind London it became the practice for the banks to grant privilege money to the discount houses until the daily amount of such bills became known.

[3] The discount houses balance their books each evening.

[4] The amount of security for bills provides a margin sufficient to cover the discount at current rates, e.g., with discount rate at 6 per cent the margin provided on three months bills would be $1\frac{1}{2}$ per cent. In the case of bonds it is usual to provide a 5 per cent margin of security at current prices over the money borrowed, e.g., for a loan of £100,000 against which bonds standing at par are lodged as security and margin, a total of £105,000 in bonds would be lodged. Were the market price of the bonds to fall, additional collateral would have to be provided to ensure that the 5 per cent margin over the money value of the loan was maintained. The security plus margin required at any time is shown by the formula—

$$\text{Security} + \text{margin} = \frac{100 \ (\text{amount of loan} + 5 \text{ per cent})}{\text{Market value of bonds lodged}}$$

For a good account of the collateral arrangements underlying call money see 'The Functioning of the London Discount Houses', by H. F. Goodson, in *The London Discount Market Today*, Institute of Bankers, London, 1962.

balance at the Bank of England for the previous day, is deducted the 8 per cent of estimated deposits required for cash reserves. Any positive amount for the resultant figure is available for the market, any negative amount is called in.[1] Assuming that the amount available for the market is positive the bank must still decide how it will distribute it as between lending at call and/or buying bills. This decision is usually based on two factors: the night money currently running and the state of the existing bill portfolio of the bank. If the amount of night money is already large the decision would probably be to place most of the available funds in bills, taking maturities of short or long date according to the tapering of the portfolio required. If short bills were few in the portfolio and heavy demands for cash were pending in a few days much of the money would be lent at call. In any event by the time the discount house representative makes his call at the bank (10–11 a.m.) the funds available for lending at call, for bill purchase or required for call, have been decided. The bank's offer of money (or demand) is based on the size of each house. This ensures that loans and calls are equitably spread.

To the representative of each discount house when he calls the bank's representative specifies the bank's position. He calls money and names the rate from which it is called, or he offers to buy bills or lend call money. The rate for bills or call money is a matter for quick negotiation. There is no contract; probably no formal record of the transaction. Later in the day parcels of bills are sent by messenger to the bank—either bills which the bank is buying or bills to serve as collateral for call money lent by it.

What has been said so far applies only to the clearing banks as lenders. Before 1962[2] it would also have applied at least in principle to the overseas banks. Since that date, however, the overseas banks have developed largely among themselves a new market in short money, the so-called market in 'inter-bank loans'.[3] This provides these banks with a much more lucrative outlet for surplus cash and although they still lend to the discount houses, and are included in the morning round, they only do so approximately up to an amount equal in each case to their own acceptances.

As the day proceeds adjustments take place. The banks' cash position may have to be modified in the light of events. The money position may

[1] There are other claimants besides the discount houses for the money available for lending at call. The clearing banks' published figure for 'call money' includes, in addition to the money lent to the discount market, several other items. The proportion of the total figure lent to the market is about 75 per cent.

[2] It is impossible to be precise with this date. A range, 1955–62, would be more accurate.

[3] Cf. p. 100 below.

tighten or ease. From noon onwards the discount houses are preparing to balance their books for the day and if many banks are calling rates will harden as money becomes progressively more difficult to obtain. If overnight money in sufficient amount for the close is not forthcoming from any of the many banking lenders there must be sufficient time to obtain funds from the Bank of England. Bank of England assistance to the market is never withheld but its terms and conditions vary with the Bank's current plans for conditioning the market.

It is worth while at this juncture describing in some detail the process which, with minor variations, unfolds daily in each of the discount houses. At the end of the morning the discount house's position will be revealed by a glance at the 'Money Book', a simple two-column receipts and payments book, kept in the parlour and in which is inscribed in ink (tradition demands a steel pen) on the left all money in, on the right all money out. A typical page might appear as follows:

IN	OUT
Opening balance	Discounts—pre-arranged
Maturing bills	do. —over counter
Bonds sold	Treasury bill take up
Pre-arranged borrowing	Bonds bought
Morning borrowing	Calls
Bill sales	

It is this book which, as the day proceeds and fresh entries are added, reveals continuously the house's money position. It must be balanced 'at the close', that is at 3 p.m. each day.

The morning sets the pattern. The clearing banks have lent or called at the morning round and by the time the seniors return from lunch (about 1.30) the clearing banks will have squared their daily position, making final calls or offering money. From then until the close money must come from the Scottish banks, the merchant banks or the overseas banks. Often a glance at the Money Book is sufficient, with the experience of the day's market conditions gained from the morning round, to reassure the executives that the required amount will be forthcoming before the Bank of England Discount Office closes at 2.30 p.m. It may be that £4m. is required. Telephone calls begin and 'money' is requested from this and that merchant bank. In these requests the rate for the overnight money will soften or harden with success or failure. Occasionally, on an easy day, money will be offered at a rate too high and refused. The offer may or may not be repeated minutes later according to the lender's success or failure to obtain his desired rate with other houses. As 2.25 p.m. nears a decision must be made. Is the amount of money still to be found so large that the house must borrow from the Bank? Perhaps £1m. is

G

still outstanding. Will this amount be raisable in the period between 2.30 p.m. and 3 p.m. when some banks are still balancing but when the Discount Office is closed? Here experience and an assessment of market conditions decide. With only £1m. left to get, rates easy, money plentiful and some banks still to balance there will be no question of recourse to the Bank. With £6m. still to find and rates hardening, the incoming calls few on the telephone, the decision may not be easy. It may go the other way. As each executive completes a successful negotiation he scribbles the amount and source of the loan on a small pad, tears off the sheet and throws it to an 'out' tray for collection. It tells the cashier the amount to record in the books and is the signal for the despatch of bills as collateral to the lending bank.

If by 2.25 p.m. it is evident that an amount unobtainable elsewhere in the remaining time has still to be found a member of the house hurries to the Bank of England to borrow the required amount at the Discount Office. This demand is met automatically but on the Bank's terms—either overnight at bank rate if the Bank is in stern mood, at market rate if it is not, at Bank Rate for seven days or, worst of all, if the Bank is really squeezing the market, at a rate above the bank rate.[1]

If the discount house does not borrow from the Bank of England, and if some positive amount has still to be found before 3 p.m., there is no risk for the house. They rarely misjudge the capacity of the market to cover the final tranche and if there is any slight shortfall their own banker (usually a clearing bank) will cover the deficiency overnight at an agreed rate.

The unfolding of this daily ritual differs widely in atmosphere. A glance at a typical Money Book will show that the daily amount left to find at 1.30 p.m. can vary (spring 1967) from as high as £30m. to only £2m. or £3m. The words 'hard' or 'easy' used to describe money market conditions have a literal meaning in discount house parlours in the early afternoon.

Much of the market's climate each day is shown early by the 'calling in' (or absence of it) by the clearing banks. Calls from the banks to repay short loans arise for two main reasons: changes in the cash position of individual banks; and a change in the cash holding of the banking system as a whole resulting from some one-way movement of cash, particularly to or from the government account at the Bank of England. Such a movement might be the result of large payments to the government for tax settlements which would diminish bank deposits and bank cash equally, thus lowering the banks' cash ratio. In the other direction large government out-payments—such as payments to farmers through the

[1] During 1966 advances were made to the houses by the Bank of England on 18 days.

Milk Marketing Board or cash redemption of a maturing bond issue—expand the banks' cash holdings. Calls arising from changes in the cash balances of the individual banks result only in discount houses switching their requests for call money to other banks which are likely, in such circumstances, to meet the calls;[1] calls arising from a general shortage of cash in the banking system, however, will result in discount houses being unable to obtain adequate call money and will necessitate Bank of England assistance.

The 'call money' system has been described in some detail because it is an important feature of the discount market: important to the houses as their main source of funds, important to the banks and lenders because it provides a means of reducing to a minimum the holding of cash which they must keep unemployed and sterile against the demands and potential demands of their depositors.[2] The clearing banks in their loans to the discount houses reflected in the *Money at Call* item have a first reserve liquid asset which is used to meet variations in public demand for cash and to even out variations in the flow of money as between the clearing banks themselves.

The existence of the large and well organised market in call money in London is a source of attraction to the overseas banks which are located there, serving to hold them in London and to preserve the City's position as an international financial centre. Until very recently the discount houses were the largest, indeed virtually the sole borrower in this call-money market but two changes, in the late fifties and early sixties, have enlarged and ramified this market and forced the houses to share with other borrowers. One important group of lenders, the overseas banks, have been diverted from lending to the discount houses except for token amounts by the growth of two new groups of borrowers. What in effect has happened is that the appearance of new borrowers of call money has created three distinct call money markets: the market for discount house call money which on the lending side is now dominated by the clearing banks; the market for local authority loans in which overseas banks and merchant banks are the lenders; and the inter-bank loan market in which overseas banks and merchant banks are both lenders and borrowers. To a great extent these three markets are separate and distinct, but as the most recent arrivals have had certain effects on the discount house call market it is necessary to describe them briefly.

[1] Because such a shortage of cash for one or two banks must, with an unchanged total of cash, mean cash surpluses in other banks who then become willing to lend to the discount houses.

[2] On 5th January 1964, £588m. was on loan at call to the Discount Market by the London clearing banks, earning at the then going rates about £14m. per annum.

The local authority loan market first appeared in the later fifties when local authorities, driven by high interest rates and the difficulty of raising money on the long-term capital market, sought money on a short-term renewable basis in London. Centrally organised, through a London financial house as agent, these local authorities as borrowers and overseas banks and acceptance houses as lenders have come to constitute a large call money market[1] distinct from that of the discount market. The higher rates in this market have drawn overseas banks and others to switch a part of their available funds to it. This has reduced the relative importance of the overseas banks as suppliers of funds to the discount houses, but apart from this the effect of the local authority loans market on the discount houses has been slight. The local authority market has led a distinct life of its own apart from the discount market.

The inter-bank loan market is of more recent vintage. It received its stimulus between 1955 and 1962 when the overseas and merchant banks opted out of the London deposit agreement.[2] Overseas banks tend to have small deposits since they lack the large savings and current account deposits which provide the domestic clearing banks with their great lendable resources. It was decided by the overseas banks that they would try to attract deposits by offering higher deposit rates, in order to gain funds wherewith to expand their lending business. This they have been moderately successful in doing. Meanwhile, in following the usual liquidity principles and seeking to provide a first liquid reserve to cash, they have virtually rejected the discount market whose borrowing rates for call money[3] are not now high enough to give a margin over deposit rates, in favour of short loans to other overseas and merchant banks at higher rates. Such loans, arranged mainly through money brokers, are made by bank to bank[4] on a day-to-day basis at rates higher than their deposit rates. This market has had more impact on the discount market than has the market for local authority money. The overseas banks now lend to the discount houses only token amounts usually bearing some relation to the volume of their own acceptances.

The impact of these new call markets on the discount houses has been slight in immediate practical terms. They still obtain from the clearing banks adequate working funds. They make no complaint of inadequacy,

[1] Loans are usually for 7 days renewable.

[2] By this agreement they and the clearing banks had held the deposit rate, i.e. the rate paid by the banks on deposit accounts, at 2 per cent below bank rate.

[3] The clearing banks' 'basic' rate for call money is ⅜ per cent above their own deposit rate.

[4] The clearing banks do not participate in the inter-bank loan market—the main reason being that inter-bank loans are unsecured.

actual or potential, but in wider senses their rôle is reduced and narrowed. Formerly they might claim that they and they alone were the demand side of the call-money market which held overseas banks in London. This claim is gone. Formerly they were dependent for call money on a wide group of institutions: now they are directly dependent on the clearing banks. Although there is no sign as yet that the clearing banks will exploit their monopoly position, and much to indicate the high value which these banks place upon the existence and operations of the discount houses, it is none the less a deterioration for the houses from their former position.

IV

It is now necessary to examine the processes whereby the Bank of England intervenes in the money market, exercising the influence and control which, in the British system, lies at the heart of monetary policy. This, in effect, must be a brief description of the Bank of England's day-by-day management of the market. Such a description needs a return to first principles if it is to be fully meaningful and if the Bank's tasks are to be seen in proper perspective.

In essence the Bank's management is two-sided: to manage the money market and through it the banking system, sometimes for this purpose using, and sometimes counteracting, its other function—the administration of the ebb and flow of funds through the Exchequer accounts, which, as the government's banker, it administers. An examination of the Bank's activities as they concern the Exchequer would be lengthy and intricate. It is not appropriate in this context. Readers interested in this field must consult some of the many books on public finance which deal with this. It is necessary, however, for present purposes, to give a rudimentary general account of what takes place.

An understanding of the money flows which arise from the Exchequer transactions of the Bank must be preceded by identifying the main accounts of the Bank through which these flows pass. First, the term Exchequer applies strictly to a group of accounts in the books of the Banking Department; the Exchequer, in the proper sense, and the accounts of the Revenue Departments, the Paymaster General (including the Exchange Equalisation Account) and the National Debt Commissioners. Second, there is the Issue Department of the Bank which conducts large dealings in government debt; and finally, there are a number of other balances maintained by government departments and included in the item Public Deposits on the weekly Bank Return. Ebbs and flows of funds through these Bank of England accounts have their effect on the private sector via another important item on the liabilities side of the weekly return, namely 'Other Deposits: Bankers' or, as we shall more briefly call them, Bankers' Deposits. Transactions through the government accounts (including the issue of notes) almost always result in a debit or credit to the total of Bankers' Deposits, and thus affect the general cash base of the banking system.

Within these government accounts the working balances of the departments are held at a minimum and surpluses in them are transferred or lent overnight to the Exchequer Account. This account, and its complementary account, that of the Paymaster General, is also operated in such a way as to preserve only a minimal balance of £2m. over the two accounts.[1] Since the turnover in these accounts is both large and irregular the Bank's work, which is done in collaboration with the Treasury, of making sure that money is available for each day's spending and of avoiding large surpluses, is onerous. Surpluses must be used to buy back Treasury bills from non-government holders in order to reduce National Debt servicing costs.

The other side of the Bank's control activities, that of managing the money market, and through it the banking system, is related to the administration of the government accounts. The main flow of day-to-day funds from the government accounts at the Bank is to the banking system and the discount houses; the main flow from the private sector to the public sector when it occurs is away from the banking system and to the government accounts at the Bank of England. More specifically, an excess of government payments over receipts increases Bankers' Deposits and thereby the cash base of the banks; a shortfall of government payments as compared with receipts depletes Bankers' Deposits, lowers the cash base and causes stringency in the market. When, as a result of the payment of large sums by the private sector to the Exchequer, say for taxation, the level of Bankers' Deposits falls, thus reducing the cash base, the banks renew their cash by calling from the discount market. The discount houses, finding themselves short of funds, must then seek money from the Bank of England in its capacity as lender of last resort.

In relieving stringency in the money market the Bank of England has a choice of methods. If it merely wishes to ease the shortage in the market and to relieve upward pressure on interest rates it will buy Treasury bills from the discount houses, that is, it will use the so-called 'direct method' of giving assistance. Alternatively, as it observes the shortage develop in the market it may buy bills from the banks (that is, use the 'indirect

[1] This is a very small balance in relation to the large daily turnover in these accounts of some hundreds of millions of pounds.

method'), leaving it to the banks to use the cash which is given them for the bills to make call loans to the discount houses. Finally, if the Bank wishes to use the stringency as a means of raising interest rates and inducing credit restrictions it will give no support, either direct or indirect, to the houses, allowing the market to come to it to borrow either at bank rate or over. This has the effect of raising the cost of the discount houses' borrowing, forcing them to raise their own rates for discounts and to review their bid for Treasury bills at the tender on the following Friday.

It is apparent that the Bank can work most effectively in a straitened market. When there is a shortage of funds it can relieve the shortage on its own terms and by a choice of methods. It can drive best on a tight rein. The mopping up of surplus funds in the market to prevent over-liquidity is, therefore, an important subsidiary function of the Bank's control. It can sell Treasury bills to the market to mop up surplus funds, but there is a limit to this since the houses will not wish to buy bills to such an extent as to leave themselves short and land themselves as borrowers at the Bank of England later in the day. The Bank can only expand its Treasury bill sales to the market in such circumstances by offering bills at very attractive rates. One influence which does provide a 'built-in' mopping up device for the Bank is the weekly Treasury bill tender. The bills offered at the tender allow for the Treasury's needs plus a margin for error and, since the houses must in their joint tender cover, at least theoretically, all bills offered, this tends to create a shortage of funds and tighten the market. The Treasury bill tender, although primarily a means whereby the government borrows short for its immediate needs, is secondarily a means of conditioning the market for Bank of England control.

To return to the discount houses, let us look at the same processes from their point of view and summarise the Bank's relation to them. When one or only a few banks call in their loans from the houses they will probably be able to obtain loans from other banks to balance their books, but in the event of a general pressure on the cash base springing from a rise in the public's demand for cash, all banks are likely to call in loans from the discount houses simultaneously. In this event the discount houses have the right to seek assistance from the Bank of England which the Bank, as lender of last resort, is bound to give. In such circumstances the Bank has a choice of actions. The first possibility is that the shortage of cash has been initiated by itself to produce the effect of putting the market in the Bank in order to bring about a change in interest rates. In such a case it may discount approved bills for the market at bank rate, thus raising the cost of borrowing to the discount houses. In turn the houses will raise their own rates and the increase in interest rates will generalise itself through the market. The effect will be the stronger if the Bank of England at the same time raises bank rate. This was the traditional practice and was the one which gave significance to bank rate in the nineteenth century and to the Bank's famous 'eligibility rules'. It has now been replaced by the method of lending to the houses with bills as collateral.

A second possibility and the more recent practice is that, with the market in the Bank, the Bank of England gives its assistance by loans, usually for a minimum period of seven days, at the advances rate (usually 1 per cent higher than bank rate), secured by approved bills, as collateral. This causes the discount houses to increase their Treasury bill rate at the next tender, thus raising this rate for that and probably subsequent tenders. This practice (apparently somewhat anomalous since the government is in effect putting up the rate on its own borrowing) has often been used during the fifties and sixties when the authorities have wished to single out the Treasury bill rate for an increase in order to draw short money to London to strengthen sterling and the balance of payments.[1] Finally, if the cash stringency is not one initiated by the authorities but is caused by transient circumstances the effects of which the Bank of England may wish to neutralise, the Bank may offset the shortage by help through the 'open back door', thus increasing the cash supply without interference with the structure of short-term rates.

In September 1966 the Bank of England initiated the practice, when it wished merely to alleviate shortage in the market, of lending overnight at market rate. This measure was intended to economise in the buying and selling of Treasury bills, the volume of which has fallen. The process of 'buying back' is reduced by this new practice. This method is, of course, used only when the Bank's aim is to ease the market. The alternative methods are still used in appropriate circumstances.

Variations in the cash supply and hence in the funds available to the money market are considerable. Not only do they vary seasonally but often quite sharply from day to day, and a great part of the Bank of England's activity in the market consists of compensating these movements by 'smoothing operations' and of adapting them to the trend of its longer-term monetary policy.[2] The following money market reports from *The Times* reflect rather stringent conditions and the steps taken to meet them.

[1] Such a method is politically preferable to taking the overt step of announcing a rise in bank rate—which would, of course, have much the same effect, if the market were put in the Bank.

[2] For example, in 1965 the market was in the Bank on 49 days.

For 30th August 1966

'The discount market met an acute general shortage of money. It is normal for money to be wanted on the day after the bank holiday; and in addition there were the usual end of the month factors and also the Tuesday tax transfers. Even so, conditions were surprisingly difficult, and the Bank of England had to intervene, its operations being, in all, on a very large scale indeed. There was help, mainly indirect, which met about half the need, the rest being made up by overnight borrowing at Bank rate.

From the start, clearing, Scottish and outside banks all called heavily. Fresh money could scarcely be found. The houses paid $6\frac{5}{8}$ per cent for day-to-day loans and conceded $6\frac{3}{4}$ per cent on the rare occasion of a line. By midday houses had massive sums to find. They received help which, where indirect, was passed on by the clearing banks as loans at $6\frac{3}{4}$ per cent and sometimes in the purchases of November bills. But almost every house had to borrow from the Bank, and some considered that these borrowings were the heaviest since overnight lending was introduced. Rates showed no signs of falling away and the market had a difficult finish. Some houses took final balances at $6\frac{3}{8}$ per cent, but others were still paying $6\frac{5}{8}$ per cent and even $6\frac{3}{4}$ per cent. Privilege facility was generally used to the full.'

For 11th October 1966

'Most of the discount houses found money acutely short; and the Bank of England intervened on a very large scale. It bought bills, partly from the houses but mostly from the clearing banks. It also lent money overnight, operating rather more in this way than through bill business. Houses were charged the market rate, suggesting that the authorities consider that charging 7 per cent on Monday was enough to make their point.

With the weekly tax transfers heavy—and only partly offset by Government disbursements on local authority accounts—houses ran into heavy calling from the clearing banks. In addition, many had repayments to make at the Bank. A little fresh money was found at $6\frac{5}{8}$ per cent. Outside calling also built up, and by midday most houses had far to go. In the afternoon a few large lines appeared, for which $6\frac{5}{8}$ per cent was paid. In places $6\frac{3}{4}$ per cent was asked, but seems to have been resisted. This view was justified when the clearing banks passed on the help at $6\frac{5}{8}$ per cent, and still more when the Bank charged $6\frac{5}{8}$ per cent to the half-dozen houses who borrowed overnight. Money came out late, and the close was mixed, with rates ranging from $5\frac{3}{4}$ to $6\frac{3}{8}$ per cent: more than half the privilege money was drawn.'

For the conduct of its day-to-day operations the Bank makes use of a
working sheet which is divided into two sections, one showing the
transactions in the fields appropriate to its dealings with bankers and the
money market; the other showing its Exchequer transactions. Some
transactions appear on both sections of the working sheet but with the
signs reversed. It is unnecessary to detail the entries on this working
sheet but the principle upon which it is compiled is simple. First the
banking section: three figures or sets of figures are strategic: the actual
balance with which the banks and discount houses begin the day; the
Bankers' 'target' which is the total balance which, the Bank of England
estimates, the market wishes to hold at the close of the current day; and
the known and estimated transactions which the Bank estimates will
take place during the day, for example the take-up or maturity of Treasury
bills and the Exchequer's receipts and payments. As the day proceeds the
net total of transactions for the day applied to the previous night's balance
and the resultant figure compared to the target for the day gives a measure
of the surplus or shortage of funds in the market. There is, throughout
the day, constant checking of the developing situation both by direct
contacts and through consultation with bill brokers. Funds may not be
flowing as quickly as was thought or may not be reaching the right places.
The main function of this working sheet is to keep the Bank apprised
of the developing situation so that when early afternoon comes and
decisions as to the nature of smoothing or controlling operations have to
be taken the Bank is already aware of the choice it must meet. Let us
suppose that by early afternoon the market is £20m. short. Various
courses are open to the Bank. It may do nothing, in which event some or
all of the houses will be driven into the Bank to borrow at bank rate or
above to balance their books. Alternatively, it may decide to give help,
in which event it will instruct the special buyer to purchase Treasury bills
in the market. It will select for the purpose bills of chosen maturities, for
by doing so it can influence the market's cash position at the maturity
date—a finesse of control which is useful and continually used. The funds
to purchase these bills on the Exchequer side are likely to be forthcoming since shortage of money in the market is almost always matched
by surplus in the Exchequer, payments to which are probably responsible
for the market stringency.

The Exchequer section of the Bank's working sheet operates in much
the same way as the Bankers'. Here the aim is to have the Exchequer and
Paymaster General's Accounts with a combined daily closing balance of
£2m. Here, as before, the starting point is the actual balance for the
previous night. Then follow the transactions either with Bankers' Accounts or with the Banking Department (of the Bank) which will in-

fluence the Exchequer group during the day. If, as is assumed above, the market faces on this day a shortage of £20m. it is possible that the Exchequer may have a surplus of more than this amount, say £25m. If the market shortage is alleviated by the purchase of £20m. in Treasury bills, a balance of £5m. will still remain with the Exchequer. This balance will be used to purchase Treasury bills from the Banking Department, bills again being selected with maturities suitable for smoothing cash flows in later weeks.

The working sheet of the Bank of England is then in effect a daily plan for co-ordinating Bank action in the market and the Exchequer. Without it the Bank in its conducting would be forced to play constantly 'by ear', a task beyond even its wit. Even with the best estimation available the working sheet can 'gang aft a-gley', particularly in its estimated timing of the main money flows. But it does bring to the process of daily operations by the Bank a purposive and planned element which would otherwise be lacking.[1]

So far as the Bank of England's control of the money market is concerned the discount houses play an important rôle. On them falls wellnigh the whole impact of changes either in the Bank of England's credit policy or in the public's demand for cash. In their absence the main streams of funds would flow more directly but certainly they would flow more abruptly and jerkily. The banks benefit greatly from the interposition of the houses between themselves and the Bank of England. In their absence changes in the cash flow would bear directly on their cash reserves and income-earning assets. Their balance sheet assets switches would be more frequent and disturbing. They would be preoccupied with continual balance sheet adjustment to the detriment of their wider task of dispensing and distributing credit. From the Bank of England's point of view the discount market serves not only as a focal point of the money market in which it must operate but also, through the Bank's rôle of lender of last resort, as a transmitter of interest rate variations.

The Bank of England's task as lender of last resort to the discount market is central to the British monetary system. The Bank can, at any time, create by open-market operations the cash shortage which will drive the discount houses to the Bank. Once there the Bank, by a choice of methods, may make effective the interest rate of its choice. Alternatively, if the market is driven into the Bank by a secularly produced cash famine the Bank may deal with this, with or without a rise in interest rates. Within this system the importance of bank rate, i.e. the rate at

[1] Readers anxious to explore further the intricacies of the Bank's daily working sheet should consult 'The Management of Money Day-by-Day', *Bank of England Quarterly Bulletin*, March 1963, pp. 15–22.

which the Bank is prepared to discount approved bills for the discount houses, is apparent. The fact that bills are rarely, if ever, rediscounted at the Bank nowadays does not reduce the importance of bank rate. The Bank's lending rate to the market is geared directly to it and changes with it. Other strategic rates in the banking system do likewise. Alterations of bank rate are more than barometric changes designed for the scrutiny of the financial world. They are the signal for alterations in the whole complex of interest rates.

V

In our model of the centralised banking system in Chapter 3 no distinct or essential rôle was assigned to the discount market. Indeed, within the model there is no logical imperative for its existence. A market in short-term paper is certainly necessary but that may be provided by the commercial banks and the central bank with or without the intermediacy of specialised dealers. This is achieved in banking systems other than the British. Nor is there any essential need for the interposition of a group of institutions between the central bank and the commercial banks. The central bank must fulfil the function of lender of last resort, but this it can do by lending when necessary directly to the commercial banks. It must make its interest rate effective but this it can do in various ways which do not require specialised institutions to spread the rate changes when they are made. If we are to argue that inclusion of a set of discount houses in the model facilitates its functioning we must show that all these functions are the smoother, the easier and the cheaper for this inclusion. We cannot do this. We cannot even argue that the specialised function of dealing in bills of exchange, of the operation of the market as one dealing in a financial commodity, is necessarily better done by discount houses than it would be done by banks had they a mind to do it. We can only say that within the British centralised banking system this institutional anomaly exists and that the British system may or may not be the better for it. It is in its relation to the British system that it must be judged: in the general theoretical case it is an anomalous addition.

For this reason, since no other financial system has such a mechanism and since there have been times when the Bank of England has clearly been concerned to preserve it, we must ask ourselves whether the British system is the better for the existence of the market or whether it is just one of those historical anachronisms with which the British delight to clutter up their law, their institutions and their conduct of affairs. In the broadest sense it is in search of an answer to this question that many people may read this book. While the writer cannot promise a definite answer to this question he must at least array the considerations, and a useful purpose may be served if at this stage the pros and cons of the issue are presented briefly so that the reader may have them in mind through what is to follow. No attempt will be made at this stage to do more than assemble the elements of this balance of advantage. Much of this book must inevitably be spent in assessing these elements.

The justification of the British discount market rests on six arguments.

Firstly, in the absence of such a market some institutional mechanism would have to be created to perform tasks at present performed by the market. Certainly somebody, probably the clearing banks, would have to discount commercial bills and provide the services to commerce and overseas trade which are at present provided cheaply and efficiently by the discount houses. That this is a type of business for which the clearing banks have neither taste nor ambition is amply demonstrated by their history. While at times, for example in the early thirties, their attitude towards the discount houses has not been benevolent, it has shown no sign of their seeking to acquire discounting as a remunerative additional banking service which they might provide. For this there is an obvious answer: it is not always remunerative and certainly it is always risky. The profits made by the discount houses as a result of their huge turnover and narrow margins are not impressive and no other financial group has cast covetous eyes upon them. Total published profits for the twelve houses usually averaged less than 10 per cent in the early sixties. No wonder that a discount house spokesman testifying before the Radcliffe Committee, asked whether there had been any tendency for the clearing banks to buy their way into the discount business, replied: 'No, it is not good enough business.'[1] In these days, however, when the commercial bill is staging a comeback this aspect of the market's work should not be underrated.

Secondly, in the absence of a discount market certain inconveniences would occur for the commercial banks in structuring their assets, and machinery would be needed to even out the day-to-day flow of funds amongst the various banks. The discount houses provide a short loan market of high efficiency in which the commercial banks and the Bank of England may both operate without coming into direct contact with one another. Because of this market the commercial banks have been able to work to minimum cash ratios, knowing that their second line of reserves, *Call money*, is immediately mobilisable and that their third line, *Bills*, can be held in a portfolio, which is appropriately structured. Without a discount market the clearing banks would have to find a new liquid asset

[1] Cf. Radcliffe. Minutes of Evidence, Vol. i, p. 11.

to replace their discount market call loans as a reserve to cash. This would be the more serious a deprivation in that the bill portfolios of the clearing banks would, in the absence of a discount market, be weighted at the long end, since, in such circumstances, Treasury bills would come to them direct from the tender and commercial bills for discount would come to them early in their currency and not, as at present, to the discount houses. A considerable restructuring of the reserve assets of the banks would be necessary. Even then it seems inevitable that they would at times need to hold uneconomically large cash reserves against the demands of depositors. To the extent that such cash holdings were in excess of the required ratio the Bank of England's control of the clearing banks would be retarded. It is, as we have shown in the preceding section of this chapter, necessary that for efficient control the Bank of England should run the system on a tight rein. The tightness of this rein is ensured by the discount market which makes it easy for surplus cash to be mopped up or for temporary cash famines to be relieved with only such effect on the monetary system as the Bank of England chooses to allow. At present the existence of the discount market ensures that there are no idle balances in the monetary system which is drawn taut through the call money arrangements.

Thirdly, the discount market greatly facilitates the working of the Bank of England in fulfilling its function as lender of last resort. The discount market is the point at which, in time of scarcity, the Bank injects cash into the system. This it could, of course, do without the discount market by giving assistance directly to the clearing banks but it is unlikely that, unless the visits of the clearing banks to the central bank were very frequent, the flow of assistance could be as evenly distributed among the banks as it is now by the discount market. The unwillingness of commercial banks outside Britain (for example, in Canada) to come to the central bank for aid and the rarity with which such aid is given seems to suggest that without a discount market the British clearing banks would order themselves very differently from the way they do in the knowledge that liberal aid can and does come to them quickly, frequently and usually indirectly. It is true that in recent years the discount market has not been the only point at which the Bank of England help is injected. The practice of giving help by the purchase of bills from the clearing banks has to some extent abrogated the principle of 'no direct help for the clearing banks' which since 1825 has been a notable feature of the British system. But it is a minor breach in the principle, demonstrating flexibility rather than any marked movement away from the recognition of the discount market's intermediate situation.

Fourthly, the discount houses perform useful functions in connection with the Treasury bill tender. Notably they 'cover the tender' for the government and they help to 'set a rate' in the market for Treasury bills. Through the discount market the large flows of funds to and from the Treasury are quietly canalised so as to minimise their impact on the monetary system.

Fifthly, the houses perform in the short bond market certain tasks which are of great value to the authorities. One in particular is useful to the Bank of England. The discount houses as professional dealers in short bonds continually buy from holders large blocks of near maturities, in particular from institutions which, when stocks are nearing maturity, wish to replace them by more lucrative holdings. These tend to collect in the discount market where they are readily available to the authorities when refinancing begins. To this must be added a certain shock-absorbing capacity in that the houses can absorb sales of stocks otherwise difficult to dispose of. This is, however, a qualified advantage, for when a large sale of stock, say by a clearing bank or a financial institution, occurs, the discount houses look for and get the support of the Bank of England. As a 'shock absorber' for short bond sales it is an auxiliary rather than a principal.

Finally, the activities of the discount houses, whatever their value to the system, are performed cheaply and efficiently with very modest resources. It is questionable whether, if the discount houses were to succumb, alternative arrangements could operate so cheaply, at least in their early stages.

These six claims for the utility of the London discount houses would not constitute a powerful case for creating such a group, did they not already exist. But we are not doing this. Rather we are considering whether the case justifies their continued existence. In the writer's view of the evidence this case is amply proved. A surgical operation to remove the discount houses, or a series of cataclysmic changes which swept them away, would render necessary a considerable re-orientation of the whole British system. This would not be beyond it but would be troublesome, and who is to say that the eventual product would excel in efficiency that which we now have? True, a case can be made for dispensing with the discount market. Its specialised knowledge and expertise in grading and vetting bills of exchange is much less used than formerly and discounting of commercial bills could as well be done by the clearing banks. Treasury bills could be taken up at the tender by the clearing banks, whose abstention from the tender serves merely to provide the discount houses with Treasury bill business. Finally, fussy and tidy minds may object to the 'roundaboutness' which the existence of the discount market has introduced into the British banking system. How much more logical and proper for the Bank of England in its majesty to speak loud and clear to the eleven instead of muttering in corners with a whispering throng of fussy attendants. Yet, when all has been said, one fact ensures that the discount houses will not easily be allowed to die: the fact that the Bank of England regards them as necessary. During their stormy existence they have come near to the brink on several occasions. On all of these they have been saved from oblivion by the Bank whose conviction it appears to be that they are an essential part of the British monetary machine.

Part III

HISTORICAL DEVELOPMENT

'Like the English Constitution, the English credit system is a living thing, that has grown out of its past and is growing into its future. Past, present and future are thus one continuing process, and no one can hope to understand its present, still less to peer into its future, unless he knows something of the past that is part of them.'

Hartley Withers in his introduction to the
14th Edition of Bagehot's *Lombard Street*

H

Chapter 5

THE EARLY NINETEENTH CENTURY

'My business is usually denominated that of a Bill Broker, in fact
a dealer in money, taking from those who have a surplus and
distributing it to those who require it.'

Samuel Gurney

I

THE ORIGINS of the discount market are recent. The nineteenth century
saw its birth, growth, maturity; perhaps a suspicion of its age but certainly
not of its retirement. If, in Britain, the discount houses and Lombard
Street are venerated as part of the British scene and heritage it is more
from an affection for Victoriana than because they are genuinely old.
Perhaps too, it is their strong association with the period of British
mercantile greatness which gives them their historical and antique air,
which they themselves are at pains to cherish and foster.[1]

In the period treated in this chapter—the late eighteenth and early
nineteenth centuries—the main prerequisites of a discount market all
emerged. A group of specialised dealers, trading in bills or acting as
brokers, bringing buyers and sellers together, was established. The
practice whereby these dealers operated with funds borrowed on short-
term from the commercial banks appeared and 'final resort facilities' at
the Bank of England for bill brokers when the commercial banks called
in loans were established. One major feature was yet to come, and was
slow in coming, the control by the Bank of England through its 'final
resort function' of the short-term rate of interest and through it the whole
interest rate structure. The recognition and perfection of the methods
whereby bank rate (i.e. the Bank of England's own lending rate) operated
and was made effective was to be a slow process and was to take the whole
of the nineteenth century to complete.

When the nineteenth century opened the banking system in Britain
could scarcely be described as a system at all. Many hundreds of small
banks in town and country and a few larger banks in London conducted
the day-to-day monetary transactions of the economy which were made

[1] For an amusing, yet accurate and informative account of the modern discount
market and a sly laugh at its 'dark, brown-panelled leathery atmosphere', see Paul
Ferris' *The City*, Chapter 3.

either in notes issued by the banks or through the medium of bills which, in the areas in which the parties to them were known, were widely accepted in payment and acted almost as currency. The bill served not only for current transaction payments but also as the main vehicle of bank lending, for the overdraft system was still to come and did not establish itself until late in the century.

Such banking differed greatly from the joint stock banking which succeeded it and with whose maturer developments we are familiar today. The most essential difference was that prior to the 1830's private banking was based not upon deposits, on the operation of a banking service for customers and from the holding of various income earning assets against deposits, but rather from the issue of notes. The newer joint stock banks, when they appeared, concentrated from the outset on deposit banking but such banks were virtually prohibited until after the crisis of 1825,[1] and in the early years of the century the scene was one of 'a vast number of small banks with purely local experience and (generally) with inadequate reserves. Many of them, indeed, were no more than jumped-up shopkeepers with no knowledge of banking principles.'[2]

Above this congeries of banking houses stood the Bank of England, *primus inter paries*, a commercial banking house with much private business of its own but holding by reason of its statutory incorporation, its early appearance in the field, its directorate and its connection with government, a unique position in the financial fraternity. It had few powers but much influence; its responsibilities were as yet undefined. In 1797 it had been forced to suspend payments, the suspension only being ended in 1821. In 1825 it came near to suspension again. Yet its reputation for soundness was great and, significantly for the future, it sensed its responsibilities, and in the crisis of 1825, and with growing momentum as the century progressed, it was to move to its position as keystone of the banking arch. Not until the Bank Charter Act of 1844 was the Bank's unique position given statutory recognition. With that Act came monopolistic control of the note issue. Other facets of central bank control, for example, control through bank rate of the structure of short-term interest rates and experience in the art of open-market operations were slower in coming, and it was indeed 1913 before the position of the Bank of England as a central bank and understanding of its armoury of credit control weapons could be said to be complete.

Finally, in this *dramatis personae* of the early nineteenth century banking system we can distinguish even at the earliest stage a group of bill brokers

---

[1] To be precise, until May 1826 when joint stock banks were authorised outside a 65 miles' radius of London. Cf. Geo. IV, c. 46.

[2] Cf. King, op. cit., p. 37.

who were the antecedents of the discount houses of later years.[1] Discounting was not new in England. It had been practised much earlier by the goldsmiths using their own or borrowed funds. Large numbers of financial intermediaries had existed in Tudor and Stuart England whose main function had been to bring together lender and borrower. Many of the activities of the bill broker were familiar in England but not until the early years of the nineteenth century did he emerge as an integral figure in the financial field. When he did so it was mainly the result of the impetus given to bill broking by the rise of country banking. Country bankers found themselves—in the period 1797 onwards—progressively in possession of liquid balances for which they sought a profitable outlet. From 1825, when London banks ceased to pay interest on the deposits in London of the country banks, such banks were forced to look elsewhere for some means of profitably employing surplus funds. For this they turned to the bill brokers, who brought buyers and sellers of bills into contact, and discounting bills from elsewhere became a useful and lucrative means of employment for the surplus funds of country banks. In the first years of the century, country banking grew and with it bill broking. In 1810 there were 721 banks outside London. Many of these banks accumulated surplus deposits, while others found local demands from borrowers to be in excess of their resources. As long as the former problem predominated the country bank could usually deal with it by placing deposits in London through a London bank which acted as its agent but when, with growing industrialisation in the provinces, there was a developing demand there for bank accommodation, country bankers found the bill broker to be a convenience. With his aid it was possible for the banker seeking resources in the industrial area to have bills discounted, either in London or with the banks in agricultural areas having employable surpluses.

The function of the bill broker was important and indeed essential in a unitary banking system striving to provide money capital for a capital-hungry, industrialising economy. This 'equalisation' function served to shift surpluses of money capital to areas in which that capital was in demand, a function which in the modern British banking system is performed by the network of branch banks.

It is clear that in the period from the beginning of the century until about 1825 the relationship between the country banks and the bill brokers was a key one. For that reason it is necessary to examine it in a little more detail.

---

[1] The modern discount house practice of running a bill portfolio with funds borrowed from banks began to appear progressively after 1830.

II

If we consider discount houses in their modern form—that is as institutions which, on the strength of funds borrowed on short-term from the banks, discount and hold bills for varying periods, rediscounting them usually with banks or on occasion with the central bank itself, and making profits from the narrow difference between the rates at which they discount and the rates at which they borrow—then, in this form, they were slow in emerging and what we refer to as bill brokers in the early nineteenth century bore to them only a family resemblance.

In the nineteenth century development of the discount market it is a pardonable simplification to distinguish two distinct phases: the growth of bill broking and the early formation of a group of bill brokers and dealers —a process which began in the eighteenth century and ended in the 1860's when the failure of Overend, Gurney symbolically closed this first phase; and the formation after 1870 of the modern group of discount houses carrying portfolios of bills, to which brokering was a secondary and declining function. It is one of the necessary tasks of this historical exigesis to trace the development from the bill broker and financial intermediary, long familiar in England, to the discount house of the later nineteenth century.

Discounting and bill broking are both very old and must have developed side by side with the bill of exchange. Although the use of bills was at first slower to develop in England than in Western Europe, and the domestic bill did not appear in great numbers until after 1697, it appears from many sources that there was in England from Tudor times a class of financial intermediaries performing a variety of functions, some useful, some legal, some beyond the fringe of legality: the 'procurers' and 'inducers' who arranged loans for merchants and needy aristocrats; the 'money scriveners', originally writers of bills but, with growing knowledge and experience, brokers for commission. These, with the lending goldsmiths, formed a multifarious group against whose activities and malpractices the law and public opinion were continually at war. In Henry VIII's time an Act sought to restrict the business of exchange to persons holding the king's licence. Under Charles I brokers and 'friperers' as well as scriveners were referred to as 'taking greater sums of money for the loan and forebearance of money upon bonds and other securities, than permitted by law.'[1] An Act of 1623[2] sought to limit the maximum legal rate of interest for arranging a loan and a statute of 1660 imposed

---

[1] Cf. *State Papers Domestic*, 1637–38, p. 603.
[2] 21 Jac. I, c. 17.

further limitations. In the eighteenth century the scriveners were still active and invoked the ire of Defoe who described their tactics as 'to lodge some money in his [i.e. the borrower's] hand ... PRETENDING 'tis from a client who has some money to dispose of.'[1] Such feelings were at least partly justified for 'procuration' charges were considerable, often more than 5 per cent, although, since the interest rate on loans was very high, it is probable that the procuration charges of the seventeenth century were relatively no higher than the nineteenth century broker's commission.

One fact which undoubtedly made possible the growth of a class of financial intermediaries in the seventeenth and eighteenth centuries was the decline of the hostility and weakening of the legislation against usury. From the sixteenth century the case against usury became not primarily a moral one but a dispute as to the nature of interest and what rate of interest it was permissible to charge. An Act of 1545 repealed all existing statutes against usury, which were 'obscure and darke in sentences, words and termes ... so framed on purpose to leave room to avoid the penalties.' This Act was a protest not so much against the anti-usury laws as against their ineffectiveness but it still sought to control usury and it named penalties for excessive rates of interest and 10 per cent as the maximum rate of interest on commercial loans and mortgages. An Act of Edward VI (Act 5 and 6 Edw. VI c. 20) reacted against this early toleration and with a full return to medieval vigour it described usury as a 'vyce most odyous and detestable', and proscribed it, enacting that 'no interest is from May 1st 1552 to be taken on any loan.' But this reaction was shortlived; it was admitted by an Act in Elizabeth's time[2] that the Act of 1552 'hathe not done so muche good as was hoped it shoulde' and was evaded by 'sales of wares and shiftes of interest.' A new enactment repealed the earlier Act and stated 10 per cent as the maximum interest upon 'all bonds, contracts and assurances, collateral or other.' But the practical difficulties to which the Act gave rise were nowhere greater than to the Queen herself who, when she borrowed from the principal merchants and aldermen through the intermediary of Gresham in 1570 was forced to guard the lenders against the consequences of disobedience to the usury laws. This Act is interesting, however, in that it enumerates the various operators who might be privy to a financial loan transaction in its various stages and demonstrates how widely known it was that such intermediaries specialised each in a separate financial function and that each was remunerated for his function. Throughout the Stuart period arguments for and against legal rates of interest pro-

[1] Cf. Daniel Defoe, *The Complete English Tradesman* (ed. 1732), p. 339.
[2] Cf. 13 Eliz., c. 8.

ceeded, but usury was now within the law and the only question was that of the maximum allowable rate of interest. Whatever rate was for the moment allowable could usually be manipulatively presented and the art and practice of evasion was widespread. Although the usury laws remained to influence events even in the nineteenth century their practical influence was not great and from the beginning of the eighteenth century the banking system was free to develop virtually untrammelled. 'Once usury was brought within the pale of the law . . . the ground was prepared for the rise of banking in its modern form.'[1]

It is tempting to simplify the picture of evolutionary descent in finance and to say that the goldsmiths were the antecedents of the banks, the scriveners, money lenders and procurers of the bill brokers. Unfortunately, the facts are not so simple. Many goldsmiths did discounting and broking in addition to taking deposits while it is probable that scriveners and money lenders sometimes took deposits from landowners, merchants and others with surplus wealth to which they looked for a remuneration.[2] The most that can probably be said is that until the end of the seventeenth century, when banking as a distinct function was beginning to emerge, there existed this wide class of financial operators, large and powerful, as the attempts to control them indicate, as yet undifferentiated but from which distinct groups were later to emerge. Until about the middle of the eighteenth century financial intermediaries were concerned mainly with making contact between merchant and merchant. We may indeed describe their activities as 'money scrivening'. From 1750 onwards the intermediaries were acting increasingly between banker and merchant or banker and banker. It is this transition which brings us to the bill broker of the nineteenth century. Undoubtedly it was a transition brought about by the development of country banking.

Private banking developed with great rapidity in the eighteenth century, in spite of the monopolistic position which the Bank of England enjoyed after 1708. This monopoly, based on Acts of 1708 and 1742, prohibited note-issuing by any bank having more than six partners. Note-issuing was *de facto* the most important function of banking at that time so that to avoid the Bank of England's monopoly all new banks had either to be small (i.e., with less than six partners) or to carry on banking as a supplement to some other form of business. For this reason the development of English banking took the initial form of small and localised banks at first hardly distinguishable from merchant houses. Wealthy merchants in the provinces came to open accounts with bankers in London in order to make payments there, and this convenience the latter came to extend to

[1] Cf. E. Lipson, *Economic History of England*, London, 1931, Vol. iii, p. 227.
[2] Ibid., p. 227.

their customers and friends. Often they lent their vaults for safe custody of money placed in their care. Bagehot's picture of the country banker of the period is interesting:

'I can imagine nothing better in theory or more successful in practice than private banks as they were in the beginning. A man of known wealth, known integrity and known ability is largely entrusted with the money of his neighbours. The confidence is strictly personal. His neighbours know him and trust him because they know him. They see daily his manner of life and judge from it that this confidence is deserved. In rural districts and in former times it was difficult for a man to ruin himself except at the place in which he lived; for the most part he spent his money there, and speculated there if he speculated at all. Those who lived there also would soon see if he was acting in a manner to shake their confidence. . . . Accordingly the bankers who for a long series of years passed successfully this strict and continual investigation became very wealthy and very powerful.'[1]

Up and down the country merchants, shopkeepers and manufacturers turned bankers. Lipson gives us an impressive list of instances.[2] The Nottingham bank, one of the country's oldest, was started in the late seventeenth century by a mercer; the Gloucester bank by a chandler. Edinburgh had banks established by a corn dealer, a linen draper, a cloth merchant and a tobacco merchant. In Liverpool, not surprisingly, banks were established by merchants and drapers, while in Birmingham the iron-masters played their part.

This development of the country banks came mainly in the second half of the eighteenth century. Edmund Burke, arriving from Ireland in 1750, remarked that there were not 'a dozen bankers' shops outside London.'[3] Those country banks already in existence were probably still in process of transition and carried on banking side by side with other activities. By 1784, however, 119 banks were listed outside London.[4] Between 1791–97, 291 banks were listed for England and Wales. In 1802 the figure was 398. From 1808, when note-issuing bankers required a licence, the figures become more reliable. In 1810–11 the total was 779,

[1] Cf. *Lombard Street*, p. 252–3.
[2] Cf. Lipson, op. cit., p. 245.
[3] Cf. Edmund Burke, *Regicide Peace* (Works, ii, p. 293), cit. Sir John Clapham, *History of the Bank of England*, vol. i, p. 157.
[4] Cf. L. S. Pressnell, *Country Banking in the Industrial Revolution*, Oxford, 1956, p. 6. All statistics for numbers of banks in this period are suspect. Many country banks carried on other activities and it was common for them to trade as merchants in order to avoid banking restrictions. This section leans heavily, as any recent discussion of country banking must do, upon Mr. Pressnell's excellent book.

in 1814 it was 940. Thus the growth pattern which emerges is that from 1750 to 1784 growth was considerable; from 1784 to 1793 numbers trebled. After a slight check between 1793 and 1797 growth was resumed at a rapid rate until 1810 after which it fluctuated until the crisis of 1825 cut the numbers sharply and began the decline which was to continue and bring country banking to an end later in the century. It is, however, well to remember that even as late as 1842 there were still over three hundred country banks.[1]

The London private banker was a more impressive figure than the country banker, tracing his lineage not to merchanting but to the goldsmiths.[2] He came upon the scene about a century earlier than the country banker and he had the British-appreciated cachet of operating from London. He was, Bagehot tells us, 'supposed to represent and often did represent, a certain union of pecuniary sagacity and educated refinement which was scarcely to be found in any other part of society.'[3] Of London private banks there was no lack even in the mid-eighteenth century, but their banking was not as yet always differentiated from other activities. Some had been formed by Londoners in London, others had been started by country bankers moving to the capital. They were primarily divisible into City banks and West End banks, the former commercial, the latter dealing with the accounts of well-to-do persons and the aristocracy. As the eighteenth century proceeded these London banks tended to shed their non-banking features and become banks pure and simple. The number of London private banks doubled between 1770 and 1800. In 1810 there were forty private banks in Lombard Street who were members of the clearing house. Linking country banks with London banks was the practice whereby the former retained a London banker as agent in the capital. This agent handled the London business of the country bank, paying the country banker's notes, accepting his drafts and executing his stock orders. It was common for a London bank of standing to have twenty or thirty country banks for which it acted as agent. These agency arrangements, amounting almost to a system of correspondent banks, did something to mitigate the unitary and regional character of commercial banking in this period.

The establishment by the mid-eighteenth century of distinct sets of financial institutions—country banks, London banks and the Bank of England—enormously widened the potential scope of the remaining set, the money brokers. As long as these were engaged in placing in contact

---

[1] Cf. Pressnell, op. cit., p. 11.
[2] Even in the late eighteenth century certain eminent London bankers kept a goldsmith's shop.
[3] Cf. Bagehot, op. cit., p. 253.

those requiring money and those holding surplus balances and as long as the parties were merely merchants, private traders and capitalists, then their scope was limited. But as soon as the parties were financial institutions whose task it was to switch balances for profit and to whom the idle balance was an anathema, then the brokers' potential usefulness was much greater. Indeed, in the late eighteenth century financial scene with its many banks, widely dispersed and varying in credit standing, he was wellnigh essential. Country banking was highly localised and in the eighteenth century separation from the capital and the London banks became virtually complete as distance increased. A country bank was tied to the economic life of its area and had to accept the fact that in a developing area demand for loans and accommodation might far exceed its deposits and therefore its power to supply credit, while in a rich but economically static area it might be flooded with liquid balances for which it could find no profitable outlet. Clearly if money capital for industrial development was to be optimally distributed some equalisation of loanable funds as between areas had to be achieved. Later with joint stock branch banks this equalisation was a simple process carried on within the branch network but at the end of the eighteenth century, with a unitary banking system in a developing and capital-hungry economy, some means of distributing money capital was vital. The use of bills, discountable with the aid of financial intermediaries, was the means through which capital flowed.

These then were the various elements of the English financial system at the beginning of the nineteenth century. We must clarify their relations a little. Was this system as fragmented as might at first appear? Was it in fact a 'system' at all?

Certainly in the sense that 'system' implies fixed relations, a degree of automaticity and some centre of control, it was not systematic and would not have appeared so at the time, but looked at now from a distant perspective, the outline and main characteristics of the later system are already discernible. The groups—London banks, country banks, the Bank of England, the emergent bill brokers—were distinct but not independent groups. They touched at certain vital points. They touched for example through a common factor in their assets, namely Government stocks and short-term paper, which they all tended to hold, although in varying degree. This gave a rudimentary money market in which they joined. Moreover, a common asset group gave to the Bank of England, which controlled its supply, a special position which held the potential of ultimate control. All the main weapons of control—open-market operations, bank rate policy, the practice of commercial banks keeping accounts at the Bank of England—were still to come when the nineteenth century opened and the whole system was not to be completed until 1914. But already links were in place. One link was of importance, that between the country banks and the developing London money market. The practice whereby country banks held balances in London formed, as one writer puts it, 'a system of unit banking, but not of isolated banks. They were linked with each other and with the London money market by the common economic influences to which provinces and capital alike were subject, by long-standing practices in handling country business and by partnership arrangements. The various parts of the banking structure, if not yet closely integrated were certainly not independent of each other; at most, they were loose-jointed.'[1]

In all this the connection between the country banks and London was important. Such connection was made for each country bank through a single London agent, usually a London banker. Thus it might be said (in the modern terminology of the greatest unitary banking system) that many of the London banks had a number of correspondent banks whom they represented and for whom they did remittance and other business. This system worked well enough as long as country banks did not become too numerous but in the last years of the eighteenth century and in particular during the period of suspended payments by the Bank of England after 1797 the rapid growth of country banking was accompanied by the growth of a new group of intermediary specialists, the bill brokers, to handle the bill business between London and the country bankers. These brokers did not supersede the London agent, and in most cases they continued to function side by side with the agent who acted as banker in London for his country client. They were not principals in the purchase and sale of bills but performed at this time a purely broking function.

The seventeenth and eighteenth centuries saw a great growth in the use of the bill of exchange which for a time and in some areas became the leading means of payment.[2] The London bill was a standard means of payment between country towns and London. The cotton industry in Lancashire, the woollen trade of the West Country, the gentry in their remittances, all became users of the domestic bill.

Great growth in the use of the bill during the Revolutionary and Napoleonic wars encouraged the rise of the bill brokers, and, as Pressnell says, 'concerned with commissions, with margins rather than with

---

[1] Cf. Pressnell, op. cit., pp. 76-7.

[2] Use of bills was by no means uniform throughout the country. It was greatest in the north, especially in Lancashire, where remoteness from London and from banking centres made coin scarce. As the Industrial Revolution progressed scarcity of means of payment became a problem met largely by use of the bill on London. Cf. T. S. Ashton, *The Bill of Exchange and Private Banks in Lancashire*.

absolute rates of interest, they became increasingly important figures in the London money market from the closing years of the eighteenth century.'[1] There was, of course, nothing new in broking. It was an old 'trade'. Brokers had long existed for a variety of purposes, buying goods on behalf of merchants dealing in goods and foreign exchange. Campbell in *The London Tradesman* in 1747 described them:

> 'there are brokers of various sorts distinguished by the Goods they mostly deal in: Their Business is to transact Business for the Merchant, buy up Goods for him; procure him Bills of Exchange, for which he has a premium called Brokerage ... they are a very considerable Body of Men and of vast credit.'

But there evidently was little if any financial specialisation among brokers who spread their activities widely over the merchanting and financial fields. Produce brokers, for example, handled bills in their field. Until the last quarter of the century bill business for the country was handled in London by the agent and according to Pressnell it was not until the late 1780's that the term 'bill broker' crept into use. After 1793 there was a steady spread of specialisation into the financial side of broking but it was the expansion of credit which followed the Bank of England's suspension of cash payments in 1797 that gave the bill of exchange its full flowering and bill broking its full opportunity. Both King and Pressnell, although they disagree on the causes, agree that the years 1797–1815 were the years of swiftest growth for bill broking.

The real causes of such growth are not easy to find but a number of factors undoubtedly contributed. Firstly, the Bank of England, *potentially* the largest discounter in the market, always charged the maximum rate,[2] making it preferable for country banks to seek discount facilities elsewhere. Secondly, the Bank laid down stringent conditions which bills discounted by them had to satisfy. It would not take bills of more than 65 days' currency and every bill to pass the Committee in Waiting had to bear at least two London names. These conditions ruled out at once a great part of the country banks' paper so that such paper had to be placed elsewhere, which in practice meant through the bill brokers.[3] Thirdly, the Usury Law of 1714 laid down that the maximum legal rate of interest was 5 per cent per annum and, with a few exceptions, this was the rate at which bills were discounted. On the other hand stock exchange securities could be traded at prices which reflected a much higher yield than 5 per cent

---

[1] Cf. Pressnell, op. cit., p. 90.
[2] Bank rate remained at 5 per cent from 1746 to 1822.
[3] London bankers did not want to take bills from their country clients which they could not rediscount at the Bank of England. Bill brokers were less choosey.

without offending the Usury Laws. In order to obtain discounts at 5 per cent many discounters went initially to the Bank of England but this growing demand led the Bank in 1795 to ration its discounts and holders of bills had to go elsewhere. Fourthly, the Bank of England had not as yet developed the technique of open-market operations whereby it might in times of money shortage[1] relieve the stringency. When such conditions occurred the market rate of interest should have risen to attract fresh lenders and to repel borrowers but, under the Usury Laws, it could not do this—the rate being fixed at 5 per cent. Shortage of funds when it occurred tended, therefore, to produce conditions in which it was very difficult to find persons to discount bills. The effect of the Usury Laws was in fact to check the volume of money coming forward in time of stringency and to render the services of the broker essential to the discounter if, under such conditions, a bill was to be placed at all. Finally, there was during the period of the Napoleonic Wars an increasing demand from country bankers in the growing industrial areas for outlets in London for their bills. This demand was only met by London bankers to the extent of the country banks' balances, and although London banks were sometimes prepared to extend credit to their country cousins, their willingness was unequal to the demand which overflowed increasingly through bills placed by the bill brokers. Moreover, many of the country bills were of such long tenor as made them unacceptable to the London banks who could not rediscount such 'long bills' at the Bank of England. The bill brokers were prepared to take such bills, being concerned with their quality rather than their tenor.

All these factors working together produced a financial climate in which the broker was a person of increasing usefulness in the monetary system, and certainly by the first decade of the nineteenth century he was part of the established scene.[2] Richardson of Richardson, Overend and Company (later referred to as Overend, Gurney), giving evidence to the Bullion Committee in 1810, described how his firm took in bills from Lancashire and sent them for discount to Norfolk, Suffolk, Sussex and Essex.[3] He had built up his bill business after leaving Messrs. Smith and Holt, bankers, in 1802, and by offering to supply country bankers with good bills at the low brokerage charge of $\frac{1}{8}$ per cent. By 1810 the annual turnover in his business was seven to eight million pounds and about £1·5m. was out on loan at any one time. Richardson's firm was by far

---

[1] Such as at times of heavy tax payment.

[2] In 1800 one of a number of new wartime taxes advocated to Pitt was one on brokers, including 'brokers in discounts'.

[3] It seems from Richardson's evidence that most of the bills he dealt in had more than 65 days to run.

the largest of the bill broking firms acting for the country banks. Although Richardson spoke in his evidence of several other houses conducting a similar country bank agency business in 1810 it seems that their turnover was small. King estimates that the whole bill market at that time was employing about £10m. annually for the country banks.[1]

Since the name of Overend, Gurney will occur many times in this and the following chapter it is necessary to say something at this stage of a firm which was to have great influence on the discount market at this period. The origins of this famous house are traceable to the development of a great wool merchanting firm and country banking business—Gurney and Co. of Norwich. The family of Gurney was Norman in origin and from the time of James I the banking and merchanting functions of its business had been combined. From merchanting in wool the house had passed naturally to lending money to spinners for working capital, making loans to wealthier textile entrepreneurs and taking deposits.

In 1775 a separate banking business was established by John and Henry Gurney in the Norwich and Norfolk Bank. This bank was unable to find suitable local outlets for all of its resources and established a close liaison with Joseph Smith, a London wool factor who had long had dealings with Gurney's. Smith was able to supply the Norwich bank with bills of exchange drawn in the wool trade for which he charged a commission of ¼ per cent.

Smith did so well at his bill broking that he dropped wool-merchanting and became a bill broker, his name appearing in 1799 in the list of London bankers as Joseph Smith and Co. of Old Broad Street and later as Smith and Holt—a firm which continued in various forms until the second half of the century.

One of Smith and Holt's clerks was Thomas Richardson who in 1802 left the firm and began business on his own as a bill broker. The reason for his defection was a dispute over who should pay for the brokering of a bill. Richardson had suggested that the process of the broker charging commission to the country banker should be replaced by one under which the London merchant paid the brokerage and the country banker was relieved of the commission. This was a shrewd realisation of the principle of elasticity of demand. Money was scarce and London merchants were quite willing to accept the brokerage charge to get their bills discounted whereas country banks, relieved of the commission, were prepared to take more bills from the London brokers. Richardson's business prospered and in joint supply of bills to Gurney's with his old

[1] Cf. Select Committee on the High Price of Bullion, 1810, Minutes, p. 122, cited in King, op. cit., pp. 9–10.

firm Smith and Holt he made serious inroads on the latter's business, for Smith and Holt continued the old system. King describes a colourful dispute in the summer of 1803, when Smith and Holt accused Gurney's of engineering Richardson's resignation from them and cast some aspersions on the 'selectiveness' of his bills. Gurney's with grace and charm but also a good eye for business suggested that thenceforward all bills from Richardson should be seen and approved by Smith and Holt, a device which secured for Gurney's a double check on all bills passed to them from London.

Richardson's business prospered despite Smith and Holt's surveillance and in 1805 he was joined by John Overend, a city clerk, and the firm's style became Richardson, Overend and Company. Within the limits of honesty and probably under the influence of Richardson, the firm were smart operators. Several schemes for supplying bills to Gurney's under very favourable conditions to that firm were not accepted by Gurney's because they were near to the borders of legality. This, together with Gurney's reluctance to abandon Smith and Holt in favour of Richardson, Overend and Co. as suppliers of bills, in spite of the higher cost of brokerage of the former, indicates a humane and high-minded approach to business by the Quaker bankers which was not to be preserved in the second and last half-century of their operations.

In 1802, John Gurney, one of the Norwich partners, sent his son Samuel to London to join Joseph Fry's, the banking and merchanting house. When he completed his apprenticeship in 1807, and after Gurney's had carried out a scrupulous examination of the firm's affairs, Samuel, with his brother John, joined Richardson, Overend and Company as partners. Samuel became a well-known and respected City figure. He was a man of great ability and business acumen and clearly much of the firm's subsequent expansion was due to him. He died in 1856.

In the years which followed the bill broking business grew steadily. In 1808, Overend's was supplying 42 per cent of Gurney's bills from London, Smith and Holt being responsible for the rest. A year later Overend's were supplying the whole of an expanded Gurney portfolio. By 1813, King estimates that Overend's early bill turnover was something over £17m. In 1823, Richardson gives it as £20m.

Long before 1827 when, after the death of Thomas Richardson, the firm's name was changed to that of Overend, Gurney and Company, the firm had established itself as 'by far the biggest bill brokering firm of the day'. It was to remain so for nearly another fifty years. At 65 Lombard Street at the corner of Birchin Lane, the 'Corner House' was a City institution of household familiarity until its spectacular collapse in the crisis of 1866.

From the bill brokers' point of view the forwarding for discount of bills from the country banks in industrial districts was but a part of their business. There was not always, it seems, sufficient demand for bills from country banks in rural areas to match the bills sent to brokers from industrial districts. Other forms of business were, therefore, carried on by brokers. One notable form was of forwarding for discount at London banks bills from London merchants. 'To obtain money on discount from London bankers'[1] for merchanting houses in London itself was an important line of business for Richardson, Overend and Company and for a 'great many' others as well. Richardson stated that these operations for London merchants considerably exceeded those for country banks. King estimates that, if we include the London merchant business, the total turnover of the market from all sources in 1810 could not have been far short of £20m. per annum with £5m. outstanding at any time.[2]

Between 1810 and 1825 there was a steady expansion of bill broking in London and business increased both with the country banks (which were still growing in number) and with the merchant houses. There was a large supply of money flowing from country banks for investment and Richardson in 1810 in his evidence to the Bullion Committee declared that the sums of money which he lent for country bankers on discount were fifty times more than the sums he borrowed for such bankers. This no doubt reflected the prosperity of the rural areas in wartime and the funds they had for investment and for payments to London.

After 1810 expansion of the bill market was rapid. The number of country banks was increasing: the reliance of such banks on bills as a channel of investment was growing. Rediscounting of bills through brokers became common and assured the brokers of a continuous supply of bills. By 1813 the Bankers' and Merchants' Almanack listed the names of 19 bill broking firms. A commercial directory of 1822–23 listed twenty-five.[3] It was, however, a somewhat unstable population. Between 1811 and 1826 thirty-seven bill brokers failed. Clapham put it well when he said of bill broking: 'Men went into it, came out of it or failed at it very frequently.'[4] Pressnell, reviewing the personalities among the bill brokers of 1812–13, presents a variegated list, topped by Richardson, Overend and Company, 'a giant among the pygmies', followed by Alexander and Company and James Bruce and tailing off quickly into a rackety crew of failed bankers and others. There was, according to Pressnell, Sir Matthew Bloxham, a former partner in Sanderson's bank in Southwark who had run a 'discount bank' of his own from 1795 until

[1] Cf. King, op. cit., p. 10.   [2] Ibid., p. 10.
[3] Cf. Pigot's Commercial Directory for 1822–23.
[4] Cf. Sir John Clapham, The Bank of England, Vol. i, p. 158.

I

its failure in 1809. There was Robert Bramley whose business as a bill broker failed in 1815. A number of other names suggest that brokers in 1812–13 had formerly been in banking houses now defunct. Other intriguing names such as 'Medina Brothers' are of unknown origin and vanished from the later scene without trace. Little wonder that the crisis of 1825 produced a high mortality rate amongst them. Yet in the period 1800 to 1825 the foundations of a bill market were laid. The Bullion Report of 1810 referred to the increase in bill broking in terms which were mildly complimentary saying that the increase in discount facilities had been of assistance to the country manufacturer and had enabled London bankers to economise their cash.

The situation then before the financial crisis of 1825 can be summed up as follows. There had grown up over three to four decades in London a group of financial intermediaries who acted as brokers[1] in London for country banks and for merchants in the discounting of bills of exchange. They did not themselves discount bills but brought the holder of the bill and the discounter together for commission. They did not as yet borrow 'call money' from the banks nor had they any rights of rediscount with the Bank of England. This did not come until about 1830.

The next fifty years were to bring a great expansion in bill broking and, more important, a transition from broking to dealing. One firm— that of Thomas Richardson—was destined to grow and straddle this period and as Overend, Gurney and Company to typify all that was best (and weakest) in this early phase of the bill market.

III

Financial crises are the ruin of many but the making of a few. Certainly the crisis of 1825 wrought a transformation in the British banking system and, in particular, marked the beginning of a second and more important chapter in the history of the bill market. But without, at this stage, recounting the many changes wrought by the financial blizzard of 1825 it is as well to note one general but fundamental result: for the first time in British financial history the constituent groups of institutions were drawn powerfully together by the instinct of self-preservation. Banks, both London and country, bill brokers and the Bank of England were made more conscious than before of interdependence, of the fact that their relations one to another were important and that events seemingly only important to one group might have great consequence for others. In

---

[1] Clapham calls them 'bills merchants'. Cf. Clapham, *Economic History of Modern Britain*, Vol. i, p. 260.

particular the Bank of England was forced tacitly to admit its responsibility for pilotage in troubled and dangerous waters.

The financial crisis itself is of less importance than the changes which it produced. It was the result of speculation springing from several causes of which a series of good harvests, great trade activity, currency over-issue and unsound policies by the country banks were the main ones.[1] The Bank of England unwittingly prepared the way by extending (in December 1821) from 65 days to 95 days the currency of bills which it was prepared to discount, and (in June 1822) by reducing its discount rate to 4 per cent. With all this the whole economy was extremely liquid and ripe for the speculation which began in earnest in 1824. There was a wave of speculation in primary commodities and a host of wildcat company projects. In the 'first great nineteenth century eruption'[2] 624 schemes for companies were mooted, 143 never got to the point of applying for capital, 236 got as far as issuing prospectuses but not issuing shares; 118 got as far as issuing shares but were subsequently abandoned; and 127 were still in existence in 1827 with a total paid-up capital of £15·2m. currently valued at £9·3m.[3] There were many schemes for the development of various newly-established South American republics. In late 1824 primary commodity markets were in a very delicate state and a drain of gold had begun.

In early 1825 the Bank of England became worried and ceased to discount, a step which in itself created an atmosphere of misgiving and potential crisis. Many country banks with accounts at London banks sought funds in London. By the last month of 1825 the panic was at its height. Banks were now in trouble. In November one of the leading banks in the West country, Elford's of Plymouth, failed. Wentworth and Company, a leading Yorkshire bank, followed. There was a high mortality in Scotland. In early December, Pole, Thornton and Company, one of the leading London firms, was in difficulties. This house was London agent for many banks in Scotland and England[4] and there were frantic efforts by the Bank of England to keep it going, but to no avail. Pole's was followed by Williams, Burgess and Company, an equally famous house. Others followed.

The failure of London banks brought the crisis to its peak. It was clear

---

[1] The financial crisis of 1825 was an almost classic case of 'the boom that ran away'. An interesting and human sidelight upon it is to be found in the 'Letters from a Young Lady', published in the *Three Banks Review*, June 1950, No. 6. These personal letters of Miss Marrianne Thornton describe her brother Henry's efforts to keep the London banking firm of Pole, Thornton & Company afloat in the crisis.

[2] Cf. Clapham, *Economic History of Modern Britain*, Vol. i, p. 272.

[3] Ibid, p. 272.   [4] King gives the figure of 44. Cf. King, op. cit., p. 36.

that if swift action was not taken complete collapse of the currency and the monetary system would ensue. Prompt action was taken. The Bank of England reversed its restrictionist policy and went far in the opposite direction lending on Exchequer bills, discounting, making advances on deposits of bills, and 'by every possible means consistent with the safety of the Bank' rendering assistance to stricken financial houses. This demonstration of strength restored confidence but could not restore the numerous firms, banking and commercial, which had failed nor recoup the distress which had been caused by the widespread loss of money capital and personal savings.

Public opinion had been stirred and much criticism of the banking system and of the existing state of banking and currency law followed the crisis. Peel, Lord Liverpool and Huskisson were major contributors to the debate which produced two Acts of Parliament, one dealing with the issue of paper money and one with banking organisation. In the debates on the currency issue much was made of the over-issue of one pound notes. These, it was argued, not only tended to drive the gold sovereign out of circulation but were a standing temptation to weaker banks to over-issue. The fact that the Scottish banking system was held up on the one hand as a model of rectitude but that it also issued one pound notes was a complication. It was got over adroitly by the argument that the Scottish banks were better managed than the English and knew better how to direct the circulation of one pound notes.

By the first of these Acts, that regulating the currency,[1] no more notes below £5 were to be issued. Those already in circulation were progressively to be withdrawn. The Bank of England (accused of over-issue prior to the crisis) was ordered to keep the Treasury informed each week of the size of the circulation of notes with denominations under £5. In the second Act, which dealt with the organisation of the banking system,[2] important innovations appeared. Firstly, the Bank of England was to be allowed to open branches outside London. Secondly, banks with any number of partners were to be allowed to operate outside a 65-mile radius of London provided that they had no place of business in London and that the liability of partners was unlimited. Since an Act of the previous year[3] had abolished restrictions on joint stock enterprise the way was now open for joint stock banking in the provinces. Moreover the Act of 1826 gave joint stock banks the right to sue and be sued in the name of their officers —a convenience when the number of partners was great.

Considerable as the changes in banking law and regulations were after the 1825 crisis they were hardly more important in the long run than the changes made by the London bankers in their own practices. For the

---

[1] 7 Geo. IV, c. 6.   [2] 7 Geo. IV, c. 46.   [3] 6 Geo. IV, c. 91.

discount market these changes were crucial. Two stand out. Firstly, the London bankers, shaken by the great demands which had been made on the Bank of England during the crisis and doubting whether in a recurrence such demands could be met for long, decided in future to hold an adequate reserve of cash to deposits, the reserve to be held both in coin and in Bank of England deposits. Moreover, in order to have a second line reserve to cash, these banks now began to lend at call to the larger bill brokers. Secondly, the London bankers ceased to rediscount bills, holding them always until redemption—a practice still adhered to by the modern clearing banks. Finally, one general effect of the crisis was to change the position of the Bank of England in the English monetary system. In the eyes of its critics the Bank's mistaken actions had caused the crisis; but it was also apparent that its realisation at the eleventh hour of its responsibilities and the implications of its large-scale operations had saved the country when it was 'within twenty-four hours of barter'. It could never again be thought either by the Bank, the financial fraternity or the public that the Bank of England was just another London bank, although large, powerful and government favoured. It was now recognised that it had special responsibilities. It took the remainder of the century, however, to learn just what these responsibilities were and how they could best be met.

The significance of these crisis-born changes for the bill market was great and is discussed below. Other revolutionary changes were also taking place. The largest of the brokers were, by the late 1820's, houses of standing and were beginning to carry bills as well as doing brokering business. On the other hand, the ranks of the weaker brokers had been thinned. The crisis had strengthened the strong and removed the weak, a process of financial 'natural selection' which was to be much in evidence during the remainder of the century. By 1829 the large brokers had acquired the confidence of the Bank of England which agreed to establish for them what it now calls 'discount accounts'. This gave these dealers the right to take bills of certain specified standards to the Bank and have them discounted. This, in effect, gave to the brokers with such accounts 'final resort' facilities at the Bank. It is certain that, at first, advances to the bill merchants were confined to Overend, Gurney, the largest and most reputable. From June 1830, Clapham tells us,[1] advances were regularly made to this firm on the security of bills of exchange.

IV

By 1830 and as a result of all these changes the three pre-requisites of the

[1] Cf. Clapham, *The Bank of England*, Vol. ii, p. 135.

London discount market were all in being: a group of dealers dealing in bills; short-term credit from the banks to enable them to do so, and rudimentary final resort facilities at the Bank of England for the brokers when the banks called in their call loans. These changes and the great growth of the discount market which followed were largely the result of the institutional and procedural changes made in English banking after the 1825 crisis. Since these had such sweeping effects it is perhaps wise at this stage to set them down concisely. They were:

(a) The establishment of Bank of England branches in the provinces;
(b) The rise of joint stock banking;
(c) The establishment of the 'call-loan' system;
(d) The end of the practice of rediscounting by the London banks; and
(e) The opening by bill brokers of discount accounts at the Bank of England.

So fundamental to the discount market were all these changes that we must examine them a little more closely.

(a) The Bank of England branches when set up had beneficial effects for the bill brokers—a somewhat surprising fact in view of the blow which branch commercial banking was later to deal them. Before the end of 1826 the Bank of England exercised its powers under the new Act and opened branches in Gloucester, Swansea and Manchester and within a few years at Birmingham, Bristol, Exeter, Hull, Leeds, Liverpool, Leicester, Newcastle and Norwich.[1] By 1833 there were eleven branches. These branches issued notes but they also discounted bills at London rates which were often below the country bank discount rates. Moreover, they held out an inducement to country banks to discount with them by offering their discount facilities at one per cent under bank rate providing they reduced their note issues and replaced these by rediscounting with the branches. Since other local rates tended to move in sympathy this sometimes had the effect of reducing local rediscount rates below the London level. It is, however, probable that this diversion of business from London was not great since the note-issuing bankers had not been large discounters. Moreover, forces driving banks and others to discount with the Bank of England branches were to a great extent offset by the very exacting criteria applied by the branches in accepting bills. These criteria were daunting in the extreme and precluded most of the bills commonly in currency. Ordinary commercial discounts were open only to those of high credit standing who opened a discount account, which had to be approved by the Bank of England in London. Such an account

[1] It would appear that the branches were opened where there was large banking business to tap rather than where banking was weak.

was subject to a discount limit. All bills had to be approved by London and bills of longer than three months' tenor were not acceptable. Initially there was a scheme for classification of bills with scaled interest charges but this was soon abandoned.

Indeed, if the purpose of these branches was to provide banking facilities in competition with local banks both to strengthen the latter and to widen the Bank of England's own business then it would seem that more flexible policies would have produced better results. For example, the branches gave no interest on long-term deposits or on balances of current accounts nor did they give overdrafts. There is no indication that the local discount facilities provided by the Bank of England branches did anything to impair the business of the bill brokers as agents for the country banks. It was the country banks who complained of the Bank of England as a government sponsored monopoly. The Bank's branches were, in the eyes of their competitors in the provinces, 'privileged competitors and semi-official censors of notes.' Had the Bank of England branches succeeded in diverting to themselves any considerable volume of discount business the brokers' business might have been greatly diminished but the inflexibility of Bank policy in the branches, indeed some said its divorcement from the realities of commercial life, prevented this. They did succeed in reducing the cost of discounting since they charged no commission and country banks who had charged 5s. or 6s. per cent were forced to follow suit.

In one respect the Bank of England branches greatly assisted the bill market—in the matter of remittances. Hitherto it had been difficult, dangerous and costly to move money about the country and local financiers were to some extent cut off from the London market. The branches provided, however, an efficient and cheap remittance service and it now became possible for persons who formerly were unable to discount in London to remit their bills direct to a London bill broker with instructions for him to pay the proceeds to the Bank of England for remission back to the branch. In this way links between London brokers and provincial manufacturers and traders were forged which were beneficial to both.

(b) The joint stock banking which began slowly to appear after the Act of 1826 was not the beginning of the branch banking network we know today.[1] Had it been so its appearance would have brought the end of bill broking in the form then existing, as did indeed happen half a century later. The 'equalising' of credit supply which the bill brokers facilitated would have quickly been performed by joint stock banks

[1] The essential quality of the later growth of joint stock banking was its establishment of a branch network.

through their branch network. The new development was rather the continuation under joint stock organisation of local unit banking with all that that implied in terms of demand for the agency functions which the bill brokers supplied. One difference, however, between the new joint stock banking and the old country banking was very marked: the older private banking was based upon the issue of notes, deposits being a secondary consideration, whereas joint stock banking was essentially deposit banking. Some joint stock banks did start with note issues but in the main they were relinquished after a few years. Being deposit banks the new institutions had to build up their deposits from two sources: either by recruiting depositors from the ranks of those already with accounts at the older country banks or by attracting persons to open accounts with them who hitherto had not had banking accounts at all. To draw deposits from either source necessitated the offering of attractive interest rates on deposit balances. This was done and interest rates, and competition in interest rates as between banks, became a distinguishing mark of the new deposit banking. A further requirement of the new system was that, if a bank were to run at a profit, very complete utilisation of its deposit resources was necessary. For this reason only a minimal cash reserve was held for till-money, the banks relying on rediscounting bills to replenish cash if and when required. This practice redounded to the advantage of the brokers into whose hands this rediscounting business naturally came. It was a steady and lucrative source of dealings for, although the older country banks had rediscounted, the practice had been regarded as one appropriate only to conditions of stringency and for rare occasions, whereas the joint stock banks rediscounted almost daily and as a matter of routine. From the viewpoint of the joint stock banker there was a dangerous ease in this system. If he wished to increase the interest he allowed on deposits all he had to do was to increase his discounts, using the bills as rediscounts to replenish his cash when necessary. In some cases the necessity to obtain bills which could become scarce might result in his scrutiny of them being less than close.

Other forces drove the new bankers to the bill market. The bill of exchange was in itself becoming a more popular form of asset for banks. Not only had their knowledge of bill dealing grown with the years but the bill of exchange was seen by the joint stock banker to be a preferable asset to government securities, in particular to Exchequer Bills which were by this period tending to lose negotiability. Not only was it more liquid but it was capable of swifter switches when required. For example, an old type country banker might often, when deposits exceeded cash plus advances, be content to hold surplus balances for a period. A joint stock banker would not do this. He could not afford the luxury of idle balances. He would rather acquire bills at once, being prepared to re-discount if he needed cash or if he wished to switch funds to advances.

From all this it is apparent that this first appearance of joint stock banking was of great assistance to the bill market. The assets structure and operations of the new banks assumed the existence of a bill market and of bill brokers and the period from 1830 to 1860 was the golden age of the old form of bill broking, in which the brokers acted as agents and distributors of credit for a banking system still local and fragmented. In the period 1800 to 1825 under the old system of country banking the bill broker had been useful but by no means indispensable. In his absence country banks would have been forced to rely far more on their London agents, but with the coming of joint stock banking and its new emphasis on deposits the bill broker was an integral part of the banking system. Indeed, had a bill market not been in existence to service the needs of the new joint stock banks their development would probably have been along different lines to those which in fact were taken.

The development of joint stock banking was slow at first but soon gained momentum. Because of the provision of the 1826 Act, which still gave the Bank of England its monopoly in London, it began in the provinces. In the years following the Act there was some growth of joint stock banking but private banks looked askance at the innovation and the public was also suspicious. Joint stock banks came first in the north: in Huddersfield, Bradford and Norwich in 1827 and in Manchester, Halifax, Cumberland and Leicester in 1829. Such banking truly began in the shadow of the 'dark Satanic mills'. But after the Bank Charter Act of 1833 joint stock banks were permitted in the London area providing they did not issue notes. This opened the way for a development of joint stock banking in the City of London itself. In March 1834 the first London joint stock bank, the London and Westminster, was opened in the teeth of hostility from the Bank of England and the private banks.[1] At the end of 1833 there were 82 joint stock banks in England, mostly in the industrial areas; by 1836 there were 99, by 1841, 115, including three new ones in London. Private banks, meanwhile, were falling in number and in 1831 there were 321 as compared with 781 in 1821. Some private banks were going joint stock, others were amalgamating with joint stock banks. In addition there had been a high mortality among country banks in the financial panic of 1825.

With the growth of joint stock banking proceeding apace the bill market and the number of bill brokers grew rapidly. Samuel Gurney said in 1836 that the discount business of London had doubled in the

[1] Most of the capital for the new bank was raised in the country.

preceding five years[1] and admitted that much of the market's growing turnover was due to the practice of rediscounting by the provincial joint stock banks. Not only did this increase the number of bills but their endorsement by a reputable bank rendered negotiable many which formerly would not have been so.

(c) No feature is so typical of the bill market or so necessary to the bill broker as the 'call loan'. If a broker, i.e. one who acts merely as agent, bringing the holder of a bill and a willing discounter together, is himself to act as discounter and to carry bills, he must be able to borrow money at rates of interest at least marginally lower than those at which he discounts. In essence development from broker to dealer depends on constant access to adequate money working capital. With the narrowness of dealing margins the bill dealer's turnover must be large—larger than he can ever finance out of his own capital resources—and he must borrow to finance his bill portfolio. It was from the changes in banking practice occurring after 1826 and contingent upon the rise of joint stock banking that bankers' call loans to bill dealers were born.

How or when the practice of call loans began is uncertain. From a variety of evidence it is clear that, by the mid-1830's, the practice was well established. In all probability it began with an arrangement, which appears to have been widespread, whereby brokers agreed to take from provincial bankers a certain value in bills each week. In return brokers had the right to expect not less than this amount in bills and on occasions when cash requirements of the banks were less than would be forthcoming from the bills rediscounted it was an obvious convenience to leave the surplus 'on call' with the bill broker, it being understood that he would turn it over to the bank if and when the state of the bank's cash reserve required it. From this arrangement it was but a step to the purposive lending of money to bill brokers on a day to day basis—this again to be for the lending bank an immediate second line reserve to cash. The practice in the provinces of lending to bill brokers on call was probably stimulated also by the fact that provincial banks got no interest on their balances with their London agents. These balances they therefore cut to a minimum and all surpluses were kept with the bill brokers. Finally, the diminishing popularity of Exchequer Bills after about 1835, and their declining negotiability, led bankers to look in other directions when placing their assets. The great convenience and liquidity of call loans commended them to bankers as the convenience of other assets declined. Thus, so far as provincial banks were concerned, there were considerable influences making for extension of the call loan practice during the

[1] Cf. Evidence before *Select Committee on Joint Stock Banks*, 1836, QQ. 2551–618, cited in King, op. cit., p. 43.

1830's. As for the London joint stock banks they had granted call loans from their beginning.[1] They were deposit banks and apart from a small cash reserve they had to find interest earning outlets for their deposits. Demands for loans from customers were rarely large enough to employ all their resources so that a substantial amount might be available for lending at call. This source of call money was not, however, a large part of the total. There were only a few London banks and competition among them for deposits was not acute in their early years.

(d) The ending of rediscounting by the London private bankers had a great and lasting effect upon the bill market, probably more fundamental than any of the influences we have reviewed above although at the time the results were not perhaps so apparent. For the change engendered here was structural, tending to transform the nature of the bill market from an agency and brokering service to a discount market of the modern type.

The force prompting the London private bankers to end a practice of such long standing was simply that of caution, not to say fear, of too deep a reliance on the Bank of England. The crisis of 1825 when the pressure of their country clients had driven them to rediscount at the Bank of England demonstrated how their very existence could rest upon the Bank of England's decision to lend or not to lend, to rediscount for them or not to rediscount. For those who survived, the crisis had been a salutary experience from which they determined to profit. They established cash reserves of their own and, to avoid holding too large a part of their resources in the form of cash, a sterile asset from the point of view of income, they cast about for second and even third line reserves for their deposits. For their main liquid asset (apart from cash) they used bills of exchange where formerly they had used government securities. These bills they bought through the London bill brokers. But not even a three-month self-liquidating asset satisfied their new thirst for liquidity. There must be some quickly mobilisable reserve to cash itself. For this secured loans to the brokers themselves at rates of interest fractionally below bill rates were ideal assets. Thus the liquid assets structure of the London banks begins from this period to look very like the liquid assets structure to which we are now accustomed although at that stage it was much less bound by convention and not at all by statute or regulation. From a description by Gilbart it is evident that the banker of the period saw this structure (perhaps somewhat mistily) as:

Deposits   Cash: In tills
                           At Bank of England
      Call loans
      Bills

[1] Cf. p. 133 above.

—very much as the commercial banker of today sees it. Cash was replenishable, when necessary, by calling in loans from the brokers: surplus cash, when it appeared, was pushed out to earn its keep as call money. Behind both stood a well-tapered bill portfolio, turning over constantly, but with all bills held to maturity.

One of the main limitations to this system in the years after 1825 was, of course, the small number of bill brokers to whom the banks might lend and the dubious credit-worthiness of some of them. At the outset it seems that Gurney's was the only house favoured by the banks and that even as the years passed and others—Sanderson's, Bruce's—came into the field Gurney's still remained the major house and borrower.

Another factor which, following 1825, stimulated bill dealing (as distinct from broking) was the low rate of interest prevailing. Under the Usury Laws the maximum legal rate of interest was 5 per cent but after the crisis of 1825 the market rate dropped below this. In June 1826 it was 4½ per cent and by June 1827, 3 per cent. With such a comfortable margin between market rate and the maximum legal rate there was a good spread of rates as between call rate and bill rate and ample room for profitable dealing.

The coming of call loans to the bill market had wider implications for the banking system as a whole, in that it began the aloofness of the commercial banks from the central bank which was long to be a marked feature of the British banking system. Had the London banks maintained the practice of rediscounting with the Bank of England when necessary this would have meant that they might be driven to the Bank frequently by the mere routine fluctuations in the flow of funds. One Bank might have been rediscounting when another had surplus funds available. With the system of call loans to the bill market things were otherwise. In times of stringency banks called in their 'brokers' loans' and thus replenished their cash. If only one or two banks were calling the deprived brokers had a chance of getting accommodation from another bank which was not calling. Only if the credit shortage were general would the bill brokers be driven to the central bank. In the developed discount market, when rediscounting occurs it is the bill brokers who do it with the Bank of England: it is through them that the Bank relieves cash stringency.

The set of relationships described above was not of course clearly discernible in 1826 nor for many years after. Bill brokers were still few and the Usury Laws, which caused them to limit the size of their bill portfolios, were not repealed until 1833.[1] But such a system was latent in

[1] The attractiveness of the bill of exchange as an investment to bankers was increased by the clause in the 1833 Act which exempted bills and notes with less than three months to run from the restrictions of the Usury Laws.

the developments which were taking place. While the arrangements in London were beginning by the 1830's to have a familiar modern look it must be remembered that it was only the London banks which had ceased to rediscount. Outside London rediscounting had increased although some provincial banks did lend at call.

(e) Until 1830 bill dealers were not allowed to have discount accounts with the Bank of England. This inspired in all who had dealings with the bill brokers a certain caution. London bankers were chary of committing themselves too far in the matter of call loans so long as no 'last resort' facilities were available. As long as a bill dealer could repay call loans to Bank A by borrowing at call from Bank B all was in order, and this situation often occurred. But, if there were to be a general call-in by banks from bill dealers, what then? The shade of 1825 haunted the banking mind of the 1830's and it was no wonder that the banks limited their lending to the large and reputable houses.

By 1830, Bank of England thought had come far as compared with 1825. The crisis of that year had established the principle that when a shortage of credit developed and embarrassed or endangered the banking system it was the Bank of England's duty to ease the shortage. Since 1830 it was the means of doing this which had been the subject of discussion. Clearly the problem was one of choosing the path through which the Bank could best channel money into the system when it was required. The natural channel for this might at first sight appear to have been the London banks but, as we have seen, these had already determined that they should be independent of the Bank of England and would not, as in 1825, rediscount with it, still less borrow from it directly. The alternative was to make the bill market the channel through which additional funds should flow when required. The Bank had observed the developments in the bill market and how its rôle was changing. It was now, it seemed, in the bill market that credit stringency first showed itself and it was there that it could quickly, easily and efficiently be alleviated. If the bill dealers had the right to come to the Bank during a period of shortage then credit would be made available which would circulate through the whole financial system. Moreover, the new credit would be well distributed. The bill dealers would, by using the Bank's funds and repaying call loans, put money in the hands of the banks but would also by discounting bills for ordinary commercial purposes push money out into the economy at large. The bill market must therefore act as the channel through which the Bank would direct the flow of new funds.

With this in view, in November 1830 the Bank sanctioned the opening of discount accounts by bill brokers. At first these accounts were of importance only to Gurney's and two or three larger houses. The names of

Overend, Gurney, Sanderson and Co., Alexander, and James Bruce recur regularly. Loans were often long. Overend, Gurney had a running loan, rarely less than £100,000. In 1834 Gurney's had £250,000 for six months: Sanderson's had £500,000 for six months. In June 1836 all four of the above houses had loans ranging from £400,000 to £500,000 for six months.[1] The small brokers[2] had little need for Bank of England accommodation and carried on as before. But for the large dealers the accounts were regarded as vital and the large houses now carried on their business with the assumption that in times of stringency they could go at once to the Bank for assistance.

Another Bank of England practice begun in this period, which helped to establish the principle of help to the money market in times of stringency, was that of lending at the so-called 'shuttings'. By vote of the Court in June 1829 a plan of the Bank's Committee of Treasury was approved which sanctioned loans by the Bank on approved security to counteract 'the disturbing effects of quarterly payments on revenue account into the Bank accompanied by its closing of the government stock transfer books while preparing the dividend warrants.'[3] Thus began the 'quarterly loans during the shutting' which were to be established practice during the century.

The significance of the Bank's action in 1830 in allowing bill dealers' accounts to be opened and in establishing means of aiding the market during the shuttings and thereby admitting its own rôle as lender of last resort, was immense in the general development of British banking and in particular for the discount market. So far as the modern banking system is concerned the foundations and some of the structure were now in place. The joint stock banks, the discount market, the central bank were all discernible and linked in ways perhaps rudimentary but still similar to those with which we are now familiar. By making credit available through one channel, the discount market, the Bank of England could, and of course now does, control both the quantity and price of credit. Much water was to flow under the bridge before the significance and full responsibilities of the Bank in this monopoly position were fully realised. There were to be recantings and second thoughts. The history of this realisation is the history of bank rate and bank rate policies and is a long one extending down into the twentieth century, but the crucial first step in this history was the opening of these first discount accounts. For the discount market itself the significance was also great. Within three years two things vital to its growth had happened: the Bank's action in

---

[1] Cf. Clapham, *The Bank of England*, Vol. ii, p. 142.
[2] As distinct from dealers.
[3] Cf. Clapham, op. cit., p. 137.

1830 and the ending by the Act of 1833 of the Usury Laws which had been a confusion and complication to its working for so long. With these events behind it the market entered a new phase of development.

V

Of all financial groups the discount market is one of the closest to the central bank and the actions, policy and development of the bank have a close influence upon it. In a formative period such as that which we have been considering, central bank action determined the very existence of a bill market. It is appropriate, therefore, to pause at this stage and consider briefly the changing part played by the Bank of England during the first half of the nineteenth century in the making of the discount market.

The century opened with the Bank of England occupying a special position in a rapidly growing banking system. Although in London the number of banking firms was not increasing, all over England the so-called 'country banks' were being set up and their numbers doubled between 1797 and 1804.[1] The special position which the Bank enjoyed was founded upon prestige, its position as banker to the government and its monopoly of the London note issue. Its private banking business had grown since the suspension of cash payments in 1797 and to differentiate this business from its rôle as *primus inter paries* among the London bankers was to be a major task in the first half of the century. Already conscious of certain as yet undefined responsibilities, the Bank was feeling its way towards the beginning of a credit policy, but the aims were still undefined and the means had still to be worked out. Apart from its note-issuing and specie policies which, in the main, lie outside the scope of this book, in the field of banking the Bank of England's method until 1825 was to influence events by participating in the carrying out of ordinary banking functions. Its size, scale of operations and prestige gave to its way of conducting business a significance beyond that attaching to the trans-actions of other banks. For example, during the period of restriction from 1797 to 1821 it operated regularly in the discount market upon competi-tive terms, its motive being partly the straightforward one of profit and partly a desire to influence the terms and conditions under which dis-counting was carried on. That the mixed motive was understood outside the Bank was demonstrated by the fact that on the occasions when the Bank sought to restrict its discounts it was smartly told by London businessmen that it had responsibilities and that the financial public had

[1] From 230 to 470, Clapham tells us. Cf. *The Bank of England*, Vol. ii, p. 1.

a right to assistance and guidance and considered that 'this assistance may be derived through the old and customary channel, the Bank of England.'[1]

Discounting had been an activity of the Bank since its foundation although its development was slow. Clapham tells us that in 1695 the Committee in Waiting (the body within the Bank responsible for bill discounting) sometimes completed only one or two transactions, and rarely were there more than ten. The wars of Marlborough inhibited discount activity in the early 1700's, but as the century progressed there was an expansion of the business, although with great fluctuations. Parcels of bills were brought to the Bank by a 'Sephardic Jewish element'[2] whose exotic names—Teixeira de Mattos, Henriques, Van Loon—added colour and probably interest and excitement to the sober business of banking. In the period 1730–50 (cf. Table XI) there was no important change in the volume of discount operations. By law the rate could not rise above 5 per cent but, for favoured customers, it often was below it. Foreign trade bills which tended to bear names known to the Bank often enjoyed lower rates than inland bills, which could be dubious documents, and at times the Bank did some bad business in them. After the suspension in 1797 discounts bounded upwards, for the Bank felt it right to discount freely to induce public confidence. The figures for 1805 and 1807 were the highest in the history of the Bank. It was for the Bank a profitable business. On the demand side the Bank's customers consisted of London traders of every type and degree of importance. There is, Clapham tells us, a sense in the Bank documents of this period that the machinery for vetting bills was creaking and working somewhat laxly. All in all the discounting of bills by the Bank in the early nineteenth century must be seen primarily as a prosperous business of the Bank and only very secondarily as a manifestation of credit policy.

If any conscious credit policy can be said to have existed in the first quarter of the nineteenth century it seems to have rested on a tacit acceptance by the Bank that it should be guided by two principles: an ultimate responsibility to the public to provide credit through discounts and a responsibility to prevent speculation, overtrading and what we would now call the overheating of the economy. There was, too, always an implication in the Bank's actions and utterances that subject to these two considerations the monetary system and the economy should make its own pace and that the Bank should follow. Only if this pace became unduly great should the Bank intervene. This is demonstrated in its early attitude towards the note issue. This it preferred to make through the

[1] Resolution passed at a meeting of London merchants at the London Tavern in March 1797. Cf. King, op. cit., p. 71.

[2] Cf. Clapham, *The Bank of England*, Vol. i, p. 127.

channel of commercial discounts, believing that (*a*) by so doing it could qualitatively influence the sort of paper being discounted and (*b*) so long as this method was followed over-issue was impossible since the notes were issued for legitimate commercial business. The public, it was argued,

TABLE XI

BANK OF ENGLAND INCOME FROM DISCOUNTS, 1730-1850
YEAR—AUGUST TO AUGUST

£	
1728–29	13,225
1735–36	6,562
1740–41	4,074
1745–46	2,934
1750–51	8,153
1755–56	8,464
1760–61	30,319
1767–68	87,877
1770–71	118,918
1775–76	40,621
1780–81	84,390
1785–86	130,481
1790–91	26,520
1795–96	147,401
1797–98	229,606
1799–1800	314,000
1800–01	368,000
1802–03	478,000
1804–05	513,000
1805–06	576,000
1806–07	633,000
1808–09	708,000
1809–10	914,000
1815–16	646,000
1820–21	150,000
1825–26	303,000
1828–29	94,000

	Threadneedle St.	Branches
1830–31	54,000	52,000
1835–36	30,000	79,000
1840–41	70,000	105,000
1844–45	35,000	46,000
1846–47	219,000	127,000
1847–48	207,000	174,000
1848–49	44,000	64,000
1849–50	31,000	47,000

Source: Clapham: *The Bank of England.*
Compiled from Vol. i, Appendix E; Vol. ii, Appendix C.

K

must act upon the circulation in this way, applying for notes as they were required. A much later instance of this principle of 'following the situation' rather than leading it was the Bank's attitude in the mid-nineteenth century towards its own discount rate which it believed should follow market rate, not determine market rate. This *laissez-faire* attitude was of course in harmony with the philosophy of the period, but it is one main reason why any conscious, controlling monetary policy was slow in coming. In fact it is no exaggeration to say that so far as credit policy development was concerned the Bank was forced to move forward only by the series of financial crises with which the first half of the nineteenth century was punctuated—with the crisis of 1825 in particular.

The crisis of 1825 brought the first important developments of the century at the Bank. The passive policy of the Bank in allowing speculation and over-trading to develop in an atmosphere of credit ease and cheap money, the ill-timed panic step of ceasing to discount when the crisis became apparent and the success, in averting disaster, of the Bank's belated open-door policy—all these demonstrated the enormous influence for good or ill which its actions now had over the monetary system. The two acts which followed in 1826 sought to reform the note-issue and to improve the stability of the banking system. In effect, from the Bank of England's point of view, they had the dual result of firstly changing the Bank's powers and sphere of operations and secondly changing radically the banking system and discount market, all of which, it was becoming clear, it was the Bank's function to control.

Some of the implications of the 1826 Acts have been discussed elsewhere:[1] it is necessary here only to consider their influence upon the Bank of England's rôle as central bank. Here it is the purely banking aspects of the legislation which are of interest.

The opening of provincial branches by the Bank of England seems to have been forced upon it from without. In 1832 Horsley Palmer, then governor of the Bank, told a Parliamentary Committee[2] that a branch policy for the Bank was 'a favourite measure of Lord Liverpool' but that 'the Bank always declined it'. The purpose of the branches seems not to have been defined but it is implicit in many of the discussions that these would be used for channelling the note issue to newly developing regions of the country and would carry the Bank's authority into the provinces to discipline the ever-increasing number of country banks. The profit motive was not absent. With the quiet business forced upon the Bank by its reduction of discounts and mortgages following the crisis of 1825 it needed fresh sources of income which the branch business might well supply. Again, however, there appears in the Bank's operation of these

[1] See p. 133 above.   [2] Committee of 1832, Minutes of Evidence, Q. 466.

branches the typical reticence, the policy of following rather than leading, of adjusting to events rather than moulding them. Had the Bank's branches pursued a flexible and dynamic discounting policy in the provinces they might have drawn to themselves the bulk of the discounting business of the country with inimical results for the bill brokers and interesting effects on the monetary system's later development.

It is, however, in the changes in the organisation of the banking system after 1826 that we see the nascent central banking system. Although still a unitary banking system the sense of common interests and common problems was giving it cohesion. The growth of the discount market was establishing it as an integral group in its own right while the growth of a call loan system and the granting by the Bank in 1830 of rediscount facilities for the bill dealers was creating the framework through which a credit policy could function. The realisation by the Bank of England before 1830 of its own position as the ultimate source of cash; of the need for a means of channelling cash to the economy in times of need; and the conscious choice of the discount market as that means, marks a definite step in the direction not only of the modern discount market but of the modern banking system as a whole.

Two weapons of monetary policy were necessary to complete the Bank of England's powers of credit control as they were evolving after 1830: a discount rate policy aimed at controlling the cost of borrowing both at short- and long-term and a means of making its discount rate effective. These weapons were slow to develop and a coherent bank rate policy was not discernible until the twentieth century, while a means of making bank rate effective was equally slow to appear. This latter result could only be achieved by some mechanism which would create a scarcity of funds in the market and drive the bill dealers to the Bank for support. In such circumstances the Bank's help could be given at any interest rate of its choice and that rate would be an effective determinant of other short-term rates, and ultimately of long-term rates as well. Such a method of control was more sophisticated than anything available to the Bank in the thirties or forties. There was at that time no accepted theory, no real understanding of the processes through which interest rates worked and were related, by reference to which development might be guided. In fact development when it came in these fields was piecemeal and *ad hoc*; theory followed practice but only after some lapse of time.

During the first two decades of the nineteenth century the Bank's discount rate policy proceeded by rule of thumb and was that a constant bank rate at 5 per cent, the maximum allowed under the Usury Laws, was the appropriate one. This rate remained in force from 1797 to June

1822 apparently on the grounds that needless variations in rates were detrimental to trade. The market rate of discount was often below bank rate and at periods when money was plentiful the Bank would therefore not have much discount business—a fact demonstrated by the fluctuations in the Bank's discount income during this period (cf. Table XI).

Prior to 1844 the Bank's discount rate policy was ordered by Horsley Palmer's 'rule of 1832' which laid down new principles to govern the note issue. Briefly, these were that the Bank's liabilities (notes and deposits) should be backed one-third by gold and two-thirds by securities. The aim should be to keep the securities virtually constant so that the note issue would fluctuate only with gold flows, and this implied that discounts should not be variable since they were an integral part of the securities item. Thus the older principle that discounts should govern the note issue was abandoned after 1832 and Bank of England discounting was now seen only as an emergency measure. Bank rate should, therefore, be above the market rate and should be a true penal rate only operative in times of emergency. From 1825 to 1844 the bank rate moved between 4 and 5 per cent. If the market rate fell below 4 per cent the Bank ceased to discount until it rose to this point again. Bank of England spokesmen claimed for this policy that it prevented wide fluctuations in the rate of discount, a claim which was partly justified. Fluctuations would certainly have been wider had the Bank competed for discount business and used its rate to do so.

With a discount rate policy which tied bank rate movements to marginal shifts within the range of 4 and 5 per cent the Bank had no means of controlling the amount of its discounts through the rate but was obliged to do this by direct restriction of the demands made upon it. It did not regard bank rate as a variable price which it, as a monopolist, could charge when it had, in times of stringency, a monopoly of cash supply. In fact it regarded the price of credit as having little if any influence upon the demand for it. The easiest way of regulating the demand was to give or withhold credit at a fixed rate.

The first open market operations originated from the Bank's recognition of its responsibilities and change of policies after 1825. During the suspension period the Bank had bought Exchequer bills when it wished to expand the currency and sold them when it wished to contract it. From 1829 recognition of the principle of Bank responsibility for 'smoothing' the cash supply was strengthened and a defence mechanism was set up against the frequent shortages of cash which occurred at certain times, particularly during the weeks preceding the dividend on government bonds, when tax gathering had denuded the system of cash but dividends had not yet been paid. These periods were the so-called 'shuttings', periods of immobilisation of funds, and in an age before the cheque system were a source of difficulty. From 1829 the Bank introduced a system of secured advances for periods each before the four main dividend disbursements of the year. These loans were available to all who (a) offered suitable security[1] and (b) would take at least £2,000 for ten days. Their maximum period was about six weeks, shortening as the dividend date approached. The rate charged was at or near the market rate.

From 1832 onwards the Bank was extending these special loan facilities to periods other than the shuttings and by 1836 temporary advances were available for 280 days in the year. In 1834, when the East India Company was liquidating its commercial assets and made large special deposits with the Bank, the latter, having offered a rate of interest on the deposits, was anxious to find borrowers for this money. It approached the bill brokers and offered temporary advances at the market rate. About £4,700,000 was lent at rates varying from 2 to 3 per cent. The motive of the Bank in this action appears to have been that if they had not accepted the deposit from the Company this large supply of liquid funds would in any case have entered the money market. It was better that they should take it and thereby hold some measure of control over its use.

The principle that the Bank should act as central bank and equalise the money supply over the year came to be accepted. It was, it is true, sometimes abused—the Bank, having one eye on its dividend, was often too liberal a lender—but its acceptance marked a definite stage in the development of central bank control. It was but a step from these simple operations to ease periodic credit shortage—the forerunner of modern smoothing operations—to the more sophisticated realisation that consciously to create shortages or affluence of credit by operating directly in the markets for paper titles was the most effective way, not only to regulate the quantity of credit but also its price.

The year 1844 is generally regarded as the climacteric in the development of the modern centralised banking system. Certainly after that date the groups of financial institutions were discernible as a system and were set for the developments that have moulded them down to our own time. The Bank Charter Act of 1844 had, however, little if any direct influence upon the discount market, whose developing character was much more moulded by the legislation and banking changes of 1825 and 1826; and although the Bank Charter Act of 1844, by ordering the banking system afresh and defining the powers of the Bank of England, changed the background against which the discount houses functioned, the period

[1] Suitable security was approved bills of exchange, Exchequer bills, India bonds or approved British securities.

1825 to, say, 1858 was one of unbroken activity and development for the bill market.

One major change in the banking background created by the Act was, of course, to strengthen as never before, and define for years to come, the power of the Bank of England. In the controversies which had preceded the Act of 1844 the Bank of England's power to control the money supply had been the major issue. Unfortunately this power had been seen as exercising itself, not through the various significant changes in open market operations and credit availability, which with the hind-sight of more than a century we see to be more significant, but through the note issue. This it was the aim of the Act to control and formalise. By separating the banking and note-issuing powers of the Bank, by strength-ening its issuing monopoly and by defining precisely its limits of issue it was thought that the problem of monetary control had been solved. Thus it is not surprising that, freed from the tyranny of monetary control by having it confined, ordered and prescribed by the dichotomy of the Issue and Banking Departments, the Bank felt itself free to devote more of its energies to its purely commercial and profit earning functions. As King says, the Bank Charter Act in this sense made the Bank of England less of a central bank rather than more.[1] When, three years later, the highest of the Bank officials was asked 'do you consider that the Act . . . relieved you entirely from any responsibility as regards the circulation?' the reply was: 'Entirely.'[2] Responsibility lay now with the law. The Bank now took the view, with the approval of Peel, the Act's main architect, that as bankers they were to compete openly for business. Samuel Gurney commented that they (i.e. the Bank) began 'canvassing for discounts and fomenting transactions under the new principle that in the Banking Department they are to act on the same principle as private bankers.'[3]

Immediately the Act of 1844 became law the Bank launched itself aggressively into the field of competitive commercial banking. It was decided that all resources not required for immediate backing to liabilities should be profitably employed. For such employment two main avenues of investment were open: government securities or bills of exchange. The first of these avenues did not commend itself since the liquidity of securities was often low and the chance of capital loss considerable; so the second was chosen. The Bank now hailed bill discounting as an ideal source of highly liquid paper and, accepting the necessity of a competitive discount rate, embarked upon its 'new discounting policy'. In early

[1] Cf. King, op. cit., p. 104.
[2] Cf. Secret Committee on Commercial Distress 1847–48. Q. 2652.
[3] Cf. ibid., Q. 1098. Cited in Clapham, *Economic History of Modern Britain*, Vol. i, p. 525.

September of 1844 the bank rate was reduced by 1½ per cent to equal the market rate at 2½ per cent. In the first year of the new policy the Bank's aggregate discounts increased from £2,116,000 to £6,526,000 (cf. also Table XI) while the banking reserve fell from £9,033,000 to £5,937,000. The old Bank idea that the rate of interest charged had little or no influence on the volume of discounts was torn to shreds. The new theory was that the Bank should vary its rate freely and compete with other discounters in the market. There was even some attempt to disabuse the public mind of the idea that bank rate was a penal rate at which the Bank was forced to lend on occasions as of right. Nor was it to remain a fixed rate. It was now a variable rate which tended in practice to be a minimum rate. Bills would now be graded and would be discounted at different rates of interest according to grade and period of currency. Thus the Bank's discount rates covered a wide range from the minimum of bank rate to much higher rates for longer and lower quality paper. Another feature of the new policy was the abandonment of the direct restrictions on discounts. Checks on the amount of Bank discounts were now exercised through changes in the rates charged.

The 'new discount policy' marked a new stage in the development of bank rate as a later weapon of control. The years of active Bank of England participation and competition in the discount market gave it the experience of working and handling the market which was to be invaluable when later it retired from active commercial participation and came to use bank rate changes for purposes of real credit control. It was never to return to the old restrictionist practices with which it had sought to implement its policies before 1844.

This excursion by the Bank into the field of commercial banking had dire results. Launched as it was, at a time of speculative activity and incipient boom, and coupled as it was with an equally aggressive policy of competitive short-term lending, it was one of the main causes of the financial crisis and panic of 1847. A stream of temporary loans and discounts at low interest rates fed the mounting speculation in shaky railway schemes in 1845–46. Even the break in the boom in railway shares which occurred in late 1845 did not deter the Bank, which persisted in lending and discounting at very low rates which were matched elsewhere and had the further effects of increasing abuses in bill credit[1] and stimulating over-trading. It is hard to believe that the Bank directors did not in some measure realise that a direct link existed between their policies and the quickening pace and growing instability of the boom. To take refuge in the assertion that they were merely acting in accordance with the spirit of the Bank Act while all hell was let loose around them was blindness

---

[1] Accommodation bills were common in this period.

indeed. To what extent it was the blindness of stupidity and to what extent of wilfulness it is difficult at this distance to say. The standard justification for Bank policies by supporters of the Bank Act was that since the over-issue of currency was now precluded by the Act any possibility of an excess of credit was out of the question.

Not until March 1847, when the Bank's reserve was seen to be diminishing rapidly, was trouble anticipated. On January 14 bank rate was increased from 3 to 3½ per cent to check an outflow of gold brought on by the bad harvest of 1846 and heavy wheat imports. A further rise to 4 per cent on January 21 began to cause some misgivings. But the Bank withheld action and the bank rate remained at 4 per cent, well below the market rate, while the Bank continued until April to discount and lend freely. But in April there was a swift change. The fall in the reserves was now alarming and could not be tolerated. On April 8 bank rate went to 5 per cent. A week later the Bank changed its discounting policy, applying bank rate only to bills with a few days to run while longer bills were only discountable at much higher rates. There was some calling in of advances and a limitation was placed upon the amount of bills which the Bank would discount. These drastic measures had calamitous effects and for a time it became almost impossible to discount in Lombard Street or to borrow money even on good security. When discounting was resumed it was at rates never before known—12 or 13 per cent. There was a profound loss of confidence and a check to trade. But the crisis was not yet. An improvement in the trade balance reversed the gold flow and the Bank relented in its restrictions. The summer of 1847 passed uneasily. It was expected that the harvest would be a poor one and speculation in anticipation of a rise in grain prices was rife. In July the Bank's reserve again fell sharply and invoked counter measures in the form of hardening discount rates and more stringent discounting conditions. There began a succession of business failures which placed strain upon the discount market. On September 14 Sanderson's, which had been carrying a large portfolio of grain bills, suspended payment. Bruce and Company followed suit. The crisis reached its height in early October when a further fall in the Bank of England's reserve induced new restrictions. The Bank now refused to make advances on stock or on Exchequer bills and all bills falling due after October 15 were to be discounted only at rates above 5½ per cent, the rates to be decided at the time. Panic selling on the London Stock Exchange, fantastic rates of discount on Lombard Street, the failure of some provincial joint stock banks—all the paraphernalia of crisis followed. In all this much of the demand for credit fell upon the Bank whose reserves had by October 22 fallen so low that they were faced with the choice of infringing the Act of 1844 or of refusing further assistance. Swift negotiations with the Treasury followed and on October 25 a cryptic letter from the Treasury empowered the Bank 'to enlarge the amount of their discounts and advances . . . but that a higher rate of interest should be charged' and that 'if this course should lead to any infringement of the existing law, Her Majesty's Government will propose to Parliament, on its meeting, a bill of indemnity.' This effectively suspended the Bank Charter Act of 1844 and the Bank, thus liberated, increased its lending accordingly.

This extreme action had the desired effect. Panic demands upon the banks ceased. The demand for credit eased. Interest rates began to drop. Four weeks after suspension the bank rate was reduced from 8 to 7 per cent. By the year's end it was back to 5 per cent.

There can be little doubt that a large part of the blame for the crisis of 1847 lay with the Bank of England, which had drawn quite the wrong conclusions from the Bank Charter Act of 1844 and had repeated its errors of 1825. Instead of regarding that Act as one formalising its position in respect of currency issue and regulation and leaving it to concentrate on the working out of more sophisticated procedures for general credit control, it had regarded the Act as covering such duties as were special to it as central bank, leaving it free to pursue policies for profit and expansion in its other rôle of commercial bank. The confusion was fatal but pardonable. Neither the controversy between the Banking and Currency Schools which preceded the Bank Charter Act nor the economic knowledge of the day drew the sharp line between the processes of money creation involved in the issue of currency and the processes of credit creation—what we would now call the general condition of liquidity—which the Bank was laboriously to learn throughout the nineteenth century. In the economic thought of the day there was little guidance and that guidance played it false. Even apart from this it was, however, arguable that in pursuing its aggressive lending policy the Bank had been inept,[1] that the line between aggressive lending and foolish lending had been none too clear and that at no time during the crisis did the Bank seem capable of seeing the advancing situation with the expertise one might have expected. Indeed, the very period when the Bank's power and position as central bank were no longer in doubt was the very period chosen for what was probably the most unfortunate demonstration of its unfitness for that rôle which had yet occurred in its history.

The 1847 crisis ended the interlude of aggressive lending and market competition by the Bank. A certain amount of competition for discounting between the discount houses and the Bank remained but it was con-

[1] It had been inept in that it persevered in its aggressive lending too long and that its correctives when they came had to be sharp and destabilising.

fined mainly to periods when discounting was difficult. Bank rate now stood above the market rate[1] and the Bank's standards of bills eligible for discounting were higher than those of the market. As the crisis passed, the Bank's bill portfolio contracted considerably. From a peak of £12·738m. on 30th October 1847 it fell by 24th June 1848 to £3·636m. From then until 1853 it was very rarely above £5m. The alleged policy of the Bank was now to follow the course of the market, reducing its bank rate when the market rate fell but in general keeping about ½ per cent above market rate. Only at times of stringency when the supply of resources in the market was not up to the demand did bank rate fall below market rate. So far as any theory can be stated to have motivated bank rate policy in the decade after 1847 it can be said that there was some recognition of the principle that bank rate was important,[2] that bank rate should move flexibly behind market rate (and not remain, as prior to 1844, fixed and at a higher level) and that it should be a minimum rate of discount in periods of stringency. This, while resembling earlier bank rate procedures, and giving no hint of what was to come, implied a more active approach and a wider conception of the potential power of bank rate changes.

The picture of the Bank of England in 1850 is then of an institution in transition. The Bank Charter Act of 1844 had given to it undoubted recognition as what we now call the central bank but just what functions it had to perform as such or what were its modes of procedure were matters still uncertain to itself, to the banking fraternity and to the informed public. For the tasks which it would ultimately perform—the control of the note issue, the management of the credit situation, the conduct of debt management—much of the machinery was already in being although its importance and significance was not in most cases understood. It was the task of the Bank of England in the second half of the century to form from these apparently disparate elements through a laborious process of trial and error the elaborate system of centralised bank control which was to be a model for the world in the twentieth century.

VI

Two notable features characterised the bill market from the financial changes of 1826–30 down to the mid-century: a steady growth of the bill market as a whole; and the repeated appearance of instabilities,

---

[1] Save in 1851 when they were both equal at 3 per cent.

[2] Prior to 1847 this was denied by many bankers who claimed that bank rate was no more important than the discount rate of any other bank.

arising partly from the abuse of the bill of exchange as a credit instrument and partly from the still precarious and immature state of the market institutions themselves. Indeed, the very rate of growth of bill dealing and the improvements wrought by the changes described above were bound to produce difficulties. The engine had been well overhauled but a period of gentle running-in was necessary to avoid setbacks. The running-in was not given: the engine became at times a little overheated.

It is as well to remember that the changes in the financial system made after the crisis of 1825, while they fostered the bill market in the ways we have described, were not designed for that purpose but to strengthen the monetary system and prevent a recurrence of crisis conditions. They did not do this. Instead they pushed the development of the monetary system on to a new stage which had its own unique conditions of instability—for example the over-use of the bill of exchange made possible by the expanding discount market—and a few left over from the old system as well. It is not our purpose to examine the problems of the whole monetary system but only those which impinge on the discount market. Here we glance briefly at the difficulties which were created by the abuse of bill credit in this period.

The difficulty lay not in the new system but rather in the way it was used. We are now in a period of commercial speculation, of numerous company flotations, good and bad, in the high summer of unbridled private enterprise. The lesson which had been learned from 1825 was that in such an atmosphere of speculation and buoyancy frail banking institutions were a menace: the lesson which had not been learned was that even strong institutions require skilful handling in accordance with some tried principles of monetary policy. Skill in handling was hard-bought by experience, and by the thirties no distinct and accepted doctrine of how the monetary machine should be managed yet existed. The same error was therefore made with the new institutions as had been made before 1825 with the old. Instead of checking back the speculative and expansive tendencies in the economy by a reasonably tight credit policy, an easy credit position was fostered. For this, ultimate responsibility lay with the Bank of England but this responsibility was shared. The Bank failed to crack the whip and bring to heel other elements in the monetary system which were contributing to instability. Of these the most notable were the joint stock banks.

The besetting sin of the new joint stock banks was rediscounting. According to one contemporary[1] many banks were in the habit of endorsing rediscounts of twenty times their paid-up capital, while on the

[1] John Amery, manager of the Stourbridge and Kidderminster Bank whose evidence to the 1836 Committee is quoted in King, op. cit., p. 92.

average, he thought, rediscounts were six or eight times paid-up capital. Moreover this rediscounting was being done on top of a large portfolio holding of bills and a considerable volume of advances. The fact was that not only was there not yet any set of guiding principles for bankers in distributing their assets but that, in respect of bills of exchange, the accepted practices appeared to be the wrong ones. Bills were rediscounted long after lending and other business had reached its limit and rediscounting after endorsement followed a mode losing sight of caution and common rules.[1] Many banks discounted all that was offered them in the way of bills, rediscounting excess holdings in London when necessary. Not only was the quantity of bills rediscounted too great but their quality was questionable. Banks were often prepared to advance money on security of accommodation bills of very dubious credit, knowing that they could by law proceed against every single endorser of the bill simultaneously[2] in the event of default.

Some attempt was made at the time to fix responsibility for this credit laxity on the Bank of England, whose discounting had perhaps been too free, but the real basis of the expansion in the mid-thirties was the large number of bills drawn on acceptance credits in respect of American imports. In late 1836 these bills fell under suspicion and it became known that the Anglo-American houses would not be able to meet them if their American clients defaulted. The Bank of England then refused all such bills as collateral from the bill brokers, thus making such bills undiscountable. The result was a near panic. The ghost of 1825 walked again, and the Bank of England came to the assistance of the threatened Anglo-American houses which, nevertheless, had inordinately high acceptances outstanding for some time. High grain imports resulting from a poor harvest caused the trade balance to worsen. There was a loss of gold and in 1839 there was danger that the Bank of England would have to suspend specie payments. But, as in 1825, a severe credit restriction by the Bank saved the monetary system from collapse.

The crisis of 1839 generated a depression which lasted until well into 1842. From the middle of that year an improvement set in and by 1844 recovery was complete and the country was reasonably prosperous. In an atmosphere of cheap money and low material prices the profits of the new railway system attracted attention and new rail projects were planned on a massive scale. In the atmosphere of confidence engendered by the Bank Charter Act of 1844, which was to prevent a recurrence of the crises of the past and make cheap credit widely available, it is not surprising

[1] Cf. King, op. cit., p. 92.
[2] Joplin pointed out that even six bankrupts each paying 3/4d. in the £ would then be sufficient to cover the bill. Cf. King, op. cit., p. 93.

that the wave of investment in railways gave momentum to a new boom and became a 'railway mania' in which schemes for railway projects jostled one another for consideration by Parliament. At the opening of the session of 1845–46 there were 1,428 schemes up for consideration. The aggressive 'new discounting' policy of the Bank of England, by engendering an atmosphere of credit ease, undoubtedly contributed to the boom, and as temporary loans and discounts were made available at low rates of interest it is small wonder that the boom ran away. The spectrum of schemes shaded from the genuine to the dubious, the ill-advised and, at the far extreme, the non-existent, for there were many fictitious schemes designed merely to boost the share values of existing undertakings.

It is unnecessary to retail here the events of yet another boom, crisis and recovery. This story belongs to the general monetary history of the nineteenth century. Moreover, the crisis of 1847 was not one which was caused by the discount market nor yet was the crisis formative in the market's history. Its mention serves, however, to remind us of the sensitivity of the financial mechanism of this period. In our imagination it may appear as a world of dark brown offices and counting houses, of hunting prints, mezzo-tints and leather smells; the clip-clop of hooves on wood block streets; where comfortable fortunes were made and maintained. More truly it was in its usages and behaviour pattern a world of harsh primary colours where profits were made on unprotected margins and where bankruptcies were frequent, total and ruinous.

The period from 1840 to 1850 was one of steady growth for the discount market. During this period there were four large bill dealing houses: Overend, Gurney and Company, Alexander and Company, Bruce, Buxton and Company, and Sanderson and Company—the last-named having been reconstructed after the crisis of 1847. Of these Overend, Gurney was by far the largest, doing probably as much business as all the rest together.[1] Apart from the four large houses the London Directory of 1845 listed twenty-five firms under headings such as 'bill brokers, discount agents and discount brokers'. Five of these seem to have been established after 1840 but thirteen were at least ten years old.

This growth of discounting between 1840 and 1850 seems to have been a result of several influences, notably: the rapid increase in size and numbers of the provincial joint stock banks; the increase in trade both foreign and domestic; the widespread and still increasing use of the bill of exchange; and the need for some institution to perform the function of

---

[1] King estimates that the deposits of the four bill-dealing houses in the mid-forties were about £11m. Cf. 'The Extent of the London Discount Market', *Economica*, August 1935.

equalising lending within the structure of a still unitary banking system.

This expansion of the discount market had, moreover, been accomplished despite the arrival in the discount field of the Bank of England itself. In the provinces, competition in discounting from the Bank of England branches was not a serious matter, since these branches charged a rate slightly higher than in London and many discounters preferred to send their bills to the capital. Once these arrived in London, however, the Bank of England was a serious competitor, since many discounters preferred to take their bills to the Bank, which did not rediscount, so that bills discounted there would not later be passing to and fro in the money market. Half per cent was not a lot to swallow for the greater secrecy which dealing with the Bank ensured.

That the discount market continued to flourish despite Bank of England competition is not so remarkable. One factor making it possible was, no doubt, the growth in the number of bills and the number of joint stock banks. There was room in short for the Bank of England to enter the growing market without diminishing the business of the bill dealers.

Chapter 6

THE LATER NINETEENTH CENTURY
1850–1914

'In England everything changes except appearances.'

I

FROM 1850 the pace of change in the British monetary system quickened. Bagehot, writing in the introduction to his *Lombard Street* in 1873, drew attention to this. 'Since 1844,' he wrote, 'Lombard Street is so changed that we cannot judge of it without describing and discussing a most vigorous adult world which then was small and weak.'[1] Moreover, the period from 1850 to 1914 saw in finance, as in so many other sectors of the economy, a veritable transformation of the scene. Britain entered the second half of the nineteenth century with a currency the principles of whose issue and control were still in dispute, a banking system still unitary, dispersed and fragmentary, a bill market of rudimentary organisation and a mechanism of public finance which had hardly changed for centuries. It ended the period with a highly centralised banking system based on joint stock banks operating through branch networks, with a central bank which controlled not only domestic credit but also the gold reserve for international payments and which was the chief arbiter in the working of the international gold standard. Ancillary to all this there was a discount market, developed along highly specialised lines for the handling of short-term paper and playing a highly specific rôle in the general banking system; and there were developments in the techniques of government borrowing which were growing out of the expanded rôle of the State in economic affairs.

It was the task of the preceding chapter to describe some of the important changes which took place in the first half of the nineteenth century, in particular between 1825 and 1850. It is evident that it was during that time that several of the fundamental relationships of the later banking system were established. But if the period 1825–50 was one in which there was preparation for the 'take off', the period 1850–1914 was that

[1] Cf. Bagehot, op. cit., 14th edition, p. 3.

of the take off itself and of the spectacular changes which attended it. In this chapter we shall be concerned with processes of change rather than with seeds of change.

The first task is to single out for attention the main processes of change which were taking place. We will in doing so refrain from dwelling on great general influences which were of course working in the economic world at large, influences such as the gathering impetus of industrialisation, the great growth in population, trade and economic activity, the changes in the balance of the economy; all these had a bearing, some of them considerable, on the development of the banking and financial system and thus of the discount market. But they would carry us too far afield. We will rather confine ourselves to influences which acted directly, and in some cases specifically, to change the fields and activities in which we are interested. Here four influences are important.

Firstly, the financial institutions of the later nineteenth century swiftly came to be concerned with trade and industry in a far wider setting than hitherto. The coming of the railway, the telegraph and the iron ship brought new standards of speed and facility in trade and communication. Overseas trade, external commercial relationships, the finance, documentation and conduct of foreign trade, became matters of dominating interest over a great part of the British banking system. In 1825 a banker in London[1] was concerned primarily with his relations with two groups of institutions: the other London banks including the Bank of England; and the country banks for which he acted as London agent. In 1875 his landscape would have been wider and more populated. There would have been vestigial traces of the old relationships but with the Bank of England now looking somewhat more dominant. But, in addition, relations with London acceptance houses and merchant banks and through them with foreign banking houses would loom large and the relation of his own currency with the currency of other countries and with the universal payment's medium of gold, would be a matter of concern. In short, the growing participation of Britain in international trade and indeed her very dominance in that field was acting to transform her banking and financial system. In this internationalising of the economy occurred one thing which was of great significance for the discount market: the decline of the domestic bill of exchange was offset by the growth in the use of overseas bills for the finance of foreign trade. Had this not occurred it is entirely likely that the discount market would have decayed and died with the domestic bill. As it was the overseas trade bill gave an impetus to the continuance not only of a discount market but of a discount

[1] Save for a few notable exceptions such as Nathan Rothschild and the other very early merchant bankers with interests outside Britain.

market qualitatively different from that which existed in the first half of the century.

Secondly, the second half of the nineteenth century saw the establishment and growth of discount houses in their modern form, houses dealing in bills and carrying a portfolio of bills on the strength of call money as distinct from houses whose main function was that of brokering. While brokering remained and to a limited extent still remains an activity of the discount houses, it shrank in importance and became secondary to the active business of dealing in and carrying bills. Old and familiar names, such as that of Overend, Gurney and Sanderson drop out of our story in this period and are replaced by others made familiar in some cases by current usage.

Thirdly, a profound influence was exerted on the financial system in general and the discount market in particular by the supersession in these years of the old unified banking structure by the large branch networks of the modern joint stock banks. This process was gradual; but it accelerated in the second half of the century until joint stock branch banking on the modern model virtually replaced the old unit banking in the last two decades of the century. This transformation had many consequences but for the discount market it had two of great importance: first, it meant that there was no longer any institution or set of institutions, external to the banks themselves, required for the purpose of equalising and distributing credit over the country. In the days of unitary, country, town and London banks the bill dealer, by taking bills from one area for discount in another, had performed this function. Now it could be done easily and quickly through the branch network of the joint stock banks. Cash surpluses and loanable balances could be switched from area to area merely by accounting processes. The discount market was thus robbed of one of its fundamental early *raisons d'être*. Second, with joint stock banking through branches the modal means of payment became the cheque and thus the domestic bill, which had played such a notable part in so many trades and regions, was superseded. The commercial bill market became predominantly a market in foreign trade bills.

Fourthly, it was in the second half of the nineteenth century, more than in any other period, that the Bank of England acceded to its full status, *de facto* as well as *de jura*, of central bank. In all its fields of operations—as controller of the note issue, as manager of credit and as holder of the gold stock and link with the world of international finance—it had by 1900 recognition at home and abroad and was, somewhat self-consciously, gaining skill and dexterity. Meanwhile in the closely related field of public finance the state was realising that seventeenth and eighteenth century systems of public borrowing were no longer adequate to meet the grow-

L

ing state outlays and were striking out towards new and flexible ways of raising and carrying public debt. These, coupled with the Bank of England's methods of controlling credit and regulating interest rates, were promising, by the close of the century, a banking and public debt technique of a complexity not dreamed of in 1850.

These then are the main elements of change affecting the discount market in this most formative period. In the pages that follow we shall consider each of these elements more fully and comment on their significance.

II

As Britain entered the second half of the nineteenth century she became progressively involved in the world economy. As late as the mid-1840's foreign bills formed only about 14 per cent of the total bills outstanding. Nor was there any marked connection between interest rates in London and those elsewhere. With no telephone communication between centres and with mails still taking several days between say London and Hamburg and several weeks between London and New York, wide disparities in interest rates between centres were possible and frequent. It is true to say that up to 1850 the banking systems of individual countries were individual cells between which there were only tenuous connections and that at that stage in the development of the international economy there did not exist any large stock of mobile international funds to move from centre to centre. Such a stock of international balances required for its maintenance a much larger volume of international trade and investment than then existed.

From the early 1860's, however, the great expansion of international trade and finance made each of the leading money markets a part of the wider international money market. Not only was international trade increasing swiftly in volume, requiring an ever-growing financial service in terms of payments, exchanges and documentation, but capital was on the move. Foreign loans and overseas investment, both direct and portfolio, moved from the richer countries to the less developed and the great financial centres of the world—London, Paris, Amsterdam—became centres for the flotation of such loans. In London acceptance business and the growth of trade caused foreign held balances to accumulate and increase. Accepting houses working on account of foreign nationals demanded of their clients that they hold minimum balances. Working balances of foreigners trading habitually with London began to increase and to show variable characteristics. The political stability of Britain came to be noticed by those abroad with funds seeking a temporary home. In short, all the conditions of a mobile short-term holding of funds in London were present. In the sixties the press in London commented on the 'hot money' coming to London as a result of the American Civil War. In 1873 in his *Lombard Street* Bagehot notes the growth of foreign held deposits after the War of 1870.

In the currencies of the world the sovereign had high standing. Its peers, the French franc, the American dollar and the German mark, dropped aside as the century progressed. The dollar 'was buried under greenbacks'[1] in 1865–66; the franc lost its way after the war of 1870 and the German currency was placed on a gold basis too late to be a serious competitor with the sovereign as the leading gold-based coin and unit of account in the new international economy.

As the international economy grew so did the need for an international currency system capable of handling the growing volume of inter-currency transactions both current and capital. Since the currencies of the main trading nations were based on gold it was natural that gold should become the common international monetary medium to which and through which all the major currencies were linked. The international gold standard became in the sixties and seventies a recognised international system through which individual countries adjusted their price levels to one another in response to the ebbs and flows of gold occasioned by movements in their balances of payments. Of this impressive system England was the centre and lynchpin, the Bank of England the virtual controller. Any such system required for its working and administration some centre, preferably in one of the great trading countries, whose banking system, and in particular its central bank, was developed enough, stable enough and skilful enough to play a major part in working the system. London provided such a centre. The British banking system was then the most advanced in the world; its centre, the Bank of England, was to evolve techniques and methods for influencing gold movements, exchange rates and relative price and cost levels, which, assembled together, were to give us later an elaborate mechanism of gold standard procedures. Although at first sight somewhat removed from the specialised functional activities of the discount market, the evolution of these gold standard techniques was of great import for the market in one respect: it forced the Bank of England in about thirty years to perfect a technique of bank rate control in which the discount market was an integral part.

For the discount market the growth of external trade and the establishment of London as a leading financial centre had great significance. No longer was the market concerned with the broking and discounting of

[1] Cf. Clapham, *Economic History of Modern Britain*, Vol. ii, p. 333.

domestic bills but rather with the vetting, discounting and holding of overseas trade bills, some of which covered British import and export transactions, some of which related to transactions between foreign countries in respect of goods which never touched British shores. For as foreign trade grew and as the bill of exchange became its modal means of payment, the London discount market acquired a new function, that of accepting bills on behalf of clients, often external to the British Isles. Certain of the London private banks came to accept for a commission bills on behalf of clients. Such bills, carrying a London acceptance of approved standing, could be discounted in the market at the most favourable rates. When such a bill fell due for payment it would be paid by the accepting house, which in turn was reimbursed by its client. This acceptance business, carried on mainly by a group of the London merchant banks, became an integral part of the London discount market and 'the bill on London' a reputable form of payment in international trade. Yet it was to be a 'short flowering', for although the overseas bill replaced the domestic bill progressively, from the 1860's onwards the quickening pace of communication brought about by the telegraph was already making it possible to dispense with the bill of exchange in foreign trade. Even as early as 1877 the *Economist* drew attention to the fact that telegraphic transfers and international coupons were replacing the overseas bill of exchange as a means of payment.[1] That the overseas bill of exchange was able to rise to prominence from 1860 and remain the important staple of the discount market down to the interwar years; that, even in face of speedier forms of payment, the bill on London and those who administered it enjoyed in the period 1870–1914 their golden age, was partly due to the enormous growth in the volume of trade in that period which served to obscure longer-term influences, but no doubt also to the basic utility, safety and convenience inherent in this process of payment for those who engaged in foreign trade.

At this time too the City of London lost much of its hitherto homely atmosphere. True, there had long been a few strange-sounding foreign names among the bankers—Rothschilds, Huths, Doxats, Raphaels— but these had not done more than relieve the monotony of Scots and provincial familiarity. Now came other foreigners, Hambros in 1848, Bischoffsheim and Goldsschmidt in 1850, Speyers in 1862, and many others—Oppenheims, Schroeders, Erlangers. Some of these were not to stay. The financial crises of the fifties and the seventies were to take their toll. Even the mighty house of Baring was one day to sway precariously. But many were to become household words in merchant banking. The fact was that in the third quarter of the century just when its

[1] Cf. *Economist*, 1877, p. 1006, cited in King, op. cit., p. 269.

sphere of influence, operation and power so widened, the City of London was strengthened and made cosmopolitan by this infusion of Jewish and mid-European blood. By 1870 the old group of sixty or seventy London banks had increased to more than a hundred and twenty, the originals[1] being augmented not only by those named above but also by about forty banks, from the Empire, colonies, and dependencies, for example the Bank of New South Wales and banks from Hong Kong, Shanghai and elsewhere in the East. Foreign central banks did not establish offices in London (nor the Bank of England in foreign capitals) but Clapham reports a 'lively' correspondence with the new Reichsbank and the Bank of France in the eighties.[2]

One of the consequences of the drawing together of the financial centres of the world which took place in the sixties and seventies was to make interest rates in London and in most other centres more mercurial. Large numbers of London acceptances were constantly held in foreign countries[3] and with any change in the relative strengths of the various financial centres or any murmur of financial unease in Britain, these acceptances would be discounted in London. Many bills had a choice of venue for discount: they might equally be discounted in Frankfurt, Amsterdam or London and were highly sensitive to even slight margins in discount rates as between the capitals. Large amounts of internationally owned bonds also contributed to international monetary movements. In short, by the seventies there was a considerable volume of international funds free to move from centre to centre, sensitive to changes in relative rates and in part determining relative rates. This gave a new urgency to the Bank of England's task of controlling interest rates either so that they could influence the British balance of payments or so that they could mitigate or offset induced movements of rates in England caused by inward or outward flows of funds.

It is evident that with these many influences operating upon the discount market its position between 1850 and 1870 had fundamentally changed, in that at the beginning of that period it had been a purely domestic institution, operating in an insular setting and concerned with

[1] Such firms as Barclays, Herries, Glyn, Martin and Coutts or the joint stock Lloyds and London & County.

[2] Earnest enquiries would be made by dutiful young central banks about the statutes, constitution and practices of the founding mother. What must the eager management of the Bank of Spain have thought when told in response to a question often asked of the Bank of England, 'that its Charter would be of very little use to them; and that its relations with the Exchequer have never been codified from the relevant Acts of Parliament.'? Cf. Clapham, op. cit., p. 352.

[3] One estimate was that in 1878 from £50m. to £60m. of London acceptances was outstanding. Cf. King, op. cit., p. 270.

domestic flows of funds; whereas by 1870 it was in part an institution of international finance concerned with the relations between foreign buyers and sellers, with flows of international funds and with the relation in the international field between national rates of interest.

III

In describing the condition of the London money market in the third quarter of the nineteenth century Clapham has a telling summary passage:

'. . . the organisation by which all free British capital was sucked into the London money market was functioning almost perfectly. Compared with other national organisations, or lacks of organisation, it had been highly efficient even twenty years earlier. In the interval, Scottish and provincial branch banking had drawn in almost the last of those rustic hoards which country folk had kept in their desks and cupboards; and a smooth open channel had been cut down which the aggregated northern surpluses flowed south. The channels from East Anglia, the South West and rural England generally, had been cut long before. Wealth slipped along them easily and without sound, very often from some placid Quaker pond in the country to a more or less Quaker reservoir in town. Agriculture prospered. Country ponds overflowed. From town what was not used there ran out into the industrial districts, by way of the discount or rediscount of manufacturers' and merchants' bills. These were the greatest days of the London bill brokers, the Lombard Street Houses.'[1]

During the period of which this passage was written the early stages of the great change, which in the course of thirty years was to transform Lombard Street, were already in act. In the fifties the business of the bill brokers was to advance money on fine trade bills, which in a nicely tapered portfolio fell due for payment day by day. Already the business of the leading houses had passed well beyond mere brokerage. Overend, Gurney's, the largest house, regarded themselves not as brokers but as money dealers. Broking in the sense of 'men who found bills for money and money for bills' still existed and was to continue.[2] We are told by Clapham of the 'great go-betweens in the banking and discount community . . . men who moved about daily to ascertain what floating surpluses were available and what were likely to be the demands upon

[1] Cf. Clapham, *Economic History of Modern Britain*, Vol. ii, pp. 352–3.
[2] Even in 1931 there were still eight running brokers in the City. See Report of the Committee on Finance and Industry, Cmd. 3897 of 1931, p. 43.

them from bill brokers.' 'In the heads of these men the supply and demand curves for short-money crossed.'[1] But the days of this type of broking were numbered and the telephone dealt it its final blow. Dealing was now the function of the discount market. Dealers bought bills either to hold to maturity, to supply subsequently to banks and others who might want them or to pledge as collateral for the call money which they borrowed to conduct their dealing.

There is a perilous quality in a business which borrows money short and uses that money to buy assets of longer currency. The margin of profit is determined by the interest rate differential between call loan interest and discounting rates. This differential is very small: turnover must be large. In the interests of turnover there is the constant temptation to discount too many bills, to discount poor bills, perhaps even dubious or shaky bills. A good example of the precarious nature of discount business at this time is furnished by the National Discount Company which was formed in 1856. In its first report the company told of a net profit of £7,767 of which it distributed £6,376 in its first dividend of 5 per cent per annum for seven months' trading. Two weeks later £11,801 of bills were returned following the failure of a major firm in the Levant trade, an incident which converted the profit into a substantial loss. Any loss of confidence in a discount house may mean a call-in by lenders of call money leaving large portfolios of bills unsupported at a time when their acceptors may have difficulty in meeting them at maturity. These are the naked elements of a business which, perilous at any time, calls for great judgement and probity. In this period of a nascent banking system, a growing but lurching economy and unbridled profit-seeking, it called indeed for nerve, assurance and skill.

Until the mid-fifties the pattern of bill dealing which had existed throughout the century continued. Bill dealing was in private hands. The houses were in the main long-established, Gurney's dominating the field. But two powerful forces made for change and development from 1855 onwards: the concurrent development of the banking system which seemed to call for some expansion of the discount market; and the legislation to establish the principle of limited liability. Great profits were being made in joint stock banking to which the principle of limited liability did not apply: how much larger profits might not be made in discounting, to which it did apply? Finance appeared to be profitable business. In the period 1856–61 five new discount companies were established with limited liability, of which the National and the London were the most prominent. Of these the National, despite initial difficulties, soon established itself and within a few years was well developed. The

[1] Ibid, p. 355.

remaining four were all liquidated by the end of 1861. There were other joint stock flotations for discount companies during the same period, mostly for the purpose of taking over the business formerly operated by private firms. Of these the majority were in liquidation within three or four years. The most notable of these latter flotations was the one made to place Overend, Gurney & Company, the long-established doyen of the market, on a limited liability basis and which preceded the failure of the Company by less than a year. The sixties were then a somewhat stormy period for the discount market. The old giants—Gurney's, Bruce and Company—vanished from the scene, while the new limited liability discount companies made heavy weather of it and suffered a heavy mortality in their early days. In the seventies three companies only were of importance: the National, the General Credit and Discount Company of London and the United Discount Corporation, and of these the two latter merged in 1885 to form the Union Discount Company of London. By the mid-eighties the Union, the National and about twenty private firms made up the market, the smaller firms buying bills mainly to resell, the larger running a portfolio. If the Union's business may be taken as typical the following was the pattern at the end of the century. Loans and deposits were taken from banks, individuals and a few large commercial firms and of these about 40 per cent might be at call. Bills, rarely under £10 or longer than twelve months in tenor were sold and guaranteed to bankers at home and abroad. On occasion when call loans and deposits were insufficient a house, or houses, might borrow from the Bank, subject to the Bank's rules which before 1890 had a discretionary quality, but since when 'successive governors had shown evident willingness to advance money freely to the market.'[1] Besides the true discount houses, some few pure brokers remained. This was in principle the structure of the market down to the first world war, a new company and an honoured name being added in 1891 with the formation of Alexander's.[2]

There are several reasons for the widespread failures among the discount companies of the sixties. Undoubtedly one was that profits were, and still are, hard-won in a service so perilous and skilled as discounting. If a firm were to be operated for safety and stability its profits were not likely to be large. The assumption that the discount market at its size in the sixties and seventies could support a fair number of large discount companies was almost certainly false. A second contributory factor was poor management. Although some flotations, the National and the

---

[1] Quoted in Clapham, op. cit., p. 356.

[2] Alexander's was formed as a private company in February 1891. It became a public company in 1911.

London for example, were in skilled hands, others were not; some were barely within the bounds of legality, and when profits did not quickly appear from discounting they were sought elsewhere in apparently high-yielding finance business. These were exciting times and the boom in discount flotations was but a part of the general boom in flotations which had followed the introduction of limited liability. The excesses and failures among the new discount companies were at least no worse than could be found in many other trades and industries.

There was something symbolical about the failure in 1866 of Overend, Gurney and Company. It symbolised the end of the old discount market and the beginning of the modern type which we know today. Almost since its beginnings the market had been dominated by the dealings, operations and opinions of the 'corner house'. It had been spoken of with 'holy hush' as representing all that was wisest, safest and shrewdest in finance. Its founding fathers, Thomas Richardson and Samuel Gurney, nurtured in the traditions of Quakerism and country banking, had been legendary as individuals in their time and had built a firm of great repute which 'stood next to the Bank of England in the City of London' and 'was better known abroad than any purely English firm'.[1] Its passing in the convulsions of the sixties gave the discount market a different appearance. The climate in which the market operated was changing and if Gurney's had been going to survive it would have been necessary for it as acknowledged leader of the market to adapt itself fundamentally to the new conditions. When it did so the move was too late and was complicated by its own financial difficulties, its attempts to solve them by becoming a limited company and the poor if rather flamboyant quality of its management.[2] Its failure indicated that even wealth, prestige, and credit standing were not enough for a discount house to survive in the conditions of the sixties, particularly if it once surrendered to the temptation to seek easy profits outside the discounting field.

The story of Overend, Gurney's failure has been told elsewhere:[3] there is no need here to recount it in detail. In 1865 the firm was floated as a limited company, £500,000 being paid to the directors for the goodwill; 'a stiff price', as Clapham drily remarks. Already in informed quarters

[1] Cf. Bagehot, op. cit., pp. 17-18.

[2] Bagehot makes acid comment on the quality of the Overend, Gurney management: 'In six years they lost all their own wealth, sold the business to the company, and then lost a large part of the company's capital. And these losses were made in a manner so reckless and so foolish that one would think a child who had lent money in the City of London would have lent it better.' Cf. op. cit., p. 18.

[3] King gives an excellent account of the difficulties and liquidation of Overend, Gurney. Cf. op. cit., pp. 238-56.

there were criticisms of the firm's dealings and management. The *Economist*, for example, welcomed the flotation on the grounds that the firm 'would now have to publish an account of the nature of their business'.[1] In fact, the 'new men' who, with the survivors of the old Gurney's, now managed the business, did not follow the pious precepts on bill dealing which had been the guide of Samuel Gurney. The portfolio contained many bills of dubious character, many 'finance securities' issued in advance by promoters of companies to which the public had not yet even subscribed. Moreover, Gurney's was now deeply committed in many fields of finance outside discounting. During late 1865 and early 1866 a boom was developing and the usual nineteenth century cyclical pattern was to be repeated. In January, Gurney's suffered a cruel stroke of luck when a firm of similar name—Watson, Overend and Company—failed. This coincidence of name plus the fact that Watson's 'was known to be rich in doubtful paper', some of it placed with Gurney's, swung public confidence away from Gurney's. Their appeal for help to the Bank of England was rejected. On 10th May 1866, they failed for over five millions.

The establishment of the new joint stock discount firms and the relative decline of the old brokers was the major change in the composition of the discount market in the late nineteenth century. This shake-up established the form of the market which was to persist, with modifications, to our own day. The discount market grouping after 1911 consisted of three strong public joint stock companies, Alexander's, the Union and the National, and about twenty private firms who, on the strength of money borrowed short from the banks, bought bills for resale or to hold to maturity. Beneath these were the remaining bill brokers, the so-called running brokers, who brought together buyers and sellers of bills for a commission.

Side by side with this change in the composition of the market in the sixties was the beginning of change in its staple material. The decline in the domestic bill, on the basis of which the old firms had flourished, and which had played such a rôle not only in the history of the market but in the history of British banking and currency, began from about 1855 and by the seventies it was noticeable that the external bill was beginning to replace the domestic bill in the market. The main reason for this replacement was the ceasing of the practice by country banks of rediscounting. This abuse had played its part in the 1857 crisis and from then onwards it came to be regarded as questionable practice for banks to rediscount. The growth of the joint stock banks and of deposit banking in general provided banks with an alternative means of investing their

---

[1] Cf. *Economist*, 15th July 1865, quoted in Clapham, op. cit., p. 26.

resources. It is probable that, at first, there was not much decline in the actual number of bills but that the apparent decline in their importance was due to the fact that banks usually held bills to maturity, thus precluding their appearance in the London market. The discount houses were quick to see this and countered by competing with the country banks for discounts in the provinces but by the late sixties it was becoming apparent that the number of bills competed for was now diminishing. Other influences were also at work. Of these the greatest was the spread of branch banking which enabled money balances to be moved about the country with speed and safety and which was beginning to supersede the old 'equalising function' which the discount market had performed so well with the aid of the domestic bill. Branch banking had been developing for some time, indeed from the fifties, and any decline in the use of bills was at first offset by the expansion of trade, but by the seventies branch networks were larger and the conscious offsetting within a given branch network of deficiencies in one area by surpluses in another within the compass of a general reserve was becoming standard practice. Not only was the bill being replaced in what may be called its transmission function by the simple transfer of deposits within branch networks, but the bank loan and overdraft was replacing it as a vehicle of short-term credit. Add to all this the fact that cash payments were becoming common in business, that the cheque system was growing in importance and general acceptance, that the great regional coverage of the new branch banks was putting an end to the use of bills as local currency, and it is clear that not even the expansion of trade was sufficient to offset these powerful forces for replacement of the domestic bill.

The decline in the domestic bill which had become marked in the seventies continued and was intensified towards the end of the century by the rapid decline in the number of private banks. By 1914 the volume of domestic bills drawn and passing through the market was insignificant. The domestic bill which had brought the discount market into being and shaped its institutions had virtually disappeared. By 1900 we find a discount market concentrating on external bills, many of them acceptances of the great merchant bankers, and beginning to deal in a newcomer, the Treasury bill, which was in due course to do much to shape its destiny. But in the meantime the future looked secure. The forces making for the supersession of the bill on London were still deeply buried under the great upsurge of world trade which it was London's task to finance. Neither the future dominance of the Treasury bill nor the market's future rôle in public finance could have been guessed at by the Forsytes as they made their calm and unruffled way to their city offices in the nineties.

IV

In the forty years which followed the Bank Charter Act of 1844 the British banking system changed very little. Peel, had he been able to observe the scene in the mid-eighties, would have found it familiar. 'Things were bigger; movements were quicker and more precise; but they were much the same things and the same sort of movements'[1] as he had known in the forties. The trends in commercial banking, the rise of joint stock and branch banking, the decline in country banking continued. As between 1841 and 1875 the number of private banks declined from 321 to 252 and the number of joint stock banks rose from 115 to 120. For 1886 the figures were almost identical to 1875 at 251 and 117 respectively. Private banking remained, it can be seen, a considerable and vital group within the system. In the mid-eighties there were still about 250 private banks. About 271 banks (200 private and 71 joint stock) still had rights of note issue under the Act of 1844. Only 148 retained their note issues in 1885, some having forfeited their rights by failure or amalgamation, some having given them up voluntarily. Within the private banking group, a number of sub-groups were discernible: the old London private banks which did general banking business in London and still performed agency functions for country banks; the large and growing group of specialist firms—such as Barings, Rothschilds, the Hambros—which though described as private banks operated mainly in the fields of investment and overseas trade and finance; and the remaining country private banks, some of which showed great toughness and longevity and a propensity also to establish branches.

The figures quoted above for joint stock banks do not, however, give any indication of the spread of branch banking between 1844 and 1884. This was great because although the number of joint stock banks was not increasing markedly the number of branches was increasing very fast. In 1864 there were 744 joint stock branches and 272 private bank branches in England and Wales. In 1886 the joint stock banks alone had more than 1,500 branches. Since it had long been the Scottish policy to establish branches freely, it is possible to say that by the mid-eighties there was very considerable national coverage through the branch banking system, predominantly administered by the joint stock banks.

This great congeries of banks scattered across the country was controlled mainly from London although certain large joint stock branch networks had head offices in Liverpool and other northern cities. But it

[1] Cf. Clapham, *Economic History of Modern Britain*, Vol. iii, p. 292.

could hardly be referred to in the fifties as a banking 'system', for it had little cohesion and was plagued by excessive competition and instability. There was, as yet, little realisation that while banking might be a profit-making service industry it occupied a special position in the fabric of things and had certain special responsibilities. The greatest disruptive force was the rivalry between the old private banks and the new joint stock banks. The joint stock banks were deposit banks. They had worked as such from the outset and had offered interest on deposits which the country banks had never done. They had, with their new-fangled methods, taken business away from the country banks. There was no love lost between them. In 1854 there was a limited *rapprochement* when the country banks admitted the joint stock banks to the London Clearing House. Ten years later in April 1864 the Bank of England joined the Clearing House and the system was inaugurated whereby residual balances, after inter-bank clearing, were settled through the accounts which commercial banks held at the Bank of England. But beyond the machinery for clearing inter-bank indebtedness there was little co-operation. The joint stock banks were not at all punctilious about the size of reserves they held. The crisis of 1857 had drawn the Bank of England's attention to this but no action had been taken. Indeed, there was as yet little recognition of a need for mutual support in times of financial crisis and even the Bank of England would not have readily admitted any responsibility for fostering mutual support or maintaining stability in time of need.[1] The joint stock banks had provoked the ire of the bill brokers by their large purchases of bills and of the accepting houses by entering that field. It was true to say that spheres of operations in finance had not been clearly defined at this period and that the joint stock banks were the most vigorous group at encroaching on the preserves of others.

Between 1880 and 1914 a great number of amalgamations took place in banking and the system gradually assumed the form we know today with a small number of very large firms operating nationwide branch networks. Private banking shrank to small proportions. As industrial and commercial firms grew larger private banks could not hope to provide the volume of credit they required. Many private banks were now smaller than their customers. Their old sources of revenue, note issue and

[1] In 1866 when Overend, Gurney & Company asked the Bank for help to tide them over their difficulties it was refused on the grounds that the Bank could not discriminate by helping a single firm. This is in contrast to their later attitude to a single firm in the Baring crisis of 1890. Considerable help was then given by the Bank and Baring's survived the crisis. True, the Bank in 1890 considered that Baring's was basically solvent and for many reasons worth saving: their motives for letting Gurney's sink in 1866 are obscure.

domestic bill finance, were fading away. They had served their turn but the business environment which had produced them and which they had nourished was passing. Only country banks with great powers of adaptation and flexibility were to survive.

V

The second half of the nineteenth century saw a great increase in the prestige, powers and responsibilities of the Bank of England, and of the Bank's skill in evolving and manipulating the tools of credit policy. Apart from the note issue which is not our direct concern here, these developments fall into two fields, which were at times closely related: the management of credit flow in the banking system and the economy generally with all which that entailed in preventing stringency at some periods and boom and overtrading at others; and, after 1870, the management of the gold reserve prompted by movements in the foreign balance and the conventions of the international gold standard. So far as the techniques of management by the Bank were concerned the foundations at least were in place well before mid-century. Rudimentary open market operations to relieve credit stringency were already practised.[1] The rôle of the discount market as the channel through which cash should flow from the Bank to the banking system was acknowledged. What was lacking, and what it was the work of a whole seventy years to create, was a reasonable understanding of what Keynes later called the 'modus operandi of bank rate'. This was a sine qua non of either domestic credit policy or gold reserve policy but it was largely under the impelling force of the latter that it was evolved.

There are few branches of history in which it is more difficult to project ourselves into the period than currency and banking history. We see change a century ago in terms of the greater monetary knowledge we now possess, knowledge of the centralised banking system, its relation-

[1] The history of open-market operations goes far back. During the suspension period (1797–1821) the Bank bought Exchequer Bills on the market when it wished to expand its circulation. It sold bills when it wished to contract the currency. This practice of dealing in Exchequer Bills went on after the resumption of payments but after 1837 Consols were more often used. At the crisis of 1847 there is the first case of borrowing from the market but this practice did not recur until 1861 when we find the Bank borrowing from Messrs. Mullens in order to take funds off the market. This occurred often in the early sixties but lapsed after 1866 and was not revived until 1873 after which it became established practice. Sayers, in his 'Open Market Operations in English Central Banking' (cf. Central Banking After Bagehot, Ch. 5), gives a good description of the processes of open market operations in the later nineteenth century.

ships, processes and integral parts. We see a particular action of the past as good or bad, right or wrong, in terms of this knowledge. We cannot feel or understand the perplexities of those at the time, subject to forces and motives we do not now feel to be important, confused by events of which we now know the outcome. We see this move to be right and constructive, that move to be a wrong turning or a movement away from the evolution we see as proper. Nor do we give due weight to the forces of instability, panic and crisis which were never far from the British banking system in the nineteenth century and which gave to every decision and move a significance for those who made them which we now often miss. The process of evolution to the intricate and interlocking model of the centralised banking system we know today was hardly a process at all but far more a series of *ad hoc* moves and adjustments which seem now, in the light of the final system, to have pattern and meaning.

It has been said above that some of the tools for the Bank of England's use in implementing credit policy were forged in the period before 1850. That is so: but tools are not of use until the craftsman is of a mind to use them and the Bank of England was not so minded until much later in the century than 1850. From 1844 until the seventies it was the firm doctrine of the Bank that its uniqueness as a bank lay in its control of the note issue; that the separation of its functions by the Act into those of note issue and banking entitled the Bank to regard its banking functions as similar to those of any other bank; that it had no special banking responsibilities and was in fact 'just like any other bank'. This view, stemming from the 1844 Act, virtually precluded action and development on the banking side, precluded the working out of a bank rate policy and precluded experimentation with methods of credit control for virtually a quarter of a century.

Two things served to end this *impasse*, one intellectual and theoretical, the other practical and action-producing. The intellectual force was that of Bagehot's *Lombard Street* which was published in 1873 and which exploded for all time the fallacies in the doctrine of 1844. It would never again be possible, in the light of Bagehot's argument, to say that the Bank of England was 'just like any other bank'. Undeniably it was the holder of the ultimate reserve with responsibility for the whole banking system in time of crisis. It's responsibilities extended far beyond the mere function of note issue. The book opened the door to discussion of the whole problem of how the Bank of England could discharge the wide responsibilities in the banking field which Bagehot ascribed to it. No such discussion took place, however. Bagehot died in 1877 without exploring the detailed implications of his book for Bank of England policy.

The real impelling force making for change in Bank of England operations after 1873 (for we may take the date of publication of *Lombard Street* as a climacteric) was the internationalising of the British monetary system and the growth, with the Bank of England at its centre, of the international gold standard. This forced upon the Bank a number of practical problems in connection with the exchanges and the gold reserve, the solutions of which were to carry it far in the direction of a general credit policy. By 1914 the framework of a bank rate policy was complete and the processes of Bank control over credit variation were understood. Our task therefore in examining even briefly the changing rôle of the Bank of England in the period 1850 to 1914 is to look first at the Bank in what we may call its period of quiescence from 1850 to 1875 and then at the evolution of its bank rate policy in its most formative period, between 1870 and 1914.

We find the Bank in 1850 in passive mood. The crisis of 1847 had brought its 'new discounting policy' to an end and it now allowed bank rate to follow the market rate of discount but to remain slightly above it.[1] The only exception to this was at the quarterly shuttings when the Bank was prepared to lend below bank rate to relieve the shortage of cash. This was a recognition of the principle that at times when credit stringency was brought on by normal routine cash movements the Bank should ease the stringency by lending at a rate which was not a penal rate. This is, of course, a principle which is still a part of recognised Bank of England practice.

During what Clapham calls the 'quiet and rather lean years' of the early fifties the Bank was preoccupied with the reorganisation of certain aspects of its banking policy, among them the discount rules which were amended and tightened. The main provisions now were: discounting would be confined to customers either having their sole bank account with the Bank or having a discount account; discount accounts could be held either at Head Office, or at a branch but not at both; bills for discount were to be approved by the Governor and the Committee in Waiting—the Committee to determine rates; no bill, draft, or promissory note of more than 95 days' tenor to be considered, similarly no bill was to be payable in a place other than London or a town where there was a Bank of England branch; and finally, all bills had to bear two good names. In London, although the number of discounters had fallen greatly since the early part of the century, it still included, besides bankers, representatives

[1] As Clapham puts it: 'Without formal vote or any public declaration the Bank became rather less competitive.' It seemed that its aim was 'by keeping near market rate' to save 'its discounts from dropping to the ridiculously low level of 1842-44.' Cf. *The Bank of England*, Vol. ii, p. 217.

of all sorts of London trades and commercial activities from grocers to cheesemongers. At the branches where the connection between the Bank and the commercial life of the district was young and undeveloped the main discounters were bankers.

The fifties saw a great growth of trade and of banking activity. The gold discoveries in California and in Australia drew gold to London and this had the effect of reducing money rates. In April 1852 bank rate went down to 2 per cent and remained there for the rest of the year. The low rates of interest and abundant credit in turn fed the boom in investment and trade which included a great number of new company flotations for all sorts of projects, some of very dubious quality. Side by side with this trade and business expansion was a great increase in the volume of banking business. The volume of deposits of the London joint stock banks rose five times in the decade 1847–57. This rise was in part due to the rise in business activity but much more to the increase in the keeping of bank deposits and to the high rates of interest paid to depositors by joint stock banks. From the fifties, banks were offering 1 per cent below bank rate on deposits, a practice which turned all accounts virtually to investment accounts when bank rate was high. Only when bank rate seemed likely to rise to 9 per cent did the banks begin to reconsider this policy to which competition for deposits was driving them. Nevertheless it remained the practice even with very high bank rate levels to give deposit rates geared to bank rate.

One effect of the high deposit rates was that joint stock banks which had always been in the van in giving call loans were now anxious to put as high a proportion as possible of their deposits out as income-earning assets. This meant that they offered much larger amounts at call to the bill brokers and were prepared to take from them much larger quantities of bills. Moreover, where previously call loans had been extended only to the larger houses such as Gurney's, they were now given to a much wider range of bill brokers. In consequence the old 'brokering' dealer became an operator on short-term borrowed bank money, doing quick deals in bills as well as broking. The character of the market changed after the mid-fifties and became a 'market of bill dealers and not of brokers'.[1] At the same time the market in the fifties was still the main vehicle for equalising the flow of credit over the country. The country banks still dealt with the bill brokers who had their surplus funds to place wherever the demand was greatest. Another factor making for the expansion of bill market business in this period was the growth of acceptance credits. These had long been in use but in the fifties they came to be used on a very large scale and in trades and areas to which they were new. This was in the main the beginning of the great tide of overseas trade bills which

[1] Cf. King, op. cit., p. 175.

M

was later to become a flood, but acceptances were also given by the joint stock banks on domestic bills.

On all counts then, from the expansion of their call money and from the growth of trade in London and in the country, the bill market expanded greatly in the fifties and it was not surprising that with expansion came bill market abuses. Among the abuses was the familiar one of excessive rediscounting. The bill dealers all too frequently discounted bills purely on the strength of the endorsement of a country bank and without having any knowledge of the original parties to the bill. This had the effect of giving country banks virtually unlimited credit in London, for all that a country bank had to do was to procure a good supply of local accommodation bills and to forward them to London to its bill broker. Bill brokers were often ignorant of the poor quality of the paper they received, but it is certain that often they suspected the poor quality but did not allow it to deter them. A second credit abuse was the over-reliance of the bill dealers on call loans, and their refusal to hold adequate reserves of cash and very short bills. A reasonable financial acumen should have prompted them to hold such a reserve against the eventuality of a call-in. This was not done. The dealing margins were very narrow and required a large turnover if profit was to be made and dealers could not afford to hold idle balances. To do so would virtually have meant they were borrowing money at call at x per cent and holding it idle at no return. With a brisk demand for bills, especially from the joint stock banks, and the possibility of a large turnover it is not surprising that most bill dealers succumbed to the temptation and held only minimal liquid reserves.

A new credit abuse came with the increase in accepting house bills of which many now came to the London market for rediscount. The system whereby open credits were allowed to persons abroad to draw upon the accepting house pre-supposed goods in transit as security. Many of these bills were not so backed, however, but were backed only by other bills. The whole transaction was in fact an accommodation. As long as bill dealers could go to the Bank of England and rediscount there in times of stringency there was little risk of loss. True, the Bank of England rate was higher, and in times of stringency perhaps a good deal higher, but even this risk was partly offset by the large turnover. The consciousness of Bank of England support at only slightly greater cost was, therefore, a great encouragement to over-trading and indeed to toleration by the bill dealers of the other weaknesses in their position. General over-trading was able in the circumstances to ride high and unchecked on the wave of prosperity and financial confidence which obtained in the early fifties.

The Bank of England could have placed a strong curb on discount market over-trading by enforcing exacting criteria to govern its own rediscounting. This it did in theory but not in practice.[1] By the fifties accounts were easily opened,[2] and it seemed that the Bank cared very little whether the bills it discounted were accommodation bills or not provided they were from a reliable house. In fact the conclusion is inescapable that the Bank was concerned purely with security for the bills it bought and not with the wider implications of this affluence of very dubious paper.

Once more, in the now familiar nineteenth century pattern crisis developed.[3] Its origins were the speculation and over-trading induced by the gold discoveries. Bank rate was raised in the middle of 1853, an indication that new capital flotations were outrunning available capital. Meanwhile, in spite of new gold imports, the rise in imports was reducing the gold reserve. Prices and wages were rising and there were reports of short-time working in industry. Prices turned downwards in 1854 but despite the Crimean War the crisis did not come. Imports of Australian gold were offsetting the potential decline in the gold reserve due to the adverse balance of payments. As the speculative activity continued strain on the money market appeared with high interest rates and periodic shortages. During one shortage, in November 1856, the Bank discriminated against the bill market by restricting rediscounts for dealers to bills of thirty days or less, but the periods of stringency were alleviated by the arrivals of gold from Australia, and in this way speculation was allowed to proceed for much longer than would otherwise have been the case. As late as June 1857 (when the Indian Mutiny broke out) the Bank of England was still reducing its discount rate by one point to $5\frac{1}{2}$ per cent.

In September came the bad news from India, a drain of gold, high discount rates in Western Europe and financial crisis in the United States. There was panic both in Liverpool and Glasgow, both cities reliant on the American trade and vulnerable to bad news from the West. In London bank rate went up by a series of rises over eleven days to 8 per cent. The discount houses were forced 'to make arrangements from day to day' and even good bills taken from credit-worthy and trusted clients were rediscounted at the Bank the same day. One discount house of twenty-two years' standing, Sanderson's, failed and there was a series of commercial and bank failures. Other discount houses had to sustain heavy

[1] For the conditions of Bank discounting see p. 176 above.

[2] A smaller deposit than formerly was required.

[3] It has been said that the crisis of 1857 was the first really world-wide economic crisis in history, involving Britain, the United States, Central Europe, Australia and the Far East.

demands after the failure of Sanderson's. Bruce's (Bruce, Wilkinson & Company) ceased to discount. Gurney's had to pay out heavily and receive substantial aid from the Bank. Alexander's continued to discount only on a very limited scale. Bank rate went to 10 per cent and the general calling in of call loans put the discount market continually in the Bank. Then news from Scotland intensified the crisis. The Western Union Bank stopped payment on 9th November and on the 11th came the failure of the City of Glasgow Bank. Scotland had long been considered a tower of strength in banking and these failures had a deep psychological effect. Coupled with the failure of the bill broking firm of Sanderson & Company they were too much for the system to sustain. On 12th November the Act of 1844 was suspended.

This time, suspension did not have the immediate effects of 1847. There was a further wave of provincial bank failures and discounts by the Bank continued heavy until December. Slowly, the crisis subsided. Towards the end of November it became possible to discount again in the open market, albeit at 10 per cent. By Christmas the rate was down to 8 per cent and by 11th February 1858 to 3 per cent. Another crisis had been weathered without major disaster, but it was to have far-reaching repercussions, particularly on Bank of England thinking.

The crisis of 1857, the second since the Bank Charter Act of 1844, had a strong effect on the morale of the Bank of England and the directors were determined that there should not be a recurrence of the strain which the days of September and October had placed upon the Bank. It was no doubt recognised that in great part the crisis and that of 1847 was due to the abuses and malpractices which tended to appear directly the economy became buoyant, but these were numerous and widespread and the Bank had few if any sanctions to apply against them or their perpetrators. But for the bill market, whose over-trading had been all too manifest in the recent crisis, there was one sanction possible and it was promptly used. The discount market's right of recourse to the Bank had involved the Bank in mammoth discounting in its support and heavy calls on its reserve. That at least could be stopped. In February the bank was discussing practical measures including two very drastic ones which proposed (a) that there should be no discounting for the bill brokers or discount companies, and (b) that no advances should be made to them save those at the quarterly shuttings. These were modified somewhat but the eventual edict, announced on March 13, was tough enough. The Bank announced that bill brokers and discount houses were not to have the right of taking bills to the Bank for discount; moreover, they would not have the benefit of temporary advances, except during the 'shuttings' when quarterly advances would be made to them on the same terms as to other applicants. The door was left open a little. The precise decision by the Bank was that 'there were to be no advances by way of discount or loans to "bill brokers, discount companies or money dealers" so "habitual" as to make them rely on the Bank in time of pressure, but that they might receive the quarterly advances and loans in emergency, such loans, however, to be reported by the Governors to the Court.'[1]

Thus at one fell swoop the principle of the special position of the discount market and the principle of using their 'last resort' privileges with the Bank as a means of channelling funds to the economy in time of need was abrogated. The Bank did not, of course, see this right of 'last resort' as we see it today. They sat amid the dust and ruins of many banks and companies, assigning blame and responsibility, and on their list of precedence the bill brokers stood high. It does not seem to have occurred to them, however, that a similar result might, by less drastic means, have been achieved, but with better effects on the conduct of the discount houses, if they had left the principle of 'last resort' intact but imposed exacting criteria as to the nature and quality of the bills they would be prepared to rediscount for the market. The imposition of the 'rule of 1858' was a retrograde step although in practice the lender-of-last-resort principle was never completely repudiated by the Bank, for accommodation was never really refused to the bill brokers in time of serious pressure.[2]

The years from 1858 to 1873 were years of great and growing prosperity. Prices and wages were rising, unemployment was low and output and trade were expanding. Britain had a large favourable balance of payments on current account. Foreign investment was increasing. Britain was moving into a period of growing international trade and widening financial responsibilities.

If in 1873 at the start of the Great Depression, men of affairs had been asked what the Bank's central policy was or should be, the question would have evoked varied responses. Bagehot would have replied that the Bank's prime duty was to maintain an adequate reserve through the medium of bank rate manipulation.[3] Thomas Hankey, a former Governor of the Bank, would have invoked shades of the past and asserted that 'the more the conduct of the affairs of the Bank is made to assimilate to the conduct of every other well-managed bank in the United Kingdom, the better for the Bank and the better for the community at large.'[4] Between these extremes most moderate men would have assigned a special position

[1] Cf. Clapham, *The Bank of England*, Vol. ii, p. 235.
[2] Excepting the refusal to Overend, Gurney in 1866 for which it might be argued there were special reasons.
[3] See *Economist*, 22nd September 1866.
[4] Cf. Quotation in Clapham, op. cit., p. 285.

to the Bank, but would have been vague and indecisive as to its detailed power and aims. One thing is certain, the *modus operandi* of bank rate was now coming to be better understood. A rise in bank rate would have certain effects: it would draw funds from country banks to London and it would attract foreign funds to London; it would lower prices in Britain and improve the balance of merchandise trade; and, if prices were reduced in the world at large, which would likely happen if other central banks raised their rates, a part of the money stock would be released from circulation and would pass into central bank reserves. This relating of bank rate policy to the reserve was not an entirely hide-bound one. It was qualitative rather than quantitative. It was known that a whole host of considerations might determine whether a given change in the reserve called for a change in bank rate. The reserve changed for many reasons: for changes in government payments; for seasonal changes in the currency circulation; from changes in foreign trade. Some changes required a bank rate change, some did not. The Bank was in the eighties and nineties acquiring judgement and selectivity in assessing the causes of change in the reserve and the appropriate bank rate reaction.

But while the bank rate was by the 1870's a consciously used Bank of England tool there was the further question of linking bank rate changes to the market rate and to interest rates in general. Bank rate had to be made effective. It could only be so if the Bank of England were a large operator in the market. Then its discount rate, i.e., bank rate, would influence all other discount rates. But in the conditions which had existed since 1847 when the Bank pursued the constant policy of adjusting bank rate to follow the market rate already established in the discount market, there was no question of bank rate being a major influence. Moreover, since the Bank's 1858 decision to refuse rediscount and final resort facilities to the discount houses the market had become even more independent of the Bank. It did not seem to be part of the Bank's 'conventional wisdom' that, in times of stringency when the discount houses were short of money and required help from the Bank, this was the very time when the Bank wanted to adjust bank rate and make the adjustment effective. It could do this by lending then to the market at its own chosen rate.

In fact, in 1858 and for some time afterwards, the Bank's attitude towards the discount market was compounded of several elements of which the technical problem of making bank rate effective was not one. Firstly, they remembered the severe strain placed upon them by giving aid to the discount houses in the 1857 crisis, and if this was what was entailed in being lender of last resort they disliked and for the present abrogated the responsibility. Secondly, they felt a certain need to discipline the discount market which had its less respectable side and which was encouraging accommodation bills and discounting dubious acceptances; and thirdly, still regarding themselves as a commercial bank competing in the discount market, they regarded the discount houses as rivals.

So far as the discount market itself was concerned the Bank of England's action of 1858 was deeply resented and they had some support from other quarters.[1] A delegation from Gurney's, Bruce's and others called on the Governor to ask for a change in the edict but were given no hope of it. The larger houses tried to boycott the Bank by refusing to borrow from it even during the shuttings. Gurney's was more militant. In April 1860, in an attempt to coerce the Bank into abandoning the 1858 rule, Gurney's withdrew at one swoop £1,650,000 in £1,000 notes from the Bank. The only immediate response from an imperturbable Bank was to raise bank rate to 5 per cent. But much publicity was given to the incident and a question was put down for Gladstone in the House. On 17th April, the Bank received an anonymous letter posted in London which threatened darkly: 'Overend's (i.e., Gurney's)[2] can pull out every note you have; from actual knowledge the writer can inform you that with their own family assistance they can nurse (?) *seven* millions.'[3] On April 18 the establishment closed ranks. Dobrée, then Governor of the Bank, saw Gladstone and gave him an account of Gurney's transactions with the Bank over a long period. Gladstone subsequently, in what must have been an interesting interview, saw representatives of Gurney's. It seems that on the 16th, Gurney's had sent a message to the Bank through Baring's that all the notes would be returned if the Bank would modify its 1858 rule. The ultimatum had been refused. Late on the 18th when Dobrée returned to the Bank he found that the notes had been returned. They had all been cut in two, probably for reasons of security. There had been a swift *volte face* on the part of the rebel and an apology was made to the Bank by Gurney's through a Bank director. This was an extraordinary incident with a mixture of Victorian melodrama, irresponsibility by a great firm now in the last years of its life, and a futility which should have been apparent from the first. It is hard to believe that the Bank's refusal to help Gurney's in their last desperate hours in the crisis of 1866 was not in part due either to the bitterness born of this attack or to the Bank's view that Gurney's was not now worth preserving.

[1] The *Economist* disliked this harsh and undiscriminating treatment of the bill brokers as a group without considering 'the character of the house or the quality of the bills it may offer.' Cf. 20th March 1858.

[2] The full name of the firm was Overend, Gurney and Company.

[3] Quoted from the Dobrée manuscript in Clapham's *The Bank of England*, Vol. ii, p. 243.

It would be tedious and unnecessary to subject the patient reader to yet another description of crisis and recovery. The crisis of 1866 was not greatly different from those of 1847 and 1857 except, perhaps, that it involved fewer commercial and industrial bankruptcies and was limited more to the purely financial and monetary sector of the economy. It is remembered now for the failure of Overend, Gurney and Company, the largest of the discount houses, which in the previous year had become a limited liability company and for more than half a century had been regarded as well-nigh as strong as the Bank itself. In its last years its strength was, however, an illusion and its management had been faulty and reckless. Accommodation bills, advances on mortgage and many types of business extraneous to a discount house had come within its scope. It was rotten at the heart by the time it became a limited company. The events of the subsequent year only served to reveal that rottenness to an astonished world.

The failure of Gurney's brought the crisis to a head in May 1866. Bank rate went to 9 per cent and on May 12 to 10 per cent, accompanied by the usual Treasury letter suspending the Bank Act. This time the reserve of the Bank was slower to recover and the very high rate of interest persisted right into the autumn. This was due to the extreme loss of confidence, particularly abroad, and even rates as high as 8 or 9 per cent were slow to attract funds back to London either from the country or from overseas.

One interesting feature of the crisis or rather of its aftermath was a speech by Lancelot Holland, then Governor of the Bank, in which, referring to the crisis, he gave something that looked very like an assurance that the Bank still recognised that it had a responsibility as lender of last resort. He said:

> 'We could not flinch from the duty which we conceived was imposed upon us, of supporting the banking community, and I am not aware that any legitimate application for assistance which was made to this house was refused.'[1]

The development of Bank policy between 1870 and 1914 must be set against the background of the international gold standard, for much of the Bank's operations were by then conditioned by British participation and virtual leadership in that system. This period was the high summer of the international gold standard. Neither invented nor consciously planned, it had grown steadily during the eighteenth and early nineteenth centuries as countries, from a choice of different metallic standards, silver,

[1] Quoted in E. V. Morgan, *The Theory and Practice of Central Banking, 1797–1913*, Cambridge, 1943, p. 180.

gold or bimetallic, had adopted gold as their monetary base. In 1871 the German Empire made gold its standard and Switzerland and Belgium followed in 1878. Thereafter gold was the basis of international payments among the leading countries until the Great War transformed the international economy which the standard had served.

Essentially the gold standard was two things: a method of clearing international indebtedness and a system of international balance of payments adjustment. Any country whose balance of trade became favourable experienced an inflow of gold to its banking system; a country experiencing a deficit lost gold. These gold flows would, by depleting or enlarging the monetary stock, produce such price and cost changes as to alter demand for the imports and exports of the countries concerned and thus correct imbalance. In the latter years of the nineteenth century the model of national price changes induced by gold flows, in and out of central banks, was supplemented by the argument that for short-term external imbalance, changes in interest rates would produce an adjustment effect. When, for example, the Bank of England lost gold as a result of a British payments deficit a rise in bank rate would serve to draw short-term funds to London and give immediate relief to the imbalance. A rise in bank rate was in any event the first step in the process of price deflation and indeed in many cases might be the only step necessary. By the last years of the century it was agreed that central banks by their interest rate policies could go far to control world movements of gold. Full scale engineered deflations and expansions of an economy were not likely to be necessary. Any examination of Bank of England technique in the period 1870–1914 must then be primarily concerned with the development of the machinery for making bank rate effective.[1]

There were three fairly distinct phases of development: from 1870–80 when the use of the bank rate was persistent but technically inefficient; from 1880–90 when the Bank of England resorted to certain practices in the gold market which, to some extent, took the place of the bank rate changes; and from 1890–1914 when there was a swift development in the power of the Bank of England, the working out of a bank rate policy and the abandonment of the gold devices—in short a definite movement towards a more purposive and confident monetary management.

From 1870 to 1880, the techniques used were rudimentary. Reliance was placed upon the ordinary processes of expansion and contraction of

[1] There were other gold standard techniques practised by the Bank of England, for example the so-called 'gold Devices' which it used when operating in the gold market. Cf. 'The Working of the Gold Standard 1870–1914', W. M. Scammell, *Yorkshire Bulletin of Economic and Social Research*, Vol. 17, No. 1, pp. 32–46, and 'The Bank in the Gold Market', R. S. Sayers, *Papers in English Monetary History*, Oxford, 1953, Ch. 10.

the monetary base with frequent changes of discount rate. Between 1871 and 1880 changes in bank rate averaged more than ten a year. The Bank of England's influence on interest rates was at this stage slight and largely ineffective. It rested purely on the fact that the Bank was ordinarily a large buyer of bills in the market, but as the Bank's discounting diminished after 1875 and as the size of the market grew this influence weakened considerably. There were halting steps during the period towards the purposive use of interest rates by the Bank but their effective use had to wait upon certain developments in the institutional framework of the monetary system, particularly upon recognition of the Bank of England as lender of last resort and the subjection of the market rate of interest to bank rate.

In considering the development of bank rate techniques it is well to remember that changes in bank rate depend fundamentally on (a) deciding the direction and size of the change, and (b) making it effective. The first condition will be determined by the circumstances obtaining at the time and depends upon the skill and experience of the monetary authority. The second depends upon financial institutions but the primary requirement is that the central bank should be able deliberately to induce a shortage of funds in the money market and then itself make money available at the chosen rate, which is thus made effective. Since borrowers can for the moment only obtain money at this rate, they alter their own lending rates accordingly. The arrangement which ultimately evolved in England was the well-known one under which by open market operations the Bank of England created a shortage of short-term credit and drove the discount houses to borrow from it at whatever rate it chose to enforce. This system did not, however, develop until late in the period we are discussing.

Before 1870 the views of the Bank on its operations in the market were purely domestic. It insisted that the bank rate in its movements should follow and not lead the ordinary market rate and that, while bank rate should conform more or less closely to market rate, the bank should never initiate rate changes.[1] The sixties were, as we have seen, a period in which there was a marked lack of co-operation between the Bank and the discount companies. The shadow of the crisis of 1857 and the controversy of 1858 over the Bank's withdrawal of discount facilities for the dealers still lay across the City and the level of discount market borrowing from the Bank even during the shuttings fell considerably. Under such conditions the Bank felt obliged to keep its own discount rate as close to the market rate as possible so that changes were frequent and for long periods bank rate was ineffective. Moreover, when large

---

[1] This rule was supposed to demonstrate the Bank's wish to abstain from competition in the market.

foreign balances were in London the market rate and its shadowy follower bank rate were low just at a time when a rise in bank rate to protect the reserve might be necessary. Bagehot and others frequently criticised the Bank in the early seventies for this state of affairs and for failing to anticipate pressure on the reserve.[1] In 1873 bank rate was changed twenty-four times in order to keep near to the market rate. Between 1865 and 1874 bank rate changes averaged twelve a year. Between 1845 and 1859 the average had been four a year.

By the 1870's it was, therefore, clear to discerning critics like Bagehot that the main aim of bank rate policy should be to exercise a positive influence on the interest rate structure. The existing condition was chaotic. There were, in effect, two short-term discount rates in London: bank rate, controlled by the Bank of England but ineffectually following market rate, which was far more important since it was the rate at which foreign bills could be discounted and therefore the rate which drew money to or deflected money from London. The Bank was the custodian of the reserve, yet it could not control market rate which was a main determinant of the size of the reserve. Clearly responsibility for the reserve and control of the main short-term rate should both be vested in the monetary authority.

In late 1871 for the first time bank rate (at 5 per cent) was temporarily above market rate (at 3½ per cent) and despite criticism it was soon clear that the rule of conformity of bank rate to market rate was being abandoned. Henceforward, the differential between the two rates steadily widened. In 1874 bank rate was raised to deal with a potential foreign demand for gold at a time when adherence to the rule of following market rate would have meant a reduction. Moreover, there were signs that not only was the Bank pursuing a new policy in changing the rate but also that it appreciated the need to make the rate effective.

But the struggle for an effective bank rate was to be a long one and not until 1890 was the Bank able to deal with the problem of what Bonamy Price in July 1877 referred to as 'two money markets in London, two rates of interest.' The trouble was that the 1858 rule still prevailed and effectively precluded the development of a 'market in the Bank'. Not until some modification of this rule was made was progress possible. This came in the seventies when an increasing volume of Treasury business began to have its effect on the money supply and on the market, extending stringency over longer periods than the shuttings during which the Bank often found itself in unaccustomed command of the market. In 1878 the Bank announced that it would be prepared to lend to the market, at or near bank rate, not only in times of crisis and at the shuttings, but at

[1] Cf. Bagehot, *Lombard Street*, pp. 321–22.

any time. It would not discount bills but would be prepared to make advances for very short periods to discount houses and bill brokers. Bank rate became for a time not a discount rate but a loan rate for short help loans to the discount market.[1] Thus, with growing effect, the Bank relaxed the 1858 rule, giving help to the market virtually at its discretion. This discretion it often exercised powerfully. In 1883, concern by the Bank at the decline in its discount business led to a suggestion by H. R. Grenfell that the rule of 1858 should be modified, but the only extension granted was that, whereas under the rule help to the market was confined to the shuttings, it might now be given whenever 'government balances accumulate in the hands of the Bank.'

This Bank practice of lending to the market at its discretion while not effectively extending its control to the market rate was not sufficient to give it more than partial control of the market and by the early nineties the Bank was under criticism for its failure to protect the gold reserve whose movements responded not to bank rate but to the market rate. The seriousness of the problem varied with the volume of bills coming to the market and with the flow of available funds, but in general bank rate still moved ineffectually in the wake of the market rate. This was a crucial period for London's leadership of the gold standard, for such leadership depended upon the Bank of England being able to control interest rates in London and vary them in relation to rates in other financial centres, and this patently it could not do. The Baring crisis in 1890 heightened criticism of the Bank of England's lack of power to maintain the gold reserve, and the Bank, under Lidderdale's leadership, at last began to take determined steps to increase its power over the market. In that year the Bank formally annulled the rule of 1858 and readmitted the discount houses to rediscount facilities, thus recognising not only the need to fix an effective bank rate but that, for that purpose, the Bank had to be in the market and not aloof from it. In July 1890 it began to discount for its regular customers at a rate below market rate. Later in the same month it rescinded the rule of 1858 when it told the bill brokers it would discount fifteen day bills for them at not less than bank rate. This willingness to rediscount was rightly followed by a qualitative control of the bills to be taken. In 1894 the stipulated currency for bills was increased to 30 days, in 1897 to three months and in 1910 to four months. These increases gradually strengthened the Bank's hold over the market not only quantitatively but also qualitatively, for as time passed the market came to prefer those bills which were rediscountable at the Bank.

There was another approach to the problem of how the Bank might try to make the market comply with its own rate. Market rate funda-

---

[1] A situation closely akin to that now obtaining.

mentally depended on the flow of funds available. It was clear that if the Bank could increase or decrease the available funds it could lower or raise the market rate. It could reduce funds in the market by reducing its own liabilities to the banking system or alternatively by bringing about a switch of its liabilities to non-bank depositors. In fact it used both these methods, combining them in a variety of devices which, apart from open market operations in consols, involved borrowing in the market, borrowing from the clearing banks and borrowing from its own depositors. The years 1890 to 1914 form a period in which the market and the Bank taught one another the theory of centralised money market control by the use of these devices and the Bank gained by convention a fair degree of control over the market when the foreign balance required it. Yet it was only in the last years of the nineteenth century that bank rate became a swiftly variable and effective means of adjusting the interest rate structure and of influencing capital movements and the balance of payments. Certainly during the nineties bank rate changes in themselves were regarded as only one possible weapon for influencing the external balance.

One can hardly be very complimentary about the Bank of England's vision or competence during this long process of development of the bank rate weapon. One could, for example, argue that the Bank might have saved years of trial and error, not to say much ill-will and animosity, by establishing in 1858 the practice they adopted in 1878, namely that of lending to the market in last resort but not rediscounting for it, or of rediscounting but only doing so for bills of unimpeachable quality and defined currency. In fact the sureness of touch and expertise which one would have wished for in the Bank was only at times forthcoming—as with Lidderdale and his shrewd handling of the Baring crisis[1]—while at

---

[1] This crisis occurred late in 1890 when Baring Brothers, the great merchant bank, was threatened by a calamitous fall in the value of securities it held as underwriter for certain South American loans. The handling of the crisis marks the first drawing together of the banks and the Bank of England and the first real acknowledgement by the banks of the Bank of England's leadership. In 1866 during the Overend, Gurney crisis the atmosphere had been one of *sauve qui peut* and the Bank had led the rout. In 1890 the threat to Baring's resulted in Lidderdale promising a meeting of representatives of leading banks and city houses that the Bank would stand behind Baring's if the banks and the market agreed to indemnify the Bank for any losses they might incur in meeting Baring's commitments as they matured. This indemnity was quickly given. It is true that the Overend, Gurney crisis and the Baring crisis are not close parallels. Gurney's failed because its management was bad, if not corrupt, and its business 'rotten to the core': Baring's was not insolvent but temporarily embarrassed by a great fall in the value of securities which it held at a time when it had large acceptances outstanding. The real point is that Lidderdale as Governor of the Bank saw clearly the wide repercussions which would result for the whole British financial fraternity from a failure of Baring's. He acted with speed and determination to prevent it.

other times it seemed ham-fisted and incompetent. Even quite repetitive and routine matters of credit variations were often not attended to. Sayers, for example, draws attention to the Bank's failure to deal with seasonal drains of gold each autumn as a serious 'blot on its record'.[1] The fact is that one cannot, in discussing Bank of England operations in the period before 1914, 'personalise' Bank actions and policies by using the collective noun 'the Bank'. Clapham points out that all that this can refer to is a series of often unco-ordinated Board and Committee decisions which might or might not add up to a concerted view, but more likely would reflect the views of various groups within the Board of Governors. Now and then under a strong and able Governor, decisive views and forward movement is seen, but quickly that Governor 'passes the Chair' to be replaced by a man of meaner calibre and all is again in flux. The problem of what Clapham calls 'the shifting and evanescent Governor' bedevilled continuity and development of Bank policy and operations in the period we have been discussing.

Little has been said in this chapter of one development which was to have great significance for the future of the discount market: the establishment in 1877 of a new vehicle of government short-term borrowing in the Treasury bill. The foundation, establishment and development of the Treasury bill have already been dealt with[2] and need not be reiterated here but a word or two on its wider significance is appropriate.

The establishment of the Treasury bill had a fourfold significance. Firstly it provided a form of short-term paper which was highly suitable to the banking system as a liquid asset and to the Bank of England as a dealing medium for open-market operations. A market for this paper developed side by side, indeed at first almost as part of the market in trade bills. Secondly, the Treasury bill provided the discount market with a growing volume of short-term paper in which to deal at a time when other forms of paper, i.e., the domestic bill and, slightly later, the overseas bill, were declining in volume. It is no exaggeration to say that if the Treasury bill had not appeared when it did the discount market would have languished and probably, in the interwar period, disappeared altogether. Thirdly, the Treasury bill, being a vehicle of government borrowing, brought the discount market a new rôle as part of the institutional set-up for government borrowing and debt administration, a rôle strengthened later when the market came to deal also in short-term government bonds. Fourthly, the Treasury bill by becoming the main stock-in-trade of the discount houses raised for the discount market the question of its own usefulness, for these bills called for none of the

[1] Cf. R. F. Sayers, *Bank of England Operations, 1890–1914*, p. 135.
[2] Cf. pp. 37–49 above.

expertise in vetting and grading which the discount houses applied to the trade bill and which was their essential contribution. The discount houses came to deal in the Treasury bill because they, as financial houses, were there, and here was a market in which they might profitably participate, but such a market could have functioned quite satisfactorily without them and indeed does so in other and newer banking systems.

All these aspects of the coming of the Treasury bill are interesting and important but they bear upon later periods in the development of the market. Up to World War I the Treasury bill was limited in scope: later its true significance was to emerge. This will be dealt with in its place in subsequent chapters.

Chapter 7

WORLD WAR I AND ITS AFTERMATH
1914–39

I

ACROSS all historical studies that span the nineteenth and twentieth centuries the First World War cuts its wide swathe, a great dividing line. This is so of the development of the discount market, for although no immediate radical changes were wrought in the composition or structure of the market by the war itself, the whole financial and economic milieu within which the market functioned and which it served was so radically changed that the discount market could not but react to these changes. Outstanding among the war's effects on the market was that, whereas it had grown to 1914 as a financial institution geared to trade, particularly overseas trade, and was therefore commercial in outlook and interest, the war shattered the trade structure which it had served. In those four years the great and imposing trade structure of the nineteenth century and the gold standard which had regulated its payments was swept away and although much time and effort was spent after the war on plans and policies for its rehabilitation it was never restored in its original form. The old international economy based on the gold standard and relying for its efficacy on the tradition of central bank co-operation was gone for ever. Instead there emerged an international trade system dominated by economic nationalism and malformed by the regulation imposed by governments. Not only did the volume of international trade suffer from this restriction and from the effects of the world depression but the gold standard as a system of international balance of payments adjustment proved unworkable in the postwar period. With this change came the swift decline of the bill as a medium of payment in foreign trade. Forces had long been working for its replacement by new and quicker media. The war provided the interruption in its use which enabled these other media to intrude and establish themselves when international trade was resumed. Robbed for four years of its function of dealing in trade bills the discount market turned to another credit instrument, the Treasury bill. These, during the war, became its staple and even after the war, when a meagre flow of trade bills returned, Treasury bills were to remain its principal form of short-term paper.

The main feature which appeared in the war and postwar years and contrasted with the nineteenth century was the great pace of economic change. The international economy was transformed; the domestic economy changed both in its relation to the rest of the world and in its internal structure; the relation of government, industry, commerce and finance to each other altered radically; above all the participation of the state and its agencies in economic and financial affairs increased and widened. In all this the discount market's basic problem was that of survival by adapting itself to changing circumstances, pressures and influences. In this chapter we shall examine the course of this process of adaptation. For convenience we shall divide the war and inter-war years into three periods: the period of the war itself; the period 1918–31, years of reconstruction during which British economic policies were first directed towards an early return to the gold standard, and later after 1925 to producing and trading under the conditions which the new gold standard imposed; and finally the period 1932–39, the period of the depression and the limited recovery which followed it. These divisions are arbitrary but they serve to split up a lengthy and crowded period of financial history and make it reasonably manageable.

II

The outbreak of war in August 1914 not only rang down the curtain on the old nineteenth-century world, many features of which were never to appear again, but produced an immediate and sharp crisis for the city of London and in particular for the discount market. The trouble lay with the great volume of bills held in London, accepted by London accepting houses, outstanding for payments by foreign nationals and for which payment was now in question. It was estimated that approximately £350m. in bills of exchange was outstanding in London, of which most bore the name of one of the great accepting houses or of a joint stock bank. Normally a bill would be accepted for an overseas debtor by either an accepting house or joint stock bank, be discounted with a bill broker, held by him and then probably rediscounted with a joint stock bank. All these parties were, therefore, concerned in the crisis caused by the inability of foreigners to make remittances to discharge their liability.[1]

[1] It is interesting to compare this early foreign exchange crisis with the many crises of our own day. In 1914 the problem was how foreigners might make payment to us and what was the consequence of their default; latterly we have been concerned with how we may discharge external liabilities to foreigners.

N

The accepting houses were faced with the possibility of widespread default; the bill brokers were holding bills which threatened to become valueless and were equally liable for bills which they had endorsed and sold to the banks. The banks in turn were liable for large amounts of their own acceptances and were holders of bills as liquid assets which might become valueless. Moreover, they had large sums out at call to the bill brokers which were imperilled by the weakness of the brokers' position. A further complication was that the stock exchange had been closed on 31st July and it was impossible to increase liquidity by bond sales. Moreover, such loans as the banks made at short notice to stock brokers could not be called in because of the stock exchange closure.

Such a situation was potentially dangerous to the whole banking system. Had it been widely realised how vulnerable the banks were in the matter of liquid assets a general run might have developed, leading to a suspension of payments.

The banks, to improve their position, were calling in such loans as were callable, including discount market call money. The bill brokers in their extremity were turning to the Bank of England. In the few days to August 1 the Bank of England lent over £31m. to bill brokers to enable them to meet their calls. The pattern of so many nineteenth century crises was here repeated. From a base of 3 per cent, bank rate escalated to 10 per cent with the Bank still discounting even at this high rate. The Bank of England's reserve fell sharply and on August 1 the Bank requested and received the usual Treasury letter on the model of 1847, 1857 and 1866, this time from Asquith and Lloyd George, authorising them to exceed the fiduciary issue if necessary and to make discounts only at a rate of 10 per cent or more. On August 2 a moratorium was proclaimed postponing for a month payment of any bill accepted before August 4. This gave breathing space to acceptors who were unable to meet maturing acceptances and prevented a spate of bankruptcies.

The immediate crisis and danger of a run on the banks was averted, but the foreign exchange market was in confusion, for the war, by making it impossible to draw bills on London or to ship gold or make foreign payments in any way, had torn the whole fabric of international finance. This was one of the earliest casualties of war, but at least, since trade shrank to low levels, it could temporarily be ignored and put aside as one of the problems to be met when the emergency had passed. More immediate was the plight of the accepting houses, discount houses, and joint stock banks as holders of uncollectable bills. As long as this Sword of Damocles hung over the market it was impossible to predict what would happen. It was seen by authority that the only way to escape from this threat was for the government to accept liability for these bills, which clearly would not be paid until after the war, if then. On August 13 the Bank was instructed accordingly to discount all approved bills accepted before August 4 at bank rate and without any right of action against the holder should they remain unpaid and that, in its turn, the government should indemnify the Bank against any loss on the bills. By November about £20m.[1] of bills had been discounted. In September the arrangement was altered and the Bank offered advances (at 2 per cent above bank rate) to acceptors to allow them to meet bills as they matured, these advances not to be repayable until one year after the end of the war. About £60,386,000[2] was advanced for this purpose. Since it is estimated that at least £350m. in bills had been outstanding we may assume that a goodly amount of bills had been disposed of normally.

These measures eased anxiety for the joint stock banks, the discount houses and the accepting houses. There remained the problem of the disorganisation of the foreign exchange market and the closure of the stock exchange. Both of these were successfully met, the former by late 1914 and the latter early in the following year. A scheme was devised to reduce the very high rate for sterling[3] by paying sterling against gold deposited to British accounts in Canada. By November the exchanges with allied countries were almost back to normal. Meanwhile, a scheme for government assistance in respect of loans to the stock exchange enabled the outstanding end-of-July settlement to be cleared. Banks agreed not to press for repayment of Account to Account loans until twelve months after the end of the war. Under the influence of these measures prices in official dealings began to harden and the market reopened on 4th January 1915.

The discount market was, needless to say, in a somewhat tender state following these stirring events. The government measures had gone far to restore British credit abroad but acceptors in Britain were very chary about making acceptances save for goods destined for Britain. The banks showed the same disinclination. The remittance problems, although less acute with the closing of the foreign bill exchanges, remained for new bills. For some time discount market business remained at very low levels. In October 1914 it was less than 5 per cent of what had been normal before the crisis.[4]

Table XII shows the outstanding amount of bills discounted at the clearing banks during the war years.

[1] Cf. *British Finance 1914–21*, Ed. A. W. Kirkcaldy, London, 1921, p. 8.
[2] Kirkcaldy, op. cit., p.8.
[3] It went to $6·5 = £1 in August 1914.
[4] Cf. The *Economist*, 24th October 1914.

TABLE XII

BILLS DISCOUNTED AND OUTSTANDING
AT CLEARING BANKS

at December 31	Amount £m.	Increase + or Decrease −
1914	161	−7
1915	127	−34
1916	237	+110
1917	368	+131
1918	444	+76
1919	376	−68

Source: British Finance 1914–21, ed. by A. W. Kirkcaldy, p. 90.

The decrease of £41m. in bills discounted for the years 1914 and 1915 was due to the drastic decline in home and foreign trade which came with the war. The increase of £317m. for the three years to December 1918 may be attributed wholly to bank purchases of Treasury bills. The drop of £68m. in 1919 was compounded of a considerable increase in trade and bank bills purchased with the re-establishment of home and foreign trade after the war and a rather larger run-off of maturing Treasury bills. Although commercial bills came back to the market in 1919 they were never to grow again to the importance they had in 1913. 'Normal' would never come again: the great day of the bill on London was over.

It is no part of our business here to discuss the worth of the measures taken by the government during the crisis. They had their critics, Keynes among them. But in the context of the times and remembering the lack of any precedent either of type or magnitude for this crisis, they were adequate and they served to preserve the fabric of British monetary institutions from disaster. What is now apparent is their basically inflationary nature which became more and more evident as the war proceeded and wrought its changes on the economy. The problems of August and September 1914 soon merged into or were overshadowed by the more fundamental problems which the war produced in the economic field as it progressed. The length and scale of the war had widespread effects on the economy. There was an unprecedented diversion of resources from normal production and, as the years passed, consumer-goods output and the output of capital goods for normal industrial use or for social utilities shrank to the lowest possible level as resources were deployed to the war-effort. To finance the great increase in government expenditure and the budget deficit,[1] massive borrowing was resorted to and, in the years which followed, wartime monetary developments were conditioned by the borrowing methods of the Treasury and by the great expansion of the note issue. The supply of legal tender money and the credit base was increased *ad infinitum* and this in its turn led to an increase in both wholesale and retail prices of 120–130 per cent over the war period. So far as short-term rates of interest were concerned, bank rate was for the moment superseded as a regulator by the rate on Treasury bills issued through the tap.[2] In the bill market the large liquid funds which the market held since the government's measures to deal with the acceptance crisis and the very small number of bills coming forward produced a very low market rate. In February 1915 it was below 1 per cent. This did not please the government, which was anxious to increase short-term rates in order to attract foreign money to improve the balance of payments and also to get short-term rates into line with the high long rates which were being offered to attract savings into the new Exchequer Bonds, War Saving Certificates and National War Bonds. In early 1915 the tap Treasury Bill rate was increased to $2\frac{3}{4}$, later in the year to $4\frac{1}{2}$ and then to 5 per cent. In 1916 the government began to borrow from the banking system through Special Deposits which were made by clearing banks with the Bank of England and then relent to the government as Ways and Means Advances. Interest rates reached their peak in July 1916 (when bank rate was 6 per cent and tap Treasury Bills $5\frac{1}{2}$ per cent) but in early 1917 a trend to cheaper money set in and the tap Treasury bill rate moved down in a series of reductions to $3\frac{1}{2}$ per cent in February 1918. The Bank was, in the later years of the war, regulating interest rates not by the bank rate but by moving the tap bill rate and rate on Special Deposits together, with the former $\frac{1}{2}$ per cent higher.[3] Ways and Means Advances were an inflationary form of financing. As the proceeds of the Advances were spent by the government they were paid out to the private sector of the economy in cheques against the Bank of England. When such cheques were paid by firms and persons into the clearing banks this had the effect of increasing the clearing banks' deposits at the Bank and therefore of increasing the cash base, thus enabling them, in due course, to expand their deposits.

[1] In the year 1914–15 only 46 per cent of expenditure was covered by revenue; in 1915–16 only 27 per cent. Cf. E. V. Morgan, *Studies in British Financial Policy, 1914–25*, pp. 99–105.

[2] These were made available in limited amounts to banks and discount houses only.

[3] From 1st August 1914 to the end of the war there were 5 changes in bank rate, from 10 per cent on the first date to 6 on 6th August 1914 to 5 two days later, to 6 on 13th July 1916, and to $5\frac{1}{2}$ on 18th July 1917.

Probably the most significant change wrought in the financial scenery by the war was the great expansion of the floating debt (and thus of the short-term paper market) through the huge issue of Treasury bills. In July 1914, the total of Treasury bills outstanding was £15·5m.: on 4th January 1919 it stood at £1,098m. These had been issued mainly 'through the tap', i.e. to selected applicants, at fixed rates of interest, but there had been brief interludes at the beginning of the war and again after June 1917 when the bills had been offered by tender. Since the flow of commercial bills to the discount market had dwindled away to a very small amount as a result of the war this expansion of Treasury bills was for it a welcome substitute, and although regarded at the time as a temporary wartime diet, it was in fact but a foretaste of what was to be the staple fare of the market in the future and what was to change its character. It became in the war one of the main buyers of bills through the tap. Its later rôle of holder of bills in their least liquid period was not then so apparent, inasmuch as the banks and other buyers also bought at issue through the tap. Not until 1934 did the Banks inaugurate the practice of not tendering for bills at issue but of taking them from the discount houses later in their currency.

To sum up: the war years, once the initial crisis of 1914 had, with the government's help, been weathered by the discount houses, proved a period in which no significant change in the number or size of the houses comprising the market has to be recorded, but a significant change of function did take place in that the market began to deal in government short-term paper and became inextricably involved in government debt activities. For the Bank of England, new but temporary methods of interest rate regulation were evolved in the Treasury bill tender rate and bank rate as a regulator was in temporary abeyance. The clearing banks continued to lend at call to the market. The main innovation in bank lending, however, during the war was the Special Deposits lent by the banks to the Bank of England, and in turn re-lent by the Bank to the Treasury. Viewing the scene in the London money market in 1918 an observer would have seen much that was new and in contrast to the spectacle of 1913 but it is doubtful whether he would not have looked on the innovations as mere temporary aberrations, to be dispensed with quickly as the emergency passed.

III

The aims of British economic policy in the immediate postwar period were greatly influenced by the Report of the Cunliffe Committee which was published in 1918.[1] The Committee clearly regarded the war as an unwholesome but reparable interruption of the normal business tenor. They recommended a return to the gold standard without delay at the pre-war parity of the pound with gold; balanced budgets and a cessation of government borrowing as soon as possible; the limitation of the fiduciary note issue; and the restoration of bank rate as an instrument of credit control. The Report was in effect a plea for a return to 'normal' as quickly as possible, 'normal' meaning conditions as they were before 1914. This 'back to normal' was to be the *leit motif* in the economic thinking of the early twenties and the realisation of its impracticability was to be the painful process of more than a decade. This process was the harder for Britain in that 'normal' in British eyes meant not only a return to the gold standard but to British industrial, commercial and financial leadership, with the pre-war parity of the pound with gold, restoration of the bill on London and all that was implied by a restoration of the old pre-war world. We are not here concerned with the problems of implementing the Cunliffe Report; with restoring the pre-war exchange parity, with all that that involved in price-level adjustment, with checking the potentially inflationary effects on consumption and investment of the great mass of liquidity which wartime finance had produced; with restoring British overseas trade and refurbishing a balance of payments threatened by the rundown of investments overseas, competition in foreign markets and the establishment of a rival financial centre to London in New York. But it is important for this study that the economic policies chosen for the period of reconstruction, in particular that which aimed at a restoration of the pre-war gold and exchange parity, requiring as it did a purposive deflation of the British price level, involved monetary manipulations of a major type, which made the years 1918–25 years of great significance for the discount market. Keynes, writing in October 1923, dedicated his *Tract on Monetary Reform* to the Governors and Court of the Bank of England who for the future would 'have a much more difficult and anxious task entrusted to them than in former days.'[2] In this task the discount market was closely involved.

Apart from the long-term aims of economic policy immediate problems called for attention. After slight unemployment and a minor check to activity in early 1919 (as a result of falls in government spending and swift demobilisation) a postwar boom began with steadily rising prices which continued until April 1920. The *Economist* index of wholesale prices (1913 = 100) rose from 212 in March 1919 to 310 in March 1920. Retail

[1] First Interim Report of Committee on Currency and Foreign Exchanges after the War. Cd. 9182, August 1918. First Report Cd. 464, December 1919.

[2] Cf. *Tract on Monetary Reform*, J. M. Keynes, London, 1923, Preface.

prices rose a little more slowly but the cost of living index (July 1914 = 100) rose from 205 in May 1919 to 276 in October 1920. There was a considerable boom in share prices. The control of this boom was the first major task of postwar monetary policy.

To restore the Bank of England's control over the interest rate structure and the discount and money markets was a pre-requisite of controlling the movements of the economy. This control had been exercised during the war by a variety of expedients: by controlling the rate at which Treasury bills were issued through the tap; by borrowing on Special Deposits from the clearing banks and curtailing their loanable funds, thus reducing funds available to the market; by accumulating the deposits held to the government's credit in the Bank, thus diminishing the amount held by the market; and by direct pressure on the clearing banks.[1] When the war ended the Bank could control interest rates only through the tap Treasury bill rate which stood then at 3½ per cent and the Special Deposit rate which was 3 per cent. Bank rate was 5 per cent but was ineffective since the market was almost never in the Bank.[2] If the market became short of funds, it simply abstained from buying tap Treasury Bills, in which event the government had to borrow from the Bank on Ways and Means Advances, a process which, since it was money-creating, quickly made the market liquid again. In early 1919 the clearing banks were extremely liquid with a ratio of cash and Bank of England balances to deposits of 13·9 per cent. Since there was as yet no limitation of currency note issue the banks could add to their reserves at any time by withdrawing currency notes. If the market rate of interest were to be forced up there would be an immediate switch from Treasury bills to commercial bills (which were coming back in increasing numbers), the drop in Treasury bill demand forcing the government to have recourse to Ways and Means Advances which, in turn, would renew the flow of credit to the market and nullify the original rise in the market rate.

With this excessive liquidity of the market in 1919 and in spite of a growing number of commercial bills, interest rates tended to fall and were only supported by the tap rate of 3½ per cent. When for a time in May 1919 tap sales of bills ceased the market rate on bank bills fell to just over 3 per cent. The tap issue of bills was resumed in July and restored the rate to 3½. As 1919 passed into its second half there were signs that the government was anxious to dismantle its wartime financial apparatus and to mop up the inflationary liquidity in the economy. In March 1919 the official

[1] For an account of the working of these wartime methods of Bank of England control see E. V. Morgan, *Studies in British Financial Policy, 1914–25*, pp. 173–197.

[2] The only significance of bank rate in these circumstances was that it determined the cost of borrowing from the banks, the Advances rate being fixed just above bank rate.

peg on the sterling-dollar exchange rate was removed and sterling depreciated in the exchange market. In December 1919 the currency note issue was limited by pegging the fiduciary issue for 1920 at £320·6m., any issues in excess of this figure to be backed by gold. The Special Deposit system ended in October and a progressive rise of interest rates began. Now that the measures to mop up surplus funds in the market were taking effect it was necessary to bring bank rate and the Treasury bill tap rate closer together, and when in October 1919 the Treasury bill rate went to $4\frac{1}{2}$ per cent bank rate was only $\frac{1}{2}$ per cent higher. By now boom conditions were general. Prices were still rising; the exchange rate was depreciating and the reserve was being reduced. On November 6 bank rate and Treasury bill rate were raised to 6 and $5\frac{1}{2}$ per cent respectively but no further action was taken for sixteen months until on 15th April 1920 bank rate went to 7 per cent and Treasury bill rate to $6\frac{1}{2}$ per cent. The effects of this hard money were soon everywhere to be seen. The stock exchange boom ended in March and the peak activity which many industries reached in the spring was not maintained, although activity generally remained high during the summer. Recession began in the autumn. Wholesale prices were falling[1] and there were signs of surplus capacity in industry. Unemployment went to 15 per cent by April 1921, when the 7 per cent bank rate was reduced to $6\frac{1}{2}$. Even then easing of the credit restriction was slow and it was November 1921 before bank rate reached 5 per cent and July 1922 when it fell to 3 per cent. The credit restriction which had broken the boom was perhaps too severe. Certainly it was too prolonged and provided the British economy with its first postwar slump and a foretaste of what was to come. Since the restriction was entirely monetary, responsibility can be laid on the Bank of England whose motives were difficult to interpret. In part the policy may have been dictated by the Bank in pursuit of the overriding policy aim of returning to the gold standard and a desire to reduce British prices relative to those of the United States, but as Victor Morgan points out[2] it is more likely that the behaviour of interest rates reflected the Bank's new-found control of the market. The slowness with which interest rates were raised was probably because the Bank still had little real control of the market. This allowed the boom to go uncontrolled for too long. Once they did rise the prolonged maintenance of the high rates was perhaps a reflection of the Bank's determination not to lose control once it had achieved it.

In the spring of 1921 there was a change in the method of control of interest rates. First, in March 1921 the tap Treasury bill rate was reduced

[1] Early in 1922 the *Economist* index fell to 158; the cost of living index fell to 180 by June 1922.
[2] Cf. E. V. Morgan, op. cit., pp. 202–209.

to 6 per cent, thus inducing at once a fall in market rate. At the end of April 1921, bank rate was reduced from 7 to $6\frac{1}{2}$ per cent, tap Treasury bills ceased and the tender system for the issue of Treasury bills was resumed. This restored the market situation to one in which the market rate of interest was determined by the degree of liquidity, i.e., by the resources available to buy bills and on the total supply of bills, commercial and Treasury. Bank rate resumed its rôle as the Bank of England's discount rate and as regulator of the market. Throughout the period April 1921 to March 1922 the Bank was purposively using open-market operations to expand the credit base in order to offset the deflationary effects of Treasury borrowings. As a result of these open-market operations easy money conditions persisted and the market was rarely in the Bank.

The spring of 1922 marks the return of market conditions—the relationship between the Bank and the market, the control of interest rates—to something like those which had existed in 1914. The features which had made the market abnormal during the war period and for nearly two years thereafter were two: the great issue of tap Treasury bills and the huge government borrowing by Ways and Means Advances which had made the market continually over-liquid and made effective credit control impossible. With these removed the Bank was able to resume its pre-war methods of market control. There was even one feature which strengthened it: the place which Treasury bills had now gained for themselves in the market assured the Bank of a plentiful supply of short-term paper convenient for large-scale open-market operations. There was an immediate example in early 1922 of the Bank's determination to use its new powers. When, with 3 per cent bank rate on July 15, market rate fell to $1\frac{3}{4}$ per cent the Bank carried out large open-market sales, reducing the 'Securities' item in the Bank return. The market was driven into the Bank, bank cash was reduced and market rate was increased by mid-August to $2\frac{1}{2}$ per cent.

The fall in prices ceased in the spring of 1922 and the next three years saw a gradual recovery in economic activity. Both the Bank and the government were anxious not to impede the recovery while at the same time their acknowledged policy was to return to the gold standard as soon as possible, the return being contingent on a restoration of the pre-war gold parity represented by a sterling-dollar exchange rate of $4.86 = £1. The sterling-dollar rate was $4.43 in March 1922 and from then until January 1925, when it was $4.78, it fluctuated between these figures, the movements being determined predominantly by the changing relation between the London and New York interest rates. From July 1923, when bank rate was raised to 4 per cent, until the return to gold in April 1925, the Bank was systematically conditioning the interest rate structure by open market operations which raised market rate to near the bank rate. Unofficial measures were taken to curtail foreign lending in London and for the time being foreign issues fell sharply. Bank rate went to 5 per cent in February to offset a rise in the Federal Reserve rate. In his budget speech in April, Mr. Winston Churchill announced a return to gold, by placing the currency on a gold bullion standard. In this, the year of the Locarno Pact, of the British return to gold at the pre-war parity, and with the Bank of England in confident control of the monetary situation, Englishmen might have been forgiven for believing that the world was back to 'normal'.

The working of the restored gold standard from 1925 to 1931 was an interlude which calls for only brief comment. Its great economic interest lies in the industrial rather than the monetary field. The Bank of England was now in complete and confident control of the monetary situation and proceeded to wield its refurbished weapons of bank rate and open-market operations in a determined fashion. The inherent weakness of the British economy at this time lay in the over-valuation of sterling which the return to gold at the pre-war parity had created. This weakness was in some measure concealed, so far as the balance of payments was concerned,[1] between 1925 and 1928, by the large outflow of capital from the United States and by the close co-operation in policy between the Bank of England and the Federal Reserve. It was a period of comparatively dear money. After a short period of 4 per cent at the end of 1925 bank rate was at $4\frac{1}{2}$ or 5 per cent until 1929 when it rose progressively to $6\frac{1}{2}$ in response to the flow of capital to Wall Street. To prevent high rates having too deflationary an effect and to offset fluctuations in the gold reserve, open-market operations were used extensively and the cash base of the clearing banks remained fairly uniform over the period. The sharp rise in bank rate to $6\frac{1}{2}$ per cent in late September 1929 was made, it would seem, because a rise of the Federal Reserve rate in August was drawing gold from London. Nothing in the domestic economic situation called for such a high bank rate and as events turned out the rise in the British rate was blamed for the withdrawal of funds from New York and the beginning of the disastrous slide which was to bring chaos to Wall Street in October. It is an interesting speculation as to what would have been the course of events had the Bank of England been prepared to suffer some diminution of the gold reserve. The policy of dear money pursued from 1925 to 1929 certainly did nothing to ease the relatively static economic conditions which Britain, by reason of her over-valued currency and industrial problems, suffered during this period.

[1] But not so far as industry was concerned. The over-valuation bore heavily upon the exports of the basic industries.

Only one condition in the discount market during the years 1925–31 calls for comment. The success of British Government Treasury bills as a vehicle of short-term borrowing invoked imitation in the issuing of similar bills by foreign governments, local corporations and municipalities and various public authorities. Such bills were three to twelve months in currency and their market varied with the credit standing of the issuer. Such bills were not rediscountable or acceptable as collateral at the Bank but in most cases they were acceptable assets and a welcome augmentation to the turnover of the houses. Foreign bills of this type were numerous between 1925 and 1930 and the governments of British dominions were frequent borrowers between 1929 and 1931. One source[1] estimated the volume of such bills in 1929, 1930 and 1931 as £20m., £30m. and £25m. respectively.

Concurrently with this the secular decline in the number of trade bills was continuing. In September 1928 Spring Rice estimated that there were about £240m. of bankers' acceptances in the market. Another writer in the same year put the figure at £150m.[2] Whatever may have been the figure contemporary observers then and economic historians since are agreed that the London market was now suffering 'from a shortage in supply of the genuine (goods-based) commercial bills which had constituted its bread and butter business before the war.'[3] Not only was the quantity of bills declining but there appears to have been a decline in quality as well. There were standing temptations in the use of the banker's acceptance. Before the war the drawer of a bill was almost always the seller of goods who lived in a different country to the debtor. This was the genuine reimbursement credit which had been the staple of the market until 1914. Now the drawer was often the importer, or a holding company or a bank making use of an acceptance credit here. While such bills were goods-based, the goods were often not sold, the connection was tenuous and the difference between a trade bill of this type and an accommodation bill was often blurred. Another innovation which was not for the best was that of renewal of bills. Before the war a renewal was a very rare event but after the war it became almost common practice. German bills, for example, were sometimes drawn for three months but were renewed again and again until they represented as much as three years' credit. The relations between such bills and the commodities which were supposed to be their basis were often remote in the extreme. Competition between discount markets and within the London market itself served to force this business as the twenties proceeded.

[1] Cf. *League of Nations Monetary Review, 1938–39*, p.100, note 2.
[2] It is probable that at this time there was about £450m. in Treasury bills in the market.
[3] Cf. W. A. Brown, *The International Gold Standard Reinterpreted, 1914–34*, vol. i, p. 643.

Changes were also taking place in the activities of the accepting houses. They were losing their merchanting connections and becoming purely financial. Even up to 1925 there were four or five merchant banks[1] which had built up their business by interesting themselves in particular parts of the world and who had been accustomed to finance commodities 'from planting to delivery'. But after 1925 such concentration and supervision disappeared and the contacts between accepting houses and merchants became purely financial.

In the face of these changes in the nature and supply of bills the attitude of the Bank of England as to the bills it would accept when the market was in the Bank was modified. The Bank never admitted to any lessening in the rigour of its standards but the decline in the average quality of bills and in their amount forced the Bank to take for discount bills which it would not have tolerated before the war. It was willing for example to take acceptances drawn against goods in warehouses—a practice from which it had formerly abstained. So far as finance bills were concerned it tended to be unfavourable because the demarcation here between these and trade bills was often blurred. The Bank during the later thirties must have been torn between the desire to be rigorous and selective in the bills it would take in order to maintain standards and the desire to help the discount houses who were embarrassed by the decline in numbers of commercial bills.

Although the decline between 1925 and 1931 in the volume of trade bills did not reduce the total volume of business in the discount market, for it was compensated by the increase in the volume of Treasury bills, it did have the effect, one writer asserts,[2] of narrowing the market and causing a smaller volume of foreign deposits to be held in London. With trade bills the preparation for payment by the acceptor on the due date caused a 'substantial volume' of funds constantly to be held in London for this purpose. This does not apply to the Treasury bill, although this in itself does offer an attractive form of investment for foreigners if they have some independent motive for holding funds in London.

It was in this period also that for the first time the discount market must have become conscious that it was losing some of its real *raison d'être*. With such a great volume of Treasury bills, homogeneous units of government short-term paper, and with a great increase in the number of joint stock bank acceptances coming to the market, the old discount house functions of vetting and grading bills according to quality were less

[1] The accepting houses were all 'merchant banks'. Not all merchant banks, however, did (or do) acceptance business.

[2] Cf. W. A. Brown, Jun., *The International Gold Standard Reinterpreted, 1914-34*, vol. 1, pp. 648-9.

necessary than when the market lived by dealing in acceptances of all dates, types and qualities. It is arguable that as a result of the uniformity of the bills dealt in, the discount houses were becoming unnecessary middlemen, purchasing and reselling bills for a middleman's profit.

It is arguable, too, that there was another effect of the new dominance of Treasury bills on the discount market, in this case on the effectiveness of the control by the Bank of England over credit and over the foreign exchanges via bank rate changes. As long as the discount market dealt in trade acceptances any change of bank rate affected not only the demand for bills but the supply as well. With Treasury bills the influence of a change in bank rate fell purely on demand. The supply, the amount which for the moment the Treasury wished to borrow on short-term, was not sensitive to bank rate, unless the bank rate changes were of such magnitude as to influence the whole national debt programme at the time. Lord Bradbury in his *Minute of Dissent* to the Report of the Macmillan Committee of 1931 drew attention to the technical implications for credit control of the increase in Treasury bills, asserting that:

> 'The volume of such [short] money generally since the war has been of such magnitude as to render the task of the Bank of England in controlling the supply (as distinct from the price) of the basis of credit extremely difficult. The main cause of this has been the enormous amount of Treasury bills. This has resulted not only in increasing the dimensions of the bill market (and so making larger scale operations necessary to produce a given effect) but also in altering its character. When the holdings of the market were mainly commercial bills drawn on London on foreign account, a rise in bank rate diminished the supply of these bills. Now that the market holdings are largely Treasury bills ... a restriction in the volume of bankers' cash, followed by a reduction of their market money, merely drives the market 'into the Bank'; i.e. causes the Bank of England to recreate the credit it has previously withdrawn. . . .'

Lord Bradbury had other technical criticisms which need not detain us here, and the effect of a substitution of Treasury bills for trade bills on the sensitivity of the foreign exchanges to bank rate variations is outside the scope of this book; but sufficient has been said to demonstrate that this substitution of government for private paper had far-reaching implications for the discount market, for its operations and for the part it was to play in the future in the monetary system.

In view of the great variety of experience of monetary control which the Bank of England had accumulated in the period from 1914 to 1931 and of the new factors involved in the control field, one is tempted to ask what, if any, changes in Bank of England aim and approach had taken place in this period. In 1913 the Bank of England used bank rate as a means primarily of protecting its gold reserve and of influencing market rates of interest via its own initiated changes in the short-term market. By the later twenties these aims still held good but the processes by which the Bank of England pursued them were now more 'self-conscious' and purposive. The war and the problems of war finance together with the struggle after the war to regain control of the market had given the Bank a much deeper knowledge of the processes of the market and a more critical judgement of methods and policies. In carrying its policies into effect it made increasing use of open-market operations to reinforce and make effective its bank rate operations. Moreover, the increase in the amount of government receipts and payments passing through the Bank and their periodic variation enabled the Bank to exercise additional control over the market via its smoothing operations. Normally, it carried out smoothing operations to counteract irregularities in the movement of government funds, but now, if it wished to tighten credit, it had merely to abstain from action when net payments were due to the Government. The advances in Bank of England control were in method. There was in the late twenties pursuit of the same policy aims, but it was a more strategic and planned pursuit. In the period 1925–31 the critical position of sterling in the new gold standard made the Bank hypersensitive to external influences which it placed paramount, but there was a growing realisation of the conflict between policies to maintain the gold reserves and policies to achieve industrial expansion—a conflict which was only to be resolved slowly and painfully in the thirties.

This is not the place to tell the detailed story of the great depression of 1929–32 but only of such effects as it had upon the discount market. The depression began in late 1929 but had little initial effect on Bank of England policy. By May 1930 bank rate had come down to 3 per cent. It remained there until May 1931, accompanied by drastic open-market operations to make it effective. It was reduced to 2½ per cent just before the Austrian Credit Anstalt failed on May 31. The next four months were concerned with trying to deal with a situation in which a great desire for liquidity drew funds from London while a great amount of London's assets remained frozen in Central Europe. These efforts were unavailing and the crisis of confidence in sterling that swept Europe forced the British government on September 21 to suspend gold payments. On the same day bank rate went up to 6 per cent from 4½. Some attempt to nullify the deflationary effects of such high rates and of the gold outflow during a period of depression was made by purchases of securities in the open market and by an increase in the fiduciary note issue. Unemployment was now over 20 per cent; it was no longer possible to maintain the primacy of the balance of payments as an arbiter of policy.

The crisis of 1931 did not itself seriously endanger the discount houses. It was to be during the slow and prolonged recovery and in the cheap money policy after 1932 that they were to be tested. In 1931 there were two risks for them: on their bills and on their security holdings. At the time of the crisis the contingent liability of the houses on German bills was heavy but almost all such bills were good bank or accepting house acceptances. It was clear that the position of the accepting houses was strong and the Bank of England was prepared to rediscount bills frozen by stand-still agreement during the crisis. There was therefore no real risk to the bill brokers. Their position with regard to security holdings was more difficult. By the end of 1931 there had been a heavy fall in the prices of gilt-edged, a fall which reduced both capital and reserves. But so long as there was no necessity to realise such securities the fall was in book values only, and in fact the comparative strength of the bill holdings of the discount houses made any realisation of securities unnecessary. By early 1932 gilt-edged prices were rising fast and such danger as had existed was over.

The active monetary policy of the later twenties, the energy of the Bank of England in the use of open-market operations, and the monetary activity which preceded the September 1931 crisis marked the end of an epoch. Twenty years of cheap money were to pass before the Bank again took up its monetary policy tools. The 6 per cent bank rate was a last flourish to a watching world before embarking on the new policies of cheap money and fluctuating exchange rates.

IV

Cheap money was embarked upon cautiously. Bank rate remained 6 per cent until 18th February 1932 then went to 5 per cent until March 4. Bill rates were falling from the beginning of 1932 and rising security prices reflected the falling yield on long-term paper. The easing of interest rates at first probably represented no more than a slight return of confidence. The departure from gold was not, as many had feared, being followed by inflation. The Bank of England had probably had a dual purpose in pushing bank rate to 6 per cent immediately the link with gold was cut. The first and most immediate reason was to give an impression that it was determined to repel the inflation which in the popular mind (and with the German precedent) might be a concomitant of the pound's depreciation. The second was to encourage an influx of foreign funds so that it could repay the French and American credits made before the crisis. Once the immediate crisis had passed and the credits been repaid there were power-ful arguments for cheap money. The first was that low interest rates might serve to lift the economy from the depression. The conflict of external and domestic stability was temporarily resolved in favour of the latter. The second was that, once the foreign credits were disposed of, there was no reason to strengthen the exchange rate by an influx of foreign money: better far to reap the benefits of the temporary exchange advantage which sterling's post-gold depreciation had yielded. And thirdly, a fall in interest rates would give budgetary relief by allowing conversion of the 5 per cent War Loan. These were weighty reasons. Cheap money in fact had a purpose: it was not embarked on in a fit of absence of mind. On March 4 bank rate was reduced to 4 per cent and by June it had come down in a series of $\frac{1}{2}$ per cent loops to 2 per cent where it was to remain for nineteen years.[1] Other interest rates moved lower in sympathy. Treasury bill rates fell to $\frac{1}{2}$ per cent. In June 1932, 5 per cent War Loan was converted to $3\frac{1}{2}$ per cent—open-market operations by the Bank easing the operation by creating easy credit conditions.

In February 1932 the government set up the Exchange Equalisation Account, a department of the Bank of England, charged with ironing out the more destabilising fluctuations of the sterling exchange rate by buying and selling in the foreign exchange market. It was made clear that low interest rates and a fluctuating exchange rate for sterling, under Bank of England influence, were to be the salient features of the new monetary order. Domestic price stability and industrial expansion were now to be the primary aims of economic policy and the link between the balance of payments and the domestic money supply forged by the Bank Charter Act of 1844 was cut.[2] The note issue became a matter of practical con-venience: the governance of credit a matter of domestic stability and economic recovery. The Bank of England's task was now to maintain low interest rates and easy credit conditions by ironing out the movements in the credit supply engendered by government financial operations and the transactions of the Exchange Equalisation Account. Meanwhile, in an effort to curtail growth of the floating debt a sharp check was placed upon the issue of Treasury bills.

It is unnecessary here to trace the general monetary history of the years 1932–39—the experimentation with fluctuating exchange rates abroad, the genesis of the Sterling Area, the drift towards managed money, the slow

[1] With the exception of a very brief precautionary rise to 4 per cent on the outbreak of war in 1939.

[2] The formal cutting of the link was delayed until 1939 when the Bank of England's gold stock, save for a nominal amount, was transferred to the Exchange Equalisation Account.

O

and incomplete industrial recovery at home. The economic environment
of the later thirties, while slowly improving, was far from hospitable. The
problems of the discount market during this period sprang from two
features in the situation: the decline of the bill market and the effect upon
it of cheap money—for continuous cheap money was a new condition to
which the financial world had to adjust itself.[1] For the Bank of England
there was the problem of evolving principles of currency management
and credit policy to replace the more or less automatic processes of the
gold standard. The clearing banks too had their problems. In particular
they were faced with a redistribution of their assets. The cash base was
enlarged but demand for loans and advances languished because of the
depression. The result was a great diminution of advances, which fell from
55·1 per cent of deposits in 1929 to 38·9 per cent in 1933 and 38·5 per
cent in 1935; and an expansion of investments in government securities,
investments advancing from 14·3 per cent of deposits in 1929 to 27·5 per
cent in 1933 and 30·8 per cent in 1935. Throughout the later thirties there
was therefore a considerable switch as between the main income earning
assets and a deeper involvement of the banks with the finance of government.

But it was on the discount market that the real weight of adjustment to
cheap money fell, this adjustment becoming, as time passed, a life and
death matter. The lack of demand for money in the early thirties forced
money rates to unprecedentedly low levels and the rate for bills fell in
1932 well below 1 per cent. Treasury bills yielded sometimes as little as
$\frac{3}{16}$ per cent and the average for January and February 1935 was only 0·27
per cent. The difficulty for the discount houses was that the clearing banks
would not lend on call save at their agreed rate of 1 per cent below bank
rate. This meant that, with bank rate at 2 per cent, the discount market
was paying 1 per cent for its call money and incurring a running loss on its
dwindling commercial bill business as well as on Treasury bills. For bills
were certainly dwindling in number. Commercial bills fell by half between
1929 and 1933 (cf. Table XIII) and although Treasury bills remained
fairly constant in volume their numbers were not so great as to prevent a
decline in the material of the market. The Treasury wished to curtail the
Treasury bill issue at this period, which was also marked by two features
greatly increasing the demand for such bills from outside the discount
houses: a flow of short-term funds to London which sought liquid
investment, and an increase in the clearing banks' demand for money
market assets resulting from the excessive liquidity attendant upon the
cheap-money policy. The discount market was, therefore, suffering a

[1] For a good discussion of cheap money and its problems see E. Nevin, *The Mechanism
of Cheap Money*, Cardiff, 1955.

TABLE XIII

BILLS OUTSTANDING 1918–37
(Yearly Averages)
(£m.)

Fiscal years	Trade Bills	Treasury Bills	Total
1918–19	306	—	—
1924–25	583	456	1039
1928–29	563	505	1068
1929–30	520	512	1032
1931–32	328	485	813
1933–34	245	558	803
1935–36	259	505	764
1936–37	276	580	856

Source: Computed from tables in T. Balogh, *Studies in Financial Organisation*, p. 167 and p. 202.

two-pronged attack on its livelihood: shortage of bills to deal in and, as a result of the clearing banks' call loan policy, a zero or even negative margin in dealing. From the point of view of the clearing banks their interest rate policy on call loans was highly illogical for they were lending on bills which they themselves discounted at $\frac{1}{4}$ to $\frac{1}{8}$ per cent while only being prepared to lend at call to the discount houses (on the security of similar bills) at not less than 1 per cent.

Such conditions could not long continue. Clearly if they did the result would be the elimination of the discount market. In late 1931 the house of Blydenstein repaid part of its capital and gave up bill-broking.[1] In 1933 there were two retirements, Lyon and Tucker and Baker Duncome and Co.—both dated from 1866—and one merger, King and Foa with White and Shaxson, to form King and Shaxson. It was a turning point for the discount houses. Inaction meant extinction.

From where was action to come? The discount houses are themselves a passive group depending on the movements of the mightier engines which surround them. The clearing banks were probably glad to see some reduction in the size of the discount market and might have welcomed further reduction. It was, after all, arguable that the number of discount houses was too great for the available business. Yet who could say in 1933–34 what the future would be: who could be sure that the commercial bill was dying? Bill business, the discount market's *forte*, might revive. Certainly

[1] It remained in the banking field.

the Bank of England was sure that the discount market must not perish; that as a buffer between itself and the clearing banks, as a channel for pushing cash into the monetary system it was indispensable. Adjustment, some retirements and consolidation, was perhaps desirable but that was all. City opinion favoured, probably still favours, 'roundabout' rather than direct help by the central bank in times of stringency.

Action took the form of a series of gentlemen's agreements between the discount houses and the clearing banks. The first of such agreements, made in September 1933, was arrived at painfully after much friction. It was an attempt to give the houses a margin for dealing by pushing the bill rate above the call loan rate. The clearing banks maintained their lending rate at 1 per cent but tried to jack up the rate on bills by making their Treasury bill tenders at rates which gave a profit to the market, and by settling their rate for discounting trade bills at the level of their Treasury bill tender. This agreement was unworkable. It proved impossible to sustain the higher bill rates and by the autumn of 1934 a shrinkage in the supply of bills complicated matters and the bill rate was once more below the call rate. In November 1934 a second agreement was reached whereby the banks agreed to reduce their minimum charges on loans against bills (i.e., call loans) to $\frac{1}{2}$ per cent. Loans against bonds, however, were to be at 1 per cent.[1] This too was unsuccessful. In spite of the reduced charge for call money, competition for bills, which was now intense, between banks and discount houses forced the bill rate on 25th January 1935 to a new low at less than 0·2 per cent. At this time banks were quoting $\frac{3}{16}$ per cent as a buying rate for Treasury bills.

The third agreement with the clearing banks in February 1935 was more comprehensive and covered both the Treasury bill tender and market dealing in bills. With regard to Treasury bills the banks agreed not to take part in the tender and not to buy Treasury bills until they were at least a week old. With regard to bill dealing the agreement laid down that the minimum buying rate for bills by the clearing banks was to be at least the minimum rate at which they were prepared to lend at call and not merely a minimum rate which they agreed among themselves from time to time. This agreement had more success, and bill rates in the market and the Treasury bill rate were held above $\frac{1}{2}$ per cent even when bills were scarce. Nevertheless, the margin between the call loan rate and bill rate was still very narrow and the only way to make an adequate living was by considerably increasing the turnover of bills. This led naturally to great competition for bills and it was upon Treasury bills that the main weight of demand fell. The tender became super-competitive with much 'stagging' of bills and the demand at the tender rose until it was many

[1] This was the first time that the banks agreed to lend against bonds.

times the number of bills on offer.[1] Self-defence drove the discount houses to joint action: it was decided that the discount houses should bid at the tender as a group against all other bidders, dividing between the houses the amount of bills allocated to them on their syndicated bids. This arrangement was truly one of self-defence by the discount houses for without it even the agreements with the clearing banks would not, in the straitened conditions of the market in 1935, have enabled them to survive. At first a few of the more important houses undertook to restrict their tenders to an agreed figure but the agreement was soon extended until it included all the discount houses. Under the syndicate arrangements each firm was now allotted a 'quota' proportionate to its capital resources, although the big firms agreed to accept quotas smaller relative to their capital than the small firms. The following was the basis of the syndicate division:

		Tender
Group 1	Firms with capital in excess of £1m.	120 per cent of their capital.
Group 2	Firms with capital £500,000—£1m.	226·5 per cent of capital.
Group 3	All others	410 per cent of capital.

The market syndicate total was originally about £26m. and a further £4m. was allotted to outside firms who had been invited to join the syndicate. Any firm within the syndicate which wished to avoid taking up bills could do this by tendering at a lower price than the syndicate (i.e. a higher rate of interest), providing it informed the syndicate beforehand of its intention to do this.

The price at which the syndicated members were to tender was fixed at an informal meeting each Friday between representatives of three private firms and each of the public 'discount' companies, which had previously had a meeting of their own. Representatives of the syndicate also saw officials of the Bank of England each Thursday and then reported back to the syndicate on the Bank's views which, of course, had a bearing on the settling of the syndicate bid.

In the syndicate system and the series of agreements between the discount houses and the clearing banks we see a drawing together of the main forces in the money market to deal with the conditions of the thirties —conditions which would have been likely in the absence of defensive action to make drastic and winnowing changes in the discount market. The conditions were: cheap money, contraction in the number of bills, the increasing influence of government financing on the market, the

[1] On one occasion £116m. was bid for £35m. of bills on offer.

growing use of open-market operations and rigidity in the structure of interest rates. There is no doubt that if no conscious action, such as that described, to save the discount market had been taken it would not have survived. The functions of bill discounting and dealing in trade bills would have come to be handled by the clearing banks, perhaps with the aid of some joint agency to act as running broker, while the clearing banks would have joined the foreign banks, the financial institutions and others in the Treasury bill tender. Such a system, unencumbered by history, works well enough in the Dominions and elsewhere. It would certainly have functioned in Britain. It was the joint action of 1934–35 which saved the discount market, and while it has frequently been asked and is still asked whether the discount market is worth preserving, the question is academic: it preserved itself with the help of others in the thirties. It has now acquired new functions, it makes a living; it is dispensable but it is there, and to 'tidy' the system would now necessitate an act of financial institutional surgery which none of the interested parties— clearing banks, Bank of England, Treasury or discount houses—would contemplate or tolerate. The historical opportunity for a tidier system and dispensing with the discount market passed in the thirties.

Why, we must ask, was this joint salvage operation undertaken? Was it a natural act of self-preservation such as was widespread in the monopolistic schemes for survival in British industry at this period? Was it City *esprit de corps*? Was it a conscious operation by the Bank of England to preserve a part of the financial system, which, for practical reasons, it valued and was not prepared to let perish?

Almost certainly the main force was the latter. City *esprit de corps* at this period was not notably strong. If the clearing banks took these steps to preserve the discount houses on their own initiative they did so mighty late in the day, having hitherto been content to see the discount houses squeezed 'until the pips squeaked'. The fact that the Bank of England was interested in this same period in a capital consolidation operation among the firms of the discount market, and let its wishes on this be known to the houses, indicates that the Bank had no idea of letting the market wither away before it. It seems certain that the Bank of England was the rescuer; that it quietly let its wishes be known, particularly to the clearing banks, and that the salvage operation which we have described was the result.

This view of the salvage operation is confirmed by a passage in Sir Henry Clay's biography of Montagu Norman, who at the time of the crisis was Governor of the Bank and whose views and forceful personality stamped themselves indelibly on Bank policy. Clay tells us that 'Norman had much sympathy' for the discount houses, squeezed by depression and the shortage of Treasury bills. 'The market was an essential and characteristic feature of London's organisation which he used to describe with such pride to overseas bankers, a great convenience as an intermediary and buffer between Central Bank and Clearing Banks.' On 15th February 1935 Norman spoke to representatives of the clearing banks and on 21st these came back to report to him 'a temporary agreement among the clearing bankers on bill rates; nothing below $\frac{1}{2}$ per cent and no tendering by the banks themselves, money rates to be unchanged.'

With this agreement to save the market from immediate danger, Norman proceeded to urge the 'rationalisation' of the discount houses, applying in his advice the same principles of elimination of weaker firms and concentration in larger units which were fashionable in industrial reorganisation schemes at that period. He was supported in his advice to the Houses by the Committee of Treasury at the Bank. His advice to the market in the matter of amalgamations was supported by offers of mediation between firms but this toughened to warnings and finally coercion by refusing to rediscount at the privileged rate the bills of firms which he regarded as too small for safety. In March 1936 he reported to the Committee of Treasury that the number of firms in the market had been reduced from 22 to 18 since January 1933.

Towards the end of 1937 the Committee agreed to 'refuse the Bank's special facilities to firms with less than £300,000 capital and reserves' but support was being given to the market. Norman asked the Committee on Advances and Discounts to widen the range of bills which the Bank would take—although at the same time he was warning accepting houses generally against finance or accommodation bills to repay existing debts.

Clay concludes with a passage which is worth quoting in full because it indicates the importance which Norman attached to the discount market and how anxious he was that it should not succumb to its difficulties:

'He recognised that the persistence of low short-term rates threatened the Discount Market. He told some of the members privately that they were doomed; but he could not contemplate the elimination of the Market. If it went it would be the end of the short money market; London would be like Paris and New York with no outlet for short funds except the Stock Exchange and no rate except the rate resulting from the banks' telephone conversations. He could only maintain the $\frac{1}{2}$ per cent minimum, help the Market to avoid complete dependence on the Clearing Banks and trust that its members' cunning and skill would continue to find a use. Some small firms went out of business voluntarily; but there were no bankruptcies and the Market continued to fulfil its function.'[1]

One other factor unrelated to conscious planning or relief action saved the discount market from extinction at this period—its entry into the short-term bond market. Short-term bonds had in fact been dealt in by discount houses since World War I,[2] but with the fall in interest rates in 1932 and the appreciation in bond market values which made bond dealing profitable and with the simultaneous contraction of the number of bills, the majority of the discount houses turned increasingly to this form of business and held gilt-edged on a large scale. One writer[3] alleges that by the end of 1934 bill brokers had really turned jobbers in gilt-edged to the extent of 30 per cent of their activities.

Bond dealing by the discount houses now came to be recognised by the clearing banks. In 1934 short bonds became, under the agreement between the discount houses and the clearing banks, a recognised discount market asset, the clearing banks agreeing to lend call money (at 1 per cent) on the security of such bonds. This was a mere recognition of facts.

The Bank of England had its reservations on the question of bond dealing by the discount houses. Such dealing was risky, for if the discount houses had to sell bonds at a time of rising interest rates (i.e. falling bond prices) they would incur capital losses—perhaps in excess of the gain they had from interest on the bonds. Stock jobbing on short borrowed money seemed, and of course was, a perilous business. On the other hand the Bank realised that times were difficult for the houses and that if they were to be denied bond business many of them might not survive. Later, too, the Bank came to see the usefulness to its own debt operations of discount house participation on the short bond market.[4] The Bank felt that if the new business was to be undertaken safely, strengthening of the market's capital structure was desirable, and it was in deference to this view that the amalgamations and capital expansion of the later thirties already referred to, took place.

The net effect of the gentlemen's agreements with the clearing banks, the establishment of a syndicated tender, and the provision of some margin, however narrow, on bond dealing, was to provide the discount houses with a living for the rest of the thirties. At least there would be no more losses on bill dealing and there might be a modest competence to be had

[1] Cf. Henry Clay, *Lord Norman*, London, 1957, pp. 465–6.

[2] During the twenties bonds did not often exceed more than a sixth of the assets (for the public companies) but in the early thirties this proportion had grown to about one-third.

[3] Cf. R. J. Truptel, *British Banks and the London Money Market*, p. 313.

[4] Cf. p 93 above.

in bond dealing. Once more we must try to see the situation in the thirties as it was seen by the main actors at the time. They saw the crisis of survival for the discount market as caused by two things: the decline of the commercial bill and cheap money. Neither of these was necessarily permanent, and indeed they have proved not to be. This was no permanent solution but a solution of expediency was sufficient. The market in short bonds might become unprofitable: it might disappear as the Treasury resorted to longer-dated stocks. The market's future was still in question and few discount house directors would have cared in the later thirties to forecast the future of their firms.

V

In 1914 the discount market consisted of three public companies, the Union Discount Company, the National Discount Company and Alexander's Discount Company, and about twenty private firms. No change in the structure of the market took place during the war and immediate postwar years but the number of firms was increased in the early twenties by four new arrivals. These were: Jessel, Toynbee and Co. (1922), Seccombe, Marshall and Campion (1922), Brocklebank, Hoare and Brown (1924), and Fairfax and Co. Ltd. (1925). Since, with these additions, the tally of firms in 1931 was still the same as in 1914, some retirements may be inferred. In 1931 the Macmillan Report[1] speaks of twenty-four firms including the three public companies and of eight running brokers who acted merely as agents for houses or for banks.

Data concerning the variations in the business of the discount houses in the inter-war period is hard to come by save for that of the three public companies which were obliged to publish their annual balance sheets. It is, moreover, unwise to take the information and asset/liability relationships in these as typical, for there appear to be wide variations in the practices of the different houses. Table XIV shows the summarised balance sheets of the three large discount companies in selected years between 1913 and 1938.

It will be seen from the table that there was a steady increase in capital throughout the period. Cash, an asset not much called for in the working of a discount house, remained relatively stable at approximately 2 per cent of total assets. It is probable that even this low percentage overstates the cash holding which is considerably window-dressed for the figures at the makeup date. Bills discounted, the principal asset, remained remarkably stable, varying between 80 and 89 per cent of total assets between 1913 and 1931, reflecting the decline in bills in the thirties and recovering

[1] Report of the Committee on Finance and Industry, Cmnd 3897, 1931.

somewhat just before World War II. The Bills Discounted figure probably includes short-term bonds with less than two years to run so that the
decline in bills proper is probably much more than the figures indicate.
The sharp rise in Investments from 10 per cent of total assets in 1931 to
20 per cent in 1933 and 25 per cent in 1936 also reflects the greater participation of the companies in the short-bond market in this period.

Of the seventeen private firms (not reflected in the table), only six
dealt in trade bills but even for them the proportion of trade bills in their
portfolios was small. Five firms dealt only in Treasury bills. The remaining
six firms divided their portfolios between bank acceptances and Treasury
bills. The number of bills rediscounted from the portfolio differed widely,
usually between 20 and 33 per cent. Smaller firms, who tended in the later
thirties to receive a larger share of Treasury bills from the Treasury
syndicate, usually turned over their portfolios more quickly than the
larger firms. In his evidence to the Macmillan Committee in 1930 a
discount house witness estimated that the private firms tended to work
to a ratio of 1:20 of capital to assets. The figures for the large companies
shown in Table XIV show a higher ratio and 1:25 would appear in the
later years to be usual.

The pure broking, or agency, function which was characteristic of the
early nineteenth century discount market lingered on in the eight firms
which in 1930 still got a living from this activity, but the shrinkage in the
discount market in the depression years 1931–3 thinned their ranks still
further and only five or six remained in 1939. Some of these firms acted
as agents in bond deals. One specialised in Indian bills which it sold to the
market. All the running broker firms were private companies and there
is no information as to their internal business.[1]

The composition of the market had two distinct phases of change in
the thirties: in 1933 there were a number of retirements and amalgamations; and in 1936–8 two further retirements[2] and one amalgamation took
place.[3] The result of these changes was that in 1938 the market consisted of
eighteen houses made up as follows: the three public companies,
Alexanders, Union and National; five private limited companies; four
unlimited companies; five partnerships and one company which did not
appear to be active but which was still classed as a discount firm and had
a rediscount account at the Bank of England. In 1930 the total capital
of the market was £15·840m.; in 1938 it was £11·430m.[4]

[1] Cf. T. Balogh, *Studies in Financial Organisation*, p. 147.
[2] The retirements were Henry Sherwood and Company in 1936 and William P.
Bonwright and Company in 1938.
[3] Reeves, Whitburn and Company was absorbed by the National Discount Company.
[4] Cf. T. Balogh, op cit., p. 140.

TABLE XIV

SUMMARY BALANCE SHEETS OF LONDON DISCOUNT COMPANIES—SELECTED YEARS, 1913-38

	1913	1918	1920	1924	1928	1931	1933	1936	1938
Assets									
Cash at bankers	1·7	2·0	2·3	2·5	2·5	2·4	2·7	3·1	3·3
Investments	5·0	8·8	5·4	10·4	17·3	13·7	28·4	40·7	21·2
Bills Discounted	58·0	64·0	91·5	115·0	118·9	111·2	111·5	110·6	123·7
	(87%)	(80%)	(89%)	(87%)	(84%)	(86%)	(78%)	(70%)	(81%)
Loans and sundry accounts	2·2	4·5	3·8	4·0	1·9	1·2	1·8	3·6	4·4
Total assets	66·9	79·3	103·0	131·9	140·6	128·5	144·4	158·0	152·6
Liabilities									
Capital & reserves	3·5	3·8	4·2	5·1	6·2	7·0	7·0	7·7	7·8
Loans, deposits (including undistributed profits)	46·7	59·7	70·5	85·5	93·2	86·4	111·7	121·8	124·9
Bills rediscounted	16·2	15·1	27·2	39·9	39·8	33·7	24·9	27·6	19·4
Rebate, etc.	0·5	0·7	1·1	1·4	1·4	1·4	0·8	0·7	0·5
Total liabilities	66·9	79·3	103·0	131·9	140·6	128·5	144·4	157·8	152·6

Source: League of Nations, *Money and Banking*, Vol. ii. Commercial banks, p. 149.

Chapter 8

WORLD WAR II AND AFTER

I

THE LATE thirties and the last years of peace saw the discount market organised for defence and survival in the face of adverse conditions which those employed in it and those who had helped it to survive hoped were temporary. A revival of trade and of the commercial bill might yet restore its original function and former greatness: meanwhile it had the grudging support of the clearing banks and the firm backing of the Bank of England in working out new forms of business which might, as temporary expedients, earn it a living. It was not yet fully realised that in fact the whole character of the market had been changing; that it had moved since 1914 from a set of finance houses closely allied to commercial interests and dealing in commercial credit instruments, to a group of houses in which was rapidly being embodied the administration and operation of public debt by the monetary authorities. In the thirties the transition was taking place, but most observers would have then regarded it as desirable to move back, to restore the market with its old tasks to its former rôle in the hierarchy of the monetary system. Instead the transition was to be completed by the financial policies of the war and postwar years. There was to be no going back: the market was to survive but it was to survive as a somewhat different entity and for a somewhat different purpose than had been thought or expected.

With the outbreak of war in 1939 a new threat to the discount market appeared: the emergent pattern of war finance brought the central bank into much closer direct contact with the clearing banks, by-passing the discount market. Early indications were that this trend might well continue. New forms of government short-term paper were introduced which were dealt in without the participation of the discount houses. This appeared ominous. Between 1939 and 1943, pessimism about the future of the market produced among the houses two more retirements and five absorptions. By 1943 the number of houses had shrunk to eleven.

Despite these ominous tendencies the market's turnover of Treasury bills increased during the war as did, of course, the Treasury bill issue itself. Nevertheless, the very small profit margins (sometimes shrinking almost to vanishing point) made the discount market's condition very straitened indeed. At the same time the authorities were encouraging the market to expand its bond operations. The war was being financed at low interest rates and many short bonds (or bonds soon to be short) were being issued. In due time many holders of such bonds (for example, companies holding them in depreciation accounts, trust-funds and institutions acquiring them now in the patriotic fervour of war-stimulated saving) would wish to sell them and a market would be required. The participation of the discount market would greatly assist in providing a market with assured liquidity for such bond holders.

Peace, reconstruction and a Labour government in 1945 promised little of comfort for the discount market. The new Chancellor of the Exchequer, Hugh Dalton, was a believer in simplified monetary systems, a critic and opponent of intermediary organisations and a fervent advocate of cheap money; yet circumstance and expediency overruled principle and after 1945 there was a considerable expansion in the activities of the money market. In fact it was in these unpropitious circumstances that the discount market expanded faster than ever in its history. No doubt Dalton and the monetary authorities believed that, if there were not a satisfactory market for short bonds, it would be difficult for the government to pursue successfully its policy of cheap, possibly ultra-cheap, money in the postwar period. In 1946 the first institutions to be allowed by the Capital Issues Committee to raise new capital were the discount houses. In 1946–47 every house in the discount market raised new capital, some private companies were turned into public companies, and one new formation took place.

The result of all this was an expanding discount market basing its business mainly on short bonds but with a very large turnover in Treasury bills on which, as a result of cheap money, the profit was very small. Cheap money lasted until 1951 and until that year bonds sustained the market. By mid-1951 the portfolios of the discount houses were at their peak. The twelve houses were carrying £885m. of bills of which £75m. were commercial and municipal and the rest were Treasury. The same houses carried over £300m. in short bonds. The total book was just short of £1,200m.

The postwar history of the discount market, as of most other British financial institutions, falls into two parts: the period from the war's end in 1945 to the end of Labour rule in 1951, the period of cheap money and deficit finance; and the period from 1951, in which year monetary policy was reinstated as a main regulator of the economy and since when there has been much experiment in the use of monetary techniques. Throughout the first of these periods, the rôle of the discount market hardened. It became a manipulator in company with the Bank of England of the large masses of short-term paper. In the past, for example, during World War I, the creation of a large volume of Treasury bills had raised the crucial question of how, by this or similar means, the government was to finance its borrowings; now there was the concomitant problem of how, when necessary, the monetary authority was to mop up the liquidity of the private sector. The creation of great masses of liquid and near-liquid paper raised problems of monetary control in which the discount market, as the main channel through which such liquid titles flowed, was intimately concerned.

Although during these postwar years nothing comparable to the great depression of the thirties arose to threaten the life of the discount houses, equally nothing appeared to revitalise them or assure them of their essential position in the financial system. They were in the position of ageing retainers in a somewhat decrepit household, for whom work is being found because no-one wishes brutally to dispense with their services. What they do is done cheaply and efficiently: it could equally be done by someone else. In the whole of the postwar period the tendency towards a direct linkage between clearing banks and the Bank of England has increased: the discount houses have things to do; they are not too sure, however, that some other group of financial institutions might not do them equally well. At a late point in our story the Radcliffe Committee in 1959, ending its treatment of the discount market, could only say,

'It is no service to claim that the discount market is indispensable to the functioning of the monetary system; but the fact remains that the discount market, by smoothing out irregularities in the ebb and flow of funds among the commercial banks and others, does simplify the functioning of the banks and enables them, free from the embarrassment of temporary disturbances in their liquidity, to concentrate on their major task of providing credit for the production of goods and services. It would not be beyond human ingenuity to replace the work of the discount houses; but they are there, they are doing the work effectively, and they are doing it at a trifling cost in terms of labour and other real resources.'[1]

A decade later, in 1967, the picture is less gloomy. The old business in bonds and Treasury bills remains; there has been a resurgence of the commercial bill; new forms of business in the foreign exchange field are being explored. While no-one could say that the discount houses have won back their assured position of pre-1914 days their future looks brighter now than it did to Radcliffe. The market is not only afloat, it is swimming strongly.

[1] Cf. Radcliffe, p. 64.

II

On the financial front, the war of 1939–45 began quietly and in marked contrast to its predecessor. Firstly, there was no immediate financial crisis, in part because, unlike the first World War, the second was foreseeable far in advance and was prepared for; and in part because Britain's position was not now that of an international creditor as in 1914 but of a debtor. There was some withdrawal of funds from London which caused a decline of the reserves but it did not threaten specific institutions, as the accepting houses, discount houses and clearing banks had been threatened in 1914. Secondly, the techniques of borrowing and debt management were better understood by the authorities and the long period of cheap money had enabled them to accumulate experience in monetary management which prepared them for deficit finance in World War II. Thirdly, this war was to be financed at low rates of interest.[1] It was believed that government borrowing in the first war had been mismanaged. This time we knew better. Moreover, our knowledge, academic and practical, of interest rate policies was now considerable. It was to be a 'Three per cent War'.[2] Finally, the finance of World War I had been seen by the authorities at the time as being carried on against a background of international trade and an open system. The second war was financed from the outset behind a high fence of exchange control in a closed economy.[3]

Direct physical controls and budgetary policy were the weapons of wartime economic planning. Monetary policy was relegated to the tasks of easing and cheapening government borrowing and smoothing operations. With the transference of the Bank of England's gold reserve to the Exchange Equalisation Account virtually the whole of the note issue became fiduciary and the Bank was permitted to increase the fiduciary issue whenever the reserve of the Banking Department required it. The fiduciary issue rose over the war period from £580m. to £1,350m.

As in World War I the cash base of the banking system was kept large but the authorities' method of doing this was new. Instead of borrowing by Ways and Means Advances as had been usual in World War I the government borrowed now on Treasury bills, issuing these through the

---

[1] Bank rate was raised to 4 per cent on August 24 as a precautionary measure but was back at 2 per cent by October 26.

[2] A phrase used by the *Economist* in a leading article 20th January 1940.

[3] The exchange control of September 1939 gave legal definition for the first time to the Sterling Area, described now as 'the scheduled territories'. Exchange control was at first governed by the Defence Regulations but was later given more precise formulation in the Exchange Control Act of 1947.

tap to its own departments and to the market through the weekly tender. After a short rise to 3¾ per cent during the bank rate increase of August–October 1939 the Treasury bill rate settled at 1 per cent where it was held throughout the war. This stability and the supply of adequate cash for the banks was achieved by the method of 'the open back door' whereby the Bank's special buyer stood always ready to buy bills in the market at 1 per cent. If the banks required more cash they had but to refrain from replacing maturing bills or reduce their call loans, in either of which events the discount houses sold bills to the special buyer to replenish their cash. In this way the cash supply was always ensured and the discount rate on Treasury bills was preserved at 1 per cent. This system of virtually automatic cash supply had, however, two important side effects: it meant that the rate at which Treasury bills were discounted by the special buyer, namely 1 per cent, became a strategic interest rate of comparable importance to bank rate which in some respects it superseded; and it meant that the discount market was assured of all the funds it required at this rate. The market could never now be 'in the Bank' nor could bank rate be used as a means of varying interest rates. As a temporary wartime expedient and in a situation where it was intended to maintain very low rates of interest this system was good. Later in the postwar reconstruction period it had to be looked at more critically.

In the discount market, the war caused commercial paper to shrink almost to vanishing point. This and the fear that the scale and pressure of administering war finance would draw the monetary authorities and the clearing banks into a closer and more direct relationship, to the exclusion of the discount market, caused gloom and foreboding in Lombard Street. Such gloom seemed justified when in June 1940 a new form of floating debt, the Treasury Deposit Receipt, was created. This was available only to the banks and the discount market had no part to play in its issue. Treasury Deposit Receipts (or TDR's as they came to be called) were issued directly to the clearing banks, each bank being informed by the authorities of the amount of TDR's it was expected to take up each week. By varying the amount of TDR's issued the authorities could withdraw any desired amount of cash from the banks. TDR's were not negotiable but remained with the banks throughout their six months' life. As the scale and intensity of the war became apparent it was clear that many conventions and survivals would perish. Small wonder that the discount market feared that its one justification, its rôle as distributor of credit from the Bank of England to the clearing banks, was imperilled.

The bill turnover rose, however, from the outbreak of war, the eclipse of trade bills being far exceeded by the increase in the issue of Treasury bills. These rose from £1,820m. in 1938–9 to £3,182m. in 1940 (cf.

TABLE XV

MARKET TURNOVER OF TREASURY BILLS
1938–46
£m.

1938–9	1,820*
1939 (4th qtr)	770
1940	3,182
1941	3,745
1942	3,900
1943	4,495
1944	5,470
1945	6,560
1946	7,800

* Twelve months to 25th August 1939.

Source: Computed from figures quoted in King, 'The Changing Discount Market', *The Banker*, March 1947.

Table XV), and to over £7,000m. by the end of the war. Although part of the great increase in the tender issue was absorbed by the foreign funds accumulating in London, almost all the rest was financed by the discount houses. This would have been ample fodder for the discount market had it contained any nutriment. Unfortunately, from October 1939 when bank rate resumed its long station at 2 per cent there was no nutriment to be had. With carrying bill rates down to the merest fraction over 1 per cent, with clearing bank call money at 1 per cent and bond money at 1¼ per cent, margins were such as not even the largest turnover could inflate. The ghost of 1933 walked again. The houses were back to wondering whether profits would cover working expenses. King said that one house reported in 1947, when bill turnover was six times that of 1938, that its bill business contributed one-third of its total expenses and nothing to its profits.

These difficulties speeded the process of consolidation among the discount houses. In the middle of 1941, the Bank of England informed the market that there was a continuing need for concentration into fewer and larger units—a view which no doubt came from the Governor, Montagu Norman.[1] In 1940–41 two firms, Brocklebank and Co. Ltd. and Fairfax

[1] In fact since as early as 1931 the Bank had followed the practice of letting its views be known when any changes were pending in the structure of the market. When a partnership broke up due to death or retirement of a partner the Bank was loath to approve the formation of a weak unit. It showed a preference for well balanced mergers into strong units.

P

and Co. Ltd., withdrew from the market, and two smaller firms, Roger
Cunliffe, Sons and Co. and Daniell Cazenove and Co., were absorbed by
larger firms in 1941 and 1943 respectively. Ryder, Parker and Co. merged
with Jones and Brown in 1940 and Gillett Bros. Discount Co. Ltd. with
Hohler and Co. These with one other amalgamation planned before the
war but implemented in October 1939—Cater and Co. Ltd. with
Brightwen and Co.—reduced the eighteen firms by seven in four years.[1]

But while bill business was becoming an unprofitable anachronism the
war was transforming bond dealing from being a transitional and scarcely
permitted activity to being 'an important and even indispensable function,
encouraged and supported by the authorities.' This was to be the market's
salvation in the war years and in the early postwar period and some of the
capital consolidation which took place was probably born of the belief that
the days of bill trading were over and that bond-jobbing was to be the
métier in the future.

The government's method of financing the war was one which
favoured bond dealing by the discount houses. Apart from the increase in
the floating debt, based on Treasury bills and Treasury deposit receipts,
the government's domestic borrowing fell into two categories: quoted
securities for the financial institutions and for the higher income savers;
and various types of bonds and securities aimed at the small saver. An
early attempt at long-term borrowing, the 3 per cent War Loan 1955–59,
was not very successful and from thenceforward the government offered
securities on tap. These were of two main types: six successive series of
2½ per cent National War Bonds of six- to ten-year currencies; and three
series of 3 per cent Savings Bonds with currencies of twenty-four to
thirty years. Between 31st March 1939 and 31st March 1946, £3,410m.
was raised through National War Bonds alone, this being the largest
single item in government war borrowing, with the exception of Treasury
bills.

The early success of National War Bonds[2] ensured that by 1943 over
£900m. of such bonds with a remaining life of three to five years had
been added to the stock of short bonds suitable for discount market
dealing. With borrowing through short- and medium-term bonds on
such a scale it was inevitable that even the minimum turnover of bonds
holders' portfolios[3] required a very large market, larger than the jobber-
in gilt-edged within the stock exchange were able to provide. The

---

[1] Of the eleven houses in the market in 1945, five were public companies; five were
private companies; and one was a partnership. In 1944 these eleven houses formally
founded the London Discount Market Association.

[2] £1,000m. were sold within one year of the opening of the tap.

[3] Due to death, bankruptcy and the like.

institutions[1] often required to switch large amounts. They bought large blocks of bonds during the periodic savings drives organised by the National Savings Movement. They also bought extensively at the end of each tap series in order to acquire at par the shortest bonds in each series. To make room for these large acquisitions they needed to sell substantial blocks of shorter dated bonds. These were large operations and were beyond the scope of the gilt-edged jobbers in the stock market who had already to cope with expansion in the supply of medium- and long-term securities. Some supplementation of the normal market facilities was therefore required if the short bond market was to be a smooth and regular one. The discount market could help to meet this need. It had the ability to tap surplus funds wherever they might be within the banking system and its own right of borrowing from the Bank of England, when necessary (via the open back door), gave an ideal means of providing a market for short bonds on the scale required. Moreover, the discount houses were already in the bond market: they had been in it for some time, they had the expertise, they had evolved techniques. So, with the blessing of the authorities, the short bond market was quickly developed. The discount houses were told by the Bank of England that they could borrow from the Bank on the collateral of bonds of less than five years' maturity. The necessity for capital consolidation was once more urged upon them, £1m. being regarded as the eventual minimum capital for each house. Only short-dated bonds were to be carried, especially by the smaller houses.

Bond dealing was a profitable activity for the houses. The existing policy ensured a steadily rising market for bonds, with no fear of capital depreciation and almost certain capital profits when the bonds were sold. Running yields on bonds were as high as $2\frac{1}{2}$ per cent as against call money at $1\frac{1}{4}$ from the clearing banks. It was rare, however, for discount houses to borrow their bond money from the clearing banks. Clearing bank money was used for bills while money for bond dealing was raised from the outside banks at the keener rate of $1\frac{1}{8}$ for bonds and 1 per cent for mixed parcels of bills and bonds. So profitable did bond business become as the war went on that capital began to come into the market—'probably the first concentrated movement since the company flotations boom of the early 1860's'.[2] In 1942-43 seven houses issued new capital and there was also some capitalising of reserves. Money from outside the discount market was subscribed for preference capital by insurance companies and merchant banks. By early 1944 as a result of this new capital and of the amalgamations, each of the eleven houses (except Seccombe, Marshall and Campion which acted—and still acts—as special buyer) had reached the

[1] Banks, insurance companies, building societies, etc.
[2] Cf. King, 'The Changing Discount Market', *The Banker*, March 1947, p. 178.

minimum objective for capital which the authorities had set as a target. In 1944 the resources of the eleven houses were approximately £22m. as compared with just over £20m. for eighteen houses in 1939.

As the war progressed and more and more bonds came within the range of money market operations, the demand for market facilities in short bonds grew rapidly. The houses had by now gained expertise in the jobbing function. They took on bonds on a falling market when the institutions were selling and sold gradually when demands on a rising market began to empty the stock market jobbers' books. The larger houses with their greater resources became very expert at this. It became known that such houses, by their ability to absorb and handle larger blocks of stock than the stock market jobbers, could often quote keener prices, and professional buyers came direct to the houses and did not go to the exchange. Even stock brokers with orders to buy or sell from clients for a time dealt directly with discount houses, although the Stock Exchange Committee frowned on this practice and made a rule in 1944 that brokers were not to 'by-pass' the jobbers unless they were certain that by so doing they could get a price which was to their client's advantage. A broker with a price quotation from a discount house was bound, thereafter, to obtain a jobber's quotation before giving his order. Still, the order often went to the discount house in the end. In some cases, but only with the larger houses, direct dealing extended far beyond the 'institutions' (i.e. the professional financial circle of banks, insurance companies, etc.) to encompass industrial concerns, who bought and sold from them without the participation of any intermediary (e.g. stockbroker). In such cases the market quoted a double price in true jobbing fashion. The smaller houses, however, did very little, if any, direct dealing and even with the larger houses only a small proportion of total dealings was done in this way. The most frequent occasions for direct dealings were when the set of the market was entirely in one direction: large selling when jobbers in the exchange were choked with bonds or large buying when they were short. When the market condition was easy, bond dealings flowed naturally through the jobbers. This was because of the 'buffer function' which the discount market performed in the short bond market. It was at times of market tension that the discount market came into its own. Only in extremity were outside buyers or sellers driven directly to discount houses. Discount houses, even large ones, operate in narrow financial fields and do not often have wide connections outside the purely financial fraternity.

From the point of view of the monetary authorities the greatest advantage of the participation of the discount houses in the short bond market was, and is, that the shortest bonds tend to concentrate there. This concentration arises because the yield on very short bonds is not large enough to attract industrial firms. Such firms may hold them as an alternative to putting ear-marked money on deposit account but the yield is not high enough to justify holding them for long.[1] The shorter a bond becomes the more likely it is to have found its way into a discount house portfolio. With maturing bonds concentrated in the hands of the discount houses refinancing operations by the authorities are made easy. Large blocks of maturing bonds can be taken from the discount houses before the maturity date and in the large and complicated process of refinancing bond issues the discount market becomes almost an agent of the authorities.

By the closing years of the war this function of the discount market was regarded as primary and it was seen as a developing one. There were special grounds for this as in 1945 industry moved from war into peace. In reconstruction all of industry's liquid resources needed to be deployed in its own investment programmes, and bonds acquired for patriotic reasons during the war were disposed of. This involved the discount market in a considerable mopping-up operation. Moreover, as the government was now moving into a period in which, for more than a decade, each year would bring redemptions of war-time issues, there was likely to be continuing need for the discount market's bond gathering services. Finally, with the coming of a Labour government, Mr. Dalton as Chancellor of the Exchequer, and an intensified cheap money policy, a delicate control of the gilt-edged market would be required in which the discount market would have its part to play.

By 1945 the position of the discount houses in respect of bonds and Treasury bills was fully extended even with reference to the tolerance of wartime. Even the houses which had raised new capital in 1943 were using their resources to the limit and several, including the larger houses, had not increased their resources at all. By the close of 1945 the companies were financing a portfolio of bills and bonds twice as large, relative to their resources, as before the war. The ratio of their portfolio to published capital resources was 29:1 and it was thought that the comparable figure for the smaller houses might be more than 40:1.[2] The need for a further jacking-up of the capital position of the discount houses was very apparent.

It was made even more apparent by an incident in the autumn of 1945. In mid-September a Thanksgiving Savings Drive was launched and as usual the institutions began to sell short bonds in order to acquire the new issue. Of these the discount houses took a large amount. Then notice was given by the Treasury of withdrawal of 3 per cent Savings Bonds and

[1] Moreover, taxation renders such bonds much less profitable for a business firm than to a discount house who can, as professional dealers, charge amortisation of premiums on bond purchases against profits for taxation.
[2] Cf. King, 'The Changing Discount Market', *The Banker*, March 1947, p. 182.

there was a strong hint that, after an interval, the next issue would be at
2½. This produced an unprecedented rush to grab the last of the 3 per cent
bonds and of course huge sales of the 2½. But the discount market had by
now reached saturation point. In one week it absorbed £40m. The selling
went on and soon the market mechanism was hopelessly inadequate. In the
absence of an assured professional buyer, prices dropped and a yield was
soon established with which even the shortest bonds gave 2½ per cent—
this at a time when Dalton hoped for this rate of interest on medium- and
long-term borrowing and when he faced heavy refinancing operations.
Cheap money was clearly imperilled by the discount market's inability to
continue its jobbing rôle in the short-bond market.

In the light of this the discount market's request to the Capital Issues
Committee to be allowed to raise more capital looked more pressing.
Hitherto, with the capital needs of British industry stretching apparently
to infinity and with the Labour left-wing looking sourly upon the City,
the prospects of new capital for Lombard Street had not seemed bright.
Now this new capital for the houses appeared to be a *sine qua non* of
Labour's financial policy. Permission to raise it was quickly given and ten
of the eleven houses raised new capital while six registered as public
companies. In December 1946 a new house, the Clive Discount Co. Ltd.,
was formed, mostly from capital advanced by merchant bankers. As a
result of these operations £10·6 m. (about 50 per cent) was added to the
capital resources of the market. Table XVI summarises the capital position
of the market at the end of these operations.

With the total capital of the market in late 1945 standing at £27·7m.
the normal bond carrying capacity of the market, allowing a bonds to
capital ratio of 10:1, was £270m.; and the bill carrying capacity, with a
bills to capital ratio of 15:1, was approximately £40m.

At the end of 1945 the discount market had reached the largest size
in its history both absolutely and relatively as part of the banking system.
The deposit liabilities as a proportion of total bank deposits increased by
more than 30 per cent above 1938, 50 per cent above 1931 and 20 per cent
above 1913. As compared with 1939 the number of houses had been
reduced by a third whilst aggregate resources had been increased by 70
per cent. Yet its basic problem remained. Its expansion was built on bond
dealing, the long-term future of which was problematic: it had become
an adjunct of the stock market. Its bill business, while still considerable,
was based on government paper, in a market in which its dealing served
no really useful purpose, and which for the houses themselves was without
profit. There must have been many in 1945 who viewed the future with
some apprehension. Even the optimistic must have approached it in a
spirit of 'none goes so far as he who knows not where he goes.'

TABLE XVI

WARTIME CAPITAL EXPANSION IN THE DISCOUNT MARKET

Capital and reserves before 1942–44 increases	£11,784,000
Total known resources after 1942–44 increases	£16,751,000
Capital increases in 1946–47	£5,117,000
Increase in total known resources after 1946–47	£10,643,000

Source: Computed from table showing wartime capital expansion of 12 discount companies in King, op. cit., p. 184.

III

From the end of the war in May 1945 until November 1951, the period of Labour government, financial policy was dominated by cheap money and punctuated in 1947 by one unsuccessful exercise in ultra-cheap money. The government's refusal to use active monetary policy in the years of reconstruction sprang from several sources: first, and most important, was Labour's scepticism of the efficacy of monetary policy. Direct controls for resource allocation and fiscal policy for overall control of the economy were the chosen weapons of economic policy. Secondly, it was widely believed in the late war years that after a brief postwar boom there would be a return of unemployment and surplus industrial capacity in the postwar period and that, in face of this, cheap money would be essential. Finally, there was in the minds of Labour politicians a deep suspicion of relying too far, for the implementation of economic policy, upon the engines of the City, even if one of these engines had been brought under public ownership in 1946. Monetary mechanics were imperfectly understood. They bore the taint of the City, Montagu Norman and the establishment. More direct methods were preferred. Briefly, the government's policy for control of the straitened British economy was to increase saving (a) by rigorously controlling consumption and (b) by controlling investment priorities through licences and resource allocation. With high saving, interest rates could be kept low for the large public borrowing which would be necessary both for reconstruction and to convert the accumulated war-debt to minimum-cost securities.

Monetary operations through the banking system would consist merely of maintaining the easy credit conditions which would make cheap money possible.

The cheap money policy of the later forties was based on a two-pronged attack: firstly, the Bank of England would stand ready to provide unlimited cheap cash by buying Treasury bills at a fixed and low rate; and secondly, the government would provide support to the gilt-edged market by switching the balances of government agencies (the Bank of England, the National Insurance Funds, etc.) from short- to long-term securities. The first steps came in October 1945 when the rate on Treasury Deposit Receipts was reduced from $1\frac{1}{8}$ to $\frac{5}{8}$ per cent and the Bank of England buying price for bills was lowered from 1 per cent, which had ruled throughout the war, to a shade over $\frac{1}{2}$ per cent. Thus the Bank was providing cash at ultra-cheap rates by means of which the commercial banks and the discount market could take up more bills—so freeing departmental funds which could be switched to long-term securities. The banks, with more liquid assets (Treasury bills and TDR's) were in a position to increase their investments. Under the influence of mounting demand the price of long-term gilts was bid up. In October 1946, the issue of £482m. Treasury $2\frac{1}{2}$ per cent stock, 1975 or after, marked the achievement of a $2\frac{1}{2}$ per cent long-term rate.

But this was the limit, and success was short-lived. There was no confidence on the part of the public that the government could sustain a long-term rate of $2\frac{1}{2}$ per cent by creating bank credit. The year 1947 with its convertibility crisis, a massive balance of payments deficit and a fuel and power crisis was the nadir of our postwar economic fortunes, and gilt-edged prices fell from the summer onwards. At first the government tried to support prices by using official funds to buy gilts but this was soon abandoned. The price of Treasury stock fell steadily until at the end of the year it was 75; $2\frac{1}{2}$ per cent had failed. From then on the government intervened in the long-term market only for the purpose of smoothing operations. Prices drifted steadily downward. In late 1947 the yield on Consols was 3·5 per cent; in 1951 they were yielding over 4 per cent. Ultra-cheap money had in the long-term field not been sustainable and was reluctantly abandoned.

The government resolutely continued its policy of keeping short-term rates low and fixed. The Bank's 'open back door' still bought bills at the rates fixed in October 1945. The market could get all the cash it wanted through this door at low rates without having to borrow from the Bank in the traditional way on bills discounted at bank rate. Not only did this mean that the banking system was kept very liquid but it meant the severance of the normal relationship between short- and long-term rates.

The whole apparatus of monetary policy was in disarray. Bank rate was no longer an effective or even meaningful rate of interest. Open-market operations could not be used and the only real control on credit was that exercised over long-term borrowing by the Capital Issues Committee. Much was made of the so-called 'moral suasion' exercised by the Bank and Treasury over the clearing banks under which the banks granted advances sparingly and only to borrowers in essential industries and the export trade; but the record of this is not impressive. It seems that the banks were prepared to be persuaded when the official line coincided with their own policies. At other times divergences were many and frequent.

Throughout this period of cheap money, and indeed well down into the fifties, the discount houses continued to make a reasonable living from dealing in short bonds. Treasury bill turnover continued to be high but unprofitable and although there was a slight rise in the small volume of trade bills this could not be regarded as significant. Altogether for the discount market the six postwar years were spent exercising their function as bond dealers and possibly wondering how long this function was to be left to them. In this they were due for a rude shock when the epoch of cheap money ended.

IV

In November 1951 two decades of cheap money ended. The Conservatives came to power at a time when prices were rising steeply and the country was experiencing one of its recurrent balance of payments crises. An active economic policy was a necessity. The new government wished to re-establish a flexible market economy, to remove direct controls on resources and investment at home and ultimately to remove exchange control and make the pound freely convertible abroad. Within this framework they proposed to make use of monetary policy. Fiscal policy was not, however, to be abandoned and there was much talk of the need to co-ordinate monetary and fiscal policy.

We find the monetary history of the fifties falling, therefore, into two distinct phases: in the first phase, from 1951 to the last months of 1953, we find the authorities tentatively returning to the methods of active monetary policy, the use of bank rate and short-term interest rate variations and the variation of bank credit; but we find them in this return somewhat handicapped by the much changed financial environment in which the old weapons now had to operate (in particular the liquidity of the banking system and the great rise in the public debt) and by the ineptness which had resulted from the laying aside of these weapons for so long. The second phase began in 1954 and was characterised by a much more purposive use of monetary policy to try to bring the economy under control, in particular to purge domestic inflation and to achieve stability in the balance of payments. In general, it may be said that the weakness of sterling and the disciplines which it imposed, the necessity to protect the currency, vulnerable as it was with its large volume of quick liabilities to foreigners, from recurrent speculative raids, was the dominant feature of the fifties and conditioned all other economic policies. In this sense the return to convertibility when it came in 1959 had little significance, for under the freer conditions of convertible currencies the forces impelling monetary operations remained unchanged and indeed still do in the sixties.

Before once more using the weapons of monetary policy it was necessary to restore the machine to a workable condition. Conditions at the close of 1951 did not look propitious for the smooth working of monetary policy. There was, for example, the excessive liquidity of the banking system and indeed of the whole economy. The public was holding large balances of bank and legal tender money, far greater in relation to national income than was healthy for an economy in a condition of near-inflation. The banking system in its turn was holding excessive amounts of Treasury bills which inflated its liquid assets ratio to over 40 per cent, providing a base for further deposit expansion and making nonsense of any attempt to use open-market operations for deflationary purposes. Outside the banking system were large holdings of highly liquid assets, deposits in savings banks and building societies, National Savings certificates and the like. The 'general climate of liquidity' was not a healthy one for an economy with a balance of payments problem and the necessity to control inflation. A great deal of this liquidity would have to be mopped up as a mere preliminary to a purposive monetary policy.

One major problem lay in the size and structure of the national debt and the capital needs of the government. In 1945, 66 per cent of the internal debt was in the form of Treasury bills or dated stocks. By the late forties and fifties maturing stock issues from dated stocks of the war period added heavily to current capital expenditure. The government was faced with the problem of meeting its current and capital expenditures from taxation, saving and long-term borrowing or of adding still further to the already large Treasury bill floating debt. In the fifties, as in the forties, over-issue of Treasury bills gave excessive liquidity to the banking system. Funding operations in 1951 reduced this liquidity temporarily but by the mid-fifties it was again a problem.

In November 1951 a start was made. Bank rate, held at 2 per cent since mid-1932, was raised to 2½. This was a modest change but with it came a return to a moving pattern of money rates in general. Seven-day loans against Treasury bills were still offered at 2 per cent but it was announced that the 'special buyer' would not now automatically take bills at market rates. The bank did not close the 'back door' but it reserved the right to do so and to make the market borrow on penal terms. The occasions on which it did this were at first few, showing only how the system worked, and for the most part the special buyer was still forthcoming to take bills at about $\frac{7}{8}$ per cent. There was at the same time an attempt to mop up some of the surplus liquidity in the clearing banks. The government offered three issues of funding stock maturing in 1952, 1953 and 1954 to a total of £1,000m. in exchange for Treasury bills. The banks were in effect instructed to take about £500m. of this stock[1]—this switch from the liquid assets group to *Investments* serving to reduce the liquid assets ratio temporarily to just over the conventional 30 per cent. The method of 'moral suasion' for influencing bank advances received a new twist when in November the Committee of London Clearing Bankers wrote to *The Times* stating that the clearing banks would subject applications for advances to a very severe scrutiny. The first 'credit squeeze' in the long series which was to punctuate the economic activity of the fifties and sixties had begun. A technical change was made in February 1952 when the last Treasury Deposit Receipts ran out and their issue was ended. In March 1952 bank rate went to 4 per cent (with loans against Treasury bills at $3\frac{1}{2}$ per cent). The differential between bank rate and the borrowing rate against Treasury bills was intended to convenience the market but at the same time to prevent borrowing via trade bills (a practice which began to appear as soon as bank advances became difficult to negotiate) and to keep commercial rates in this country aligned with those abroad. A package deal of restrictive economic measures in the autumn of 1951 was followed by a deflationary budget in the spring of 1952, which included a tightening of hire-purchase conditions.

There were soon signs that credit restriction was beginning to work. Between November 1951 and March 1952 the advances of the clearing banks rose only by £21m. as compared with £144m. and £120m. in the same period for the two previous years. With the wartime food subsidies now removed, an end to many of the direct controls on resource allocation and a return to monetary policy, the Conservative experiment in flexibility and the price mechanism was well launched in the first year of office.

For the discount houses the first effect of the new monetary policy was to bring a profit on bill business. Houses discounted only at a rate higher than that at which they could get call money. Rates became more flexible and the risks and rewards of bill dealing became greater. The risks in bonds (now that interest rates were trending upwards) were greater and

[1] Cf. *Report of the Committee on the Working of the Monetary System*, Radcliffe Report, para. 406.

in 1955 the market suffered through depreciation. Another unfavourable feature which began to manifest itself at this time was the entry into the tender of new bidders for Treasury bills. Private companies in particular began to use Treasury bills as a profitable repository of liquid reserves at the higher interest rates. The discount houses from now on might make a profit on their Treasury bills but they could not be at all certain that they could get as many of them at the tender as they would wish.

Between March and December 1952 there was a very marked tightening of credit. Credit directly extended by the banking system to private borrowers fell by over £300m. in the nine months March–December 1952. From the point of view of monetary policy there was a technical anomaly here in that while credit was so restricted bank liquidity rose[1] and there was a rise of £468m. in the deposits of the clearing banks—this reflecting a fall of £307m. in advances and bills (other than Treasury bills) discounted and a rise of £775m. in Investments, Treasury bills and cash. This excessive liquidity of the banking system was the result of heavy government borrowing. The exchequer required to raise £998m. for budgetary and extra-budgetary requirements and to finance an increase in the exchange reserves but in getting this large sum the tight rein placed on the banking system by the funding operation in 1951 was seriously loosened. There was some improvement in early 1953. A surplus on revenue enabled some net repayment of Treasury bills to take place and between January and the end of the fiscal year they were reduced by £269m., although over the year 1952–53 the increase was £401m. By April 1953 the liquidity ratio of the clearing banks was reduced to just under 33 per cent. Again, however, the pendulum swung. General budgetary requirements led to an increase of £498m. in Treasury bills of which the rise in the clearing banks holding was £370m. In spite of the great liquidity of the clearing banks and the strongly expanding economy advances fell by £136m. between April and September 1953 and over the whole of the fiscal year 1953–54 showed no advance.

So far as interest rates were concerned there was some argument for reduction in 1953. Rates abroad were declining and the market rate for commercial bills at home was tending to fall due to a decline in the number of trade bills. It was, moreover, becoming harder to maintain the differential between Treasury bill rates (dictated by the so-called Special Rate of 3½ per cent) and commercial bill rates (dictated by bank rate at 4 per cent). Moreover, the government, with its eye on the Collective Approach[2] and an early return to sterling convertibility, was anxious not

---

[1] The liquidity ratio of the clearing banks rose to 36 per cent.

[2] The 'collective' approach was the name then in vogue for a joint Anglo-American plan to make sterling convertible for current payments abroad.

to give any hint to observant foreigners of a return to easy money. The real problem was covertly to give flexibility to interest rates and to create conditions in which they could be raised or lowered quickly for reasons either of credit control or of public finance. The duality of interest rates which had been operated since 1951 with bank rate and the special rate both being used for control of two short-term paper markets which the authorities wished to keep separate and distinct, was now abandoned and bank rate was, in September 1953, reduced from 4 to 3½ per cent and the special rate abolished. This had the appearance of a technical adjustment and gave the operation a more innocent appearance. At the same time it considerably narrowed the differential between commercial and Treasury bill rates. Long-term rates and equity yields continued on a gently falling trend. In May 1954 bank rate was further reduced to 3 per cent and to underline the fact that disinflation was for the moment at an end, restrictions on bank lending for bill purchase and hire purchase controls were lifted in September.

This restoration of bank rate to its old position of penal rate and regulator of all other short-term rates seemed to bring to an end the disparity in interest rates which had existed since the failure of Dalton's ultra-cheap money policy in 1947 had separated long- and short-term rates. We seemed in 1953 to be back to that old condition in which bank rate was the controlling rate and in which a change in bank rate caused short-term rates to move at once and long-term rates to move more slowly in sympathy with the change. But one never goes all the way back. The authorities had learnt the usefulness of operating on several rates of interest rather than on one and although in the later fifties and the sixties bank rate did play the main controlling part in interest rate policy there were to be times when, for balance of payments or other reasons, the Treasury bill rate might be moved without a change in bank rate or vice versa.[1] Moreover, while access to the 'open back door' over more than a decade had demonstrated that its indiscriminate use was detrimental to sensitive credit control, it was now realised that its discriminate use could add considerably to the alternative weapons in the hands of the authorities. There were two ways in which it could do this: firstly, by allowing the

[1] For example the difference between short-term rates in London and New York is clearly of great importance to short-money movements and the balance of payments. With the U.S. experiencing a balance of payments problem of her own there were times in the early sixties (e.g. 1963) when a rise of bank rate appeared un-neighbourly. What more easy than to push the Treasury bill rate up leaving bank rate unchanged, for the Treasury bill rate is important to foreigners holding balances in London in Treasury bills. Such a movement of the Treasury bill rate could be accomplished by leaving bank rate unchanged, by driving the market into the bank, refusing to discount at bank rate but agreeing to lend against bills at the Advances Rate—1 per cent above bank rate.

special buyer to operate in the market in times of credit stringency, taking up bills from either the clearing banks or the discount houses, the authorities could relieve that stringency at rates of their choice rather than at the penal bank rate. Thus, smoothing operations were greatly eased and could be carried on without putting the market into the Bank. Secondly, the operations of the Bank of England, acting in its capacity of national debt administrator, were facilitated in that, through the operations of the special buyer, the Bank could gather into its hands just those Treasury bill maturities which it required. Dates of these maturities would be conditioned by the authorities' knowledge of future cash flows. For example, the anticipation of an affluence of cash on a given future date, due to, say, a bond issue repayment, would lead the special buyer on behalf of the authorities to collect in advance Treasury bills due for repayment on or near that date. In this way other and contributing sources of cash supply at that time would be closed in advance. The open back door of the forties and early fifties was then the antecedent of the special buyer whose operations now give 'official help' to the market or facilitate the Bank's debt operations.

By the close of 1953 the instruments of the new monetary policy were in place and what might be regarded as a period of experiment in their restoration, adaptation and use was at an end. In the years which followed and to the present time monetary policy has been used continuously in the dreary succession of 'stop-go' policies to which, we are told, in the interests of the balance of payments, the British economy has been subjected. It is not our purpose to justify these policies but a brief account of the pattern they have established is in order.

As the year 1954 went on signs of inflation and pressure appeared in the British economy: unemployment fell well below the level of unfilled vacancies; prices were rising; delivery dates were lengthening; imports were buoyant; ordinary share prices were rising and the rate for sterling in the free market was falling. How familiar these symptoms were to become each time the government sought to expand the economy in the late fifties and early sixties. How stereotyped too the reaction was to become. In November 1954 open market operations forced the discount houses to go to the Bank and the Treasury bill rate rose in consequence, narrowing by $\frac{1}{2}$ per cent the gap between that rate and bank rate. This method of raising the Treasury bill rate whilst leaving bank rate untouched seems to have been adopted because the authorities were anxious not to create a crisis atmosphere and increase the pressure on sterling which they feared raising the bank rate would do. This may also have been an early example of a policy later to be pursued frequently: that of attempting to attract foreign short-term capital by raising the return on Treasury

bills, the main repository in Britain of such capital, without the publicity
and psychological reactions of raising bank rate. Nevertheless, in this case,
a rise in bank rate followed. In January 1955 the rate was raised to $3\frac{1}{2}$ per
cent and at the end of February it went to $4\frac{1}{2}$ and was accompanied by the
reimposition of hire purchase controls.[1] The discount market continued
under pressure and the Treasury bill rate rose higher in the direction of
bank rate. This had the effect of reducing the liquidity of the banks; for
some persons and institutions who normally held their 'near cash' in
deposit accounts now found it more profitable to hold bills[2] and switched
from deposits to bills. This pressure on bank liquid assets was increased by
a revenue surplus and by the government's receipts from the sale of gold
by the Exchange Equalisation Account. As the demand for bank advances
rose, there was some selling of investments, but by the summer, the banks
were again reducing their advances for certain purposes in response to
moral pressure from the Bank of England. In July the Chancellor, after a
'package deal'[3] which included tightening of hire purchase conditions and
investment cuts, exhorted the banks to restrict their advances generally.
The inflation was slow to yield and an autumn budget with tax increases
came in October; in January 1956 bank rate went to $5\frac{1}{2}$ per cent. This
rise affected overdraft rates for the first time since the new monetary
policy began[4] and the monetary policy had begun to look much more
businesslike with active open-market operations and the market frequently
in the Bank. It was at this time also that the so-called 'liquid assets ratio' of
the clearing banks emerged into the light of day as a regulator of bank
liquidity and monetary policy. It had for long, even before the war, had
recognition as a rule of thumb but just at what stage it passed from being
a 'rule of thumb' to being a convention as binding as, and more important
than, the cash ratio it is very difficult to say. In 1957 we find the Bank of
England in a memorandum of evidence to the Radcliffe Committee
saying that 'as a general rule the banks will be very reluctant to see the
ratio to their deposits of their cash plus other liquid assets—their liquidity
ratio—fall below 30 per cent.'[5] By the later fifties economists were tacitly

[1] A high Treasury official once remarked: 'It is always wise to take off hire purchase
controls because you give yourself the immediate power to put them on again when they
are needed.'

[2] The deposit rate is normally linked to bank rate which in this case was not increasing.
Treasury bill rate was now more profitable than deposit rate.

[3] A term used by the Radcliffe Committee to describe a collection of economic
measures, other than the budget, introduced by a Chancellor for expansionary or contractionary purposes.

[4] Since overdraft rates are traditionally one point above bank rate with a minimum of
5 per cent, bank rate has to go beyond 4 per cent before they are affected.

[5] Cf. Radcliffe, Principal Memoranda of Evidence, vol. i, p. 9.

assuming that the liquid assets ratio was the most strategic regulator of bank asset distribution and there was talk not only of making it legally binding rather than conventional but of giving the power to the monetary authority to raise it above 30 per cent or lower it below, according to whether the authorities were pursuing an expansionary or contractionary monetary policy. Even while desultory discussion of 'statutorily variable reserve ratios' was going on, the Bank of England began to use the method, on the merits of which it had long been silent, but in a loose and flexible fashion, simply indicating to the clearing banks from time to time what the Bank considered their liquid assets ratio ought to be.

The British economic situation in 1956 and 1957 permitted no easing of monetary pressure. There was some improvement in the balance of payments in early 1956 but in October the Suez adventure put the clock back and there was speculative pressure on sterling—which was met by drawing on the IMF. In February 1957 bank rate was reduced to 5 per cent but later in the year, in September, the condition of certain European currencies caused sterling to fall under suspicion of impending devaluation.[1] There were heavy withdrawals of foreign balances from London and during August and September £186m. ebbed away from the British reserves. On 19th September bank rate was raised to 7 per cent—the first time it had attained this level since 1920. This very high rate achieved its purpose, speculation against sterling ceased for the moment, and short-term funds began to flow back to London. As soon as the gold loss was regained in March 1958 bank rate was reduced to 6 per cent and then downward in half per cent steps to 4 per cent by November.

By the spring of 1958 the economy was already showing signs of recession and once more the process of expansion was begun with the customary package deals easing hire purchase restrictions and restoring investment cuts. One notable feature of this expansion was the removal of the control of the Capital Issues Committee from domestic borrowing. With this went the last control on free investment and from then forward the banks were free to lend as much as they wished, to whom they wished, subject only to the discipline of their reserve ratios.

The problem of over-liquidity of the banking system had dogged the authorities in their monetary policy throughout the fifties. Excessive issue of Treasury bills made it difficult to hold the bank's liquidity ratio at or near the 30 per cent level, where open-market operations could begin

[1] The French franc was *de facto* devalued by 20 per cent in August 1957. There were strong rumours that the German Mark would be revalued and heavy buying of this currency developed. This weakened sterling and gave rise to fears for its future. There was deep suspicion abroad of the policies of the British government and heavy selling of sterling resulted.

to be effective.[1] Funding in 1951 had reduced it temporarily but then and subsequently it had risen again. Monetary policy was sluggish in such an over-liquid banking system. There were various ways out of this impasse. The government might create an interest rate structure at which it could finance its borrowing at acceptable long-term rates. To do this would mean a conflict between the aims of interest rates for borrowing and interest rates for other purposes. Alternatively, it could create some new form of government borrowing from the banks, outside the normal market in short-term paper and outside the liquid assets ratio; finally, it could take to itself the right to vary the liquid assets ratio at will and make it obligatory for the banks to honour the stated ratio at any time.

The second alternative was chosen and a system of 'special deposits' was created whereby the Bank could call upon the clearing banks to make special deposits with it—the amount in each case to be proportionate to the bank's own deposits—which would bear interest.[2] These deposits the Bank of England would relend to the government which would then be in a position to retire Treasury bills. From the point of view of the clearing banks the special deposits would not be included in the liquid assets group and any expansion of special deposits would have to be matched by a contraction of investments or advances. The special deposits, although announced in 1959, were not used until April 1960 when calls for 1 per cent of gross deposits from the clearing banks were made.

There was from 1959 onwards a new tautness in the operation of the monetary machine which it had hitherto lacked. This was demonstrated in late 1959 and early 1960 when a fresh check was being imposed on the economy. In order to expand advances and still preserve their liquidity ratios the banks were selling large blocks of government securities. The authorities acted quickly and forcefully. Hitherto the government broker had been supporting the gilt-edged market but at the end of February support was withdrawn and there were sharp falls in the gilt-edged prices. The banks could now only switch from income-earning assets (in this case Investments) to liquid assets at the cost of incurring capital loss on their sales of gilt-edged. They had therefore to curtail advances. 'The need to maintain a given liquidity ratio is only a real deterrent to new lending if the switch from illiquid to liquid assets involves a penalty.'[3] Up to 1960

[1] Of what use were open-market operations if the ratio was 37 per cent? Open-market operations might reduce the ratio to 35 per cent but still there was no compulsion on the banks to restrict credit. Only at, or near, 30 per cent would credit restriction begin to bite. There seems to be a case, with such excessive liquidity, for a statutorily variable reserve ratio.

[2] There were of course precedents for this innovation, as the special deposits of World War I and the TDR's of World War II.

[3] Cf. *The Pound Sterling*, A. Feaveryear, 2nd Edition, p. 413.

Q

the penalty for a switch had been slight, but now with any expansion of advances, involving as it did a sale of investments, the penalty was heavy and not worth incurring. It was clear that the authorities were learning fast the technique of controlling credit through the liquidity ratio of the clearing banks.

So far as the discount houses were concerned the new monetary policy of the fifties brought a change of emphasis for them—away from bond business and back to bill business. During the period of cheap money in the forties and the relatively stable interest rates of the early fifties they had done well out of their bond business. There had been a good working margin between yields and call money and little risk. When, however, interest rates became more volatile, in particular when the authorities in their new militancy began to force swift and sharp changes in short rates, profits dwindled and sometimes vanished while risks became considerable. With higher bill rates the trading margins on bills became more profitable and the houses did all in their power to expand their bill business while curtailing their bond dealing. The year 1957, as we have seen, was one of considerable activity in the use of monetary policy and the pushing of bank rate to 7 per cent was a sharp shock for the discount market's bond portfolios. In 1957 the houses were extremely loath to operate in bonds in a market where capital values were so unstable and dangerous.[1] There was contraction of their bond business and of the large jobbing rôle which they had played in the gilt-edged market for well over a decade. Much of that rôle was taken over by the government broker, the broker acting in the stock market for the Bank of England in its open-market operations. A rise in the price of bonds late in 1958 drew the houses into the market again and since that time their bond holdings have fluctuated about a rising trend to an all-time high of nearly £700m. at the end of 1967.

The discount houses have maintained a short-bond turnover sufficient in size to preclude the necessity of the clearing banks operating in the market. This they could do in the absence of the discount market just as, in the bill market, they could if necessary take up bills directly at the tender. Neither of these functions attracts them, however, and they are well satisfied to delegate them to the discount houses.

V

The period 1945–59 saw the restoration of the Bank of England to full power as controller of the monetary system. However technically dex-

[1] It is an 'open secret' in the market that some firms had to receive help in the form of unsecured loans in 1957–58 when the jump in interest rates (fall in bond values) caused their asset values to slump sharply. Revaluation of collateral became a vital problem and according to one writer, some 'discount house directors had to transfer money from their own bank accounts.' Cf. Paul Ferris, *The City*, London, 1960, p. 66.

terous and intricate may be the tasks involved in maintaining continuous credit and cash supply at minimal rates of interest, there is reason to believe that a central bank is only truly fulfilling its destiny and function when it is using all its power and skill to regulate the level of resources, prices and activity in the economy through variations in the credit and money flow. The postwar years saw the restoration of monetary policy with the bank as its centre, but it was a monetary policy which bore only a family likeness to that which we have discussed in earlier chapters of this book. To some extent in aims and quite markedly in methods it differed from the monetary policies of pre-1913 or of 1918 to 1932. Since we have already touched on the chronological developments of the new monetary policy in earlier sections of this chapter it is now upon the innovations, the discontinuities, the breaks with the past in aim and method that we shall touch.

First, to deal with aim. At first sight it might appear that the aim of British monetary policy has been unchanged throughout the three periods when it has been freely used: before 1914; from 1918 to 1932; and from 1951 to the present. In all these periods the equilibrium of the balance of payments has been the central policy aim. But while this has been the theme each period has provided its own variation: in the first, protection of the Bank's gold reserve, by domestic credit adjustment and bank rate change, the maintenance of a gold parity, the primacy of the external over the domestic situation; in the second, the establishment (i.e. to 1925) and maintenance (1925–31) of a gold bullion standard doomed from the outset to failure; in the third, the guiding of an economy ever teetering on the border of inflation and, if checked, swinging to recession, yet all the while conscious of a balance of payments the movements and condition of which were not appropriate to a country administering an international currency with slim reserves and large quick liabilities. In this last period it is, more than anything else, the narrowness of the tolerances which distinguishes it. Between the unemployment rates of $1\frac{1}{2}$ per cent and 3 per cent, the one near to inflation, the other dubbed by a watchful electorate 'depression', the tasks it poses for monetary control have called for a delicacy and precision absent and unnecessary in previous periods. Coupled with this necessity for delicacy and precision is the much wider scope of operation which, in the light of modern knowledge, is seen to be necessary in the monetary sphere. Before World War II and in the nineteenth century the central bank saw its rôle as that of controlling the total money supply and of influencing inflows and outflows of short-term capital. Now, whilst these tasks remain and are clearly important, it is also seen to be necessary to influence the whole state of liquidity within the economy, thus involving control over many intermediary institutions outside or only on the periphery of the banking system. In some cases, as in that of hire purchase, the control is not exercised by the Bank of England but by the government. Thus the monetary control is now merged with governmental control of general economic policy in a way which is entirely new. There are problems of timing and co-ordination here which still await attention, but which lie far outside the scope of this book.

Another feature which distinguishes the new monetary policy of the 1950's from that of earlier periods is that while balance of payments policy still motivates much of the action of monetary policy, institutionally the domestic banking system is now to a great extent sealed off from the effects of the balance of payments. The establishing of the Exchange Equalisation Account, the transfer of the Bank of England's gold reserve from the Issue Department of the Bank to the Exchange Equalisation Account and the establishing of a note issue which is entirely fiduciary achieved at least a mechanistic separation. No longer would an adverse balance of payments cause a gold outflow which had immediate repercussions on the domestic money supply. The connections between the external balance and the domestic money and credit supply obviously still exist and are of vital importance, but they are qualitative policy relations which have to be weighed and considered and which are matters of judgement and opinion, not structural connections, direct, quantitative and functional.

Within this new environment two aspects of Bank of England policy in the fifties interest us since they bear closely on the discount market: interest rate policy, at the heart of which bank rate policy still lies; and the use of reserve ratios and open-market operations to control clearing bank liquidity.

The Bank's interest rate policy in the postwar years falls into three phases: from 1945 to 1951 when bank rate was not operative, being pegged at the 2 per cent at which it had stood since 1932; from 1951 to 1953 when, the cheap money policy over, a tentative interest rate policy was emerging and bank rate was being used and varied in concert with other rates, but when its rôle of penal rate and determinant of all short-term rates was still only partial; and from 1953 onwards when, with bank rate fully restored to its focal position in the interest rate structure, principles for its manipulation and its relation to other rates were being worked out. The first of these periods need not concern us here. What is of interest has already been commented upon. Upon the second two periods some comment is required.

The problems in connection with interest rates facing the authorities in 1951 were two: the first, to restore order to the structure of interest rates. This meant getting a graded structure of short-term rates which could be controlled by the authorities through bank rate and also restoring a proper relationship between short- and long-term rates—a relationship which had become blurred in the preceding cheap money period. The second problem was to find out how the economy, now very different from that of pre-1932 and, in particular, the monetary institutions, would react to monetary policy, to manipulations of interest rates and checking and easing of the credit flow. Had reactions to monetary control become dulled by the years of cheap money: would the new manipulators of monetary weapons have the skill and touch of their fathers? In face of these questions it is not surprising that the first years of the new monetary policy were tentative and at times halting. This tentativeness can be seen in several aspects of the policy. For example, it was initially thought to be wise to make few movements in bank rate itself on the ground that these might alarm foreign observers and overseas holders of sterling. This view was in contrast to the old nineteenth century view that a high bank rate would draw gold powerfully into the country, and in contrast to the view which prevailed later in the fifties and in the sixties when speculative runs on sterling were met by 7 per cent bank rates, and an important indicator of the need for a bank rate increase was a rise in the rate of the Federal Reserve. Another example was that of open-market operations. Not until 1953 did the authorities seem to have the confidence to use these with vigour; to put the market in the Bank and make their chosen rate structure effective. Up to that time they seem to have been experimenting with market reaction to quite minor changes in interest rates and open-market operations. For example, the period from November 1951 to September 1953, when the 'open back door' system still operated, was punctuated by periodic, rather shy and self-conscious shuttings of the door which gave the impression of being minor trials of strength to accustom the market to control by bank rate.

After 1954 movements of bank rate were made with more assurance and the policy of the authorities gave a greater appearance of vigour and self-confidence. Bank rate changes were used either to steady the foreign exchange reserves by fitting the rate for sterling balances appropriately into the world pattern of short money rates and short-term capital movements or as part of the alleviating expansion and contraction policies forced on the authorities by the balance of payments.

As a new weapon to control the distribution of clearing bank assets and thus the general liquidity situation, the recognition and use of the liquid assets ratio by the Bank of England from the late fifties is notable. In a truly British fashion, without announcement or apparent official recognition, we woke up to the fact, towards the end of the fifties, that the cash ratio as a controller of bank credit was no longer in its place and that it had been succeeded by this new upstart. A constant cash ratio of 8 per cent meant that the 30 per cent liquid assets ratio spanned the entire list of bank assets in its influence and made the penalties of switching between liquid and earning assets very real indeed.

In the prevalent postwar situation, where surplus liquidity in the clearing banks was a major stumbling block to central bank control, the temptation to make the reserve ratio mandatory and to vary it widely from time to time must have been great. Why was this practice not adopted by an authority which was clearly at that time in the mood for experiment? There seems little doubt of the reason. However rigorous and experimental the authorities were in their post-1953 operations they were also well aware of the need stressed above for delicacy and precision. The credit weapon of compulsorily variable reserve ratios was (and still largely is) untried. Although provision for its use exists in several foreign and Commonwealth banking systems comparatively little use has been made of it and there has been little experience upon which to draw. The speed of reaction by the clearing banks to a sudden announcement of the change of liquid reserve ratio from 30 to 35 per cent might look at first sight attractive to an authority seeking to control a system choked with Treasury bills but it is also possible, indeed likely, that the reaction would be too quick and too violent when the weapon was used in a deflationary direction. Such a raising of the rate would have two results: a sale of investments, with all that that implied for the banks in potential loss, and/or a sharp and immediate call-in of advances with all that that implied for business confidence. To pioneer such a new weapon was no doubt deemed by the Bank to be a long and cautious business. With the Bank announcement in 1961 that the clearing banks might with advantage reduce their liquid assets ratio to 28 per cent, a start was made to try out this new weapon, wisely starting with reduction of the ratio to promote expansion, the direction of movement in which least harm could be done. It seems probable that we shall see in the next decade a growing use of the ratio by the Bank in this gentle persuasive way, unless it is not justified by results, in which case it will slip out of everyone's notice. An institution which cheerfully took half a century to pioneer and establish control through bank rate is not going to boggle at a decade to test this tricky-looking mechanism.

One significant innovation in the Bank's relations with the discount market occurred in the postwar period and became normal routine in the fifties. Traditionally the Bank of England's function as lender of last resort has been exercised through the discount market. In many other countries the central bank stands ready to lend directly to the commercial banks but in Britain a shortage of cash drives the clearing banks to call in loans from the discount houses who then have the right to obtain assistance from the Bank of England. In this way help to the clearing banks is indirect, the discount houses acting as a buffer between them and the central bank. Since 1953, when the open back door as an automatic source of funds was abolished, use has been made of the special buyer to give assistance to the banking system by buying bills of chosen maturity date at the open back door. In this way three forms of last resort assistance may be given. The first is the old traditional form, whereby the discount houses rediscount bills at the Bank of England at bank rate. The second is the method now used, and more penal in effect, whereby seven-day loans are made to the discount houses at the Advances rate. Finally, there is the method described above whereby the special buyer gives 'official assistance' by buying bills of chosen maturities at market rates either from the clearing banks or the discount houses, according to where the maturities are held. By this third method the authorities can relieve any temporary cash stringency without enforcing a penal rate of interest and without effect on the existing structure of interest rates. It is an ideal method for day-to-day smoothing operations. The old traditional method of supplying cash to the market via the discount houses has been broken, however, and direct help is often given to the clearing banks should it be they who hold the particular maturities which the special buyer is seeking. In fact this is most usually the case since the authorities most often require for their own purposes very short bills which are in the last part of their currency. Such bills are much more likely to be in the hands of the banks than of the discount houses, so that it is more often the former to which the special buyer gives help by buying bills. From the general monetary standpoint it is not important whether the help is given to the discount houses to meet their calls from the clearing banks or whether it is given to the clearing banks who cancel their call demands on the discount houses. It is, however, interesting that this method of official help by forging in many cases a direct link between the clearing banks and the lender of last resort contravenes the century-old tradition of indirectness. It would be wrong to read into this practice any sinister significance, any plot by the authorities to render the discount houses redundant or to undermine their position. The practice is purely one of expediency. Nevertheless, occurring as it did at a time when the discount market was peculiarly sensitive about its functions, usefulness and future, it saddened some hearts.

Chapter 9

CONCLUSION

'You get into trouble if you go to the bottom of things.'
Latin-American delegate to an international conference.

I

IT IS APPROPRIATE to end this study of the discount market by glancing briefly at its present state and taking stock of its problems in the light of what has been said in earlier chapters. In particular we are concerned in this brief review with the market's relations with other parts of the monetary system. A brief comment on its business position is, however, appropriate at the outset.

During the first half of the sixties the discount houses have had stable trading, few, if any, threats to their existence and the pleasure of seeing a revival of their commercial bill business. True, their profit rate has not been high but it has been steady and declared dividends of 10–12 per cent have been the order of the day. The resurgence of the commercial bill has been a glorious windfall gain in the sixties, and if it continues and the commercial bill becomes a dealing staple again, the houses will not only be emancipated from their long total dependence on public sector financing, but may regain something of their old quality as private finance houses with wide interests and influence in the private sector.

Among the individual firms there is ample evidence of vigour and a desire to move with the times. A number of houses have begun to seek new business outlets—for example as money brokers in the inter-bank loan market, as foreign exchange dealers and as dealers in the Euro-dollar market. A recent innovation attributable to the discount houses' initiative has been the market in one-year local authority bonds. These bonds are issued by British local authorities through a broker or merchant bank who places them. They provide, for the authorities, slightly longer-term borrowing than the alternative short-term advances which have been (and still are) widely used. The discount houses provide a market for these bonds, dealing in them in much the same way as with other short bonds. Three months' local authority bills are also to be seen again, reviving memories of the use made of such bills in the thirties. All this new business is still very peripheral and it is not possible to say whether it is transient or whether it marks the beginning of a process of diversification by the discount houses. All that can now be said is that the houses are at present

248

as quick to scent and pursue new forms of business as they are to reorganise their office routines by computer and machine.

From the structural point of view the houses are stronger than ever before. The mergers and capital consolidation of the thirties have reduced their number to what must be near an optimum. The small under-capitalised houses have disappeared. Except for Seccombe, Marshall and Campion, the house which acts as special buyer for the Bank of England, no house now has a capital of under £1m., while at the same time the houses have managed to maintain their quality of smallness, personal management and low cost working. Probably at no time since 1914 has the market looked so strong and capable of survival.

To the discount houses the attitude of other financial groups, of the central bank and of the monetary authorities is important. A hostile business environment would be fatal. They live as intermediates and may be crushed or isolated by the hostility or indifference of the groups they serve. The clearing banks, for example, hold the power of life or death for the discount houses in their hands; indifference on the part of the Bank of England to their welfare would be detrimental; the belief by the informed financial world that they are a historical anachronism might be the first step towards their becoming one. On all of these fronts the position is at present reasonably secure. The clearing banks appear to have orientated themselves to the discount market in all important respects. The Treasury bill tender routines, in particular the clearing banks' abstention from the tender, are accepted without demur and help to give the market a living from Treasury bills. Since these arrangements are an expedient dating from 1934–35, when they were adopted to save a discount market in dire straits, and since they show the discount market in perhaps its least productive light, it would not be surprising if, in calmer times, the banks had called for their revision. No such call has been heard. The clearing banks now appear to regard the discount houses as institutions conveniencing them through the outlet they provide for call loans and also performing certain financial services which they themselves have no ambition to provide. There is some advantage to the banks in their continuance: several irritations and frictions of a minor character and one major problem, that of underwriting the cash reserve, would be incurred by their demise. The clearing banks, therefore, so far as they think about it, are for maintaining the present arrangements.

There is no indication that the Bank of England's favourable view of the discount market has changed since the thirties when Montagu Norman gave it succour in distress. The bank does not of course declare itself in the finer nuances of its opinion of other financial institutions but there is nothing in the record of the fifties or sixties which indicates a change in its former view and there have been some indications of its continuing appreciation of the discount houses' tasks and position.[1] Two recent instances come to mind. The first has been in the matter of credit supply. The Governor's letter of May 1965 to the London Discount Market Association calling for a curtailment of bill lending should not be seen as a rebuke to the market for excessive lending on accommodation bills during a credit squeeze but rather as an official Bank recognition of the market's promotion to a status among the suppliers of short-term credit, calling for Bank guidance and supervision. The second instance of Bank of England favour has been in the slight easing of the Bank's eligibility standards for the approval of trade bills, which took place in 1964 and 1965. The Bank's acceptance of good trade bills as collateral has given further proof of its qualified approval of the new bill business and its importance for the discount market.

It must be recognised, however, that in even a slight change of the Bank's view of the market's usefulness there would be great danger for the discount houses. A mere tolerance of them is not enough. There must exist, as there has existed, a firm belief in their high utility in the British monetary system, a determination to keep them in being and, if necessary, to bring to heel any recalcitrant group which follows policies inimical to them. It is not suggested that they now lead a pauperised existence helped only by Bank of England support and encouragement, but the fact remains that the Bank has played a major rôle in preserving them by encouraging monetary arrangements in which it was known they could continue. A change on the part of the Bank of England, even if it were a mere deterioration from enthusiasm to tolerance, might seriously shorten the lives of the smaller houses and drive the larger ones progressively into other fields of activity.

In the eyes of the informed financial world the discount houses have a confused public image. The nature of their work, the intricacy of their relations with other financial institutions, the fact that an appreciation of their real worth demands a considerable knowledge of the monetary system—all this and the somewhat patronising conclusion of the Radcliffe Committee on the question of their usefulness[2] have all contributed

---

[1] Apart from the practical signs that the Bank of England still favours a strong discount market there was a very forthright statement of the Bank of England view by Mr. L. O'Brien, then Chief Cashier of the Bank and now Governor, in evidence to the Radcliffe Committee. He said: 'The fact is that the discount market has survived. That may not be entirely due to the fact that the clearing banks like it so much. It may be because the Bank of England likes it also. We believe it to be the most highly flexible mechanism for looking after the needs for short-term money that there is in the world. I cannot say more than that.'

[2] Cf. Radcliffe, p. 64, para. 180.

to this confusion. But if few have actively joined their cause, and if the discount market itself privately sighed with relief in 1959 that the verdict of Radcliffe was at least no worse, at the same time no one cries for their blood or campaigns for their extinction. The question of the market's real usefulness and dispensability remains but it is an academic question only, for there is no way of removing the market save by a root and branch operation for which there is neither means nor justification. In the light of this, and of the market's present health, the question is an un-profitable one, and if the weary reader at this late stage requires an answer he will have to seek it in his own view of the description which has been given of the market's working and of the story which has been told of its evolution in this book. The case for and against a discount market such as the British has been summarised.[1] The fire in this con-troversy is not dead but it has burnt low and the writer does not consider it profitable or practical to rake over these ashes any further. The discount market is there; it is prosperous and vigorous. There is no sign of its decline, rather a promise in the future of the capacity for flexibility and adaptability which it has shown in the past. No government now discer-nible would inaugurate the surgery of its removal. Only a great upheaval in the financial system and a great exercise in *a priori* financial planning would bring about the discount market's elimination, and for great *a priori* plans, particularly in the financial field, the British have neither enthusiasm nor genius.

II

One task remains: that of examining the present position of the discount market in the light of the changes in monetary policy which have been taking place in recent years. Two streams of events have concerned us in this book: the evolution of the discount market itself and the part it has played in the monetary system; and, more briefly, the evolution of the system of monetary management and control into which the discount market must fit and within which it must operate. To what point has this evolution now come? This is a large question and at this late stage the answer will be brief.

Apart from its functional task of discounting bills and dealing in short-term bonds and in the wider sense as an integral part of the British monetary system, the discount market has been many things in its century and a half of life. Initially, and until almost mid-nineteenth century, it was

[1] Cf. pp. 109-111 above.

a means of evening out flows of credit in a unitary banking system. In its absence credit would have coagulated around London and in the richer areas while developing areas would have been starved of capital. Its second phase was during the late nineteenth century when, with the accepting houses, it was instrumental in making London a great international monetary centre for short-term borrowing and when it played a rôle as monetary intermediary which helped the Bank of England to establish an apparatus of control, in particular through short-term interest rates, for monetary management. A third phase began with the first World War and the making by the discount houses of the nucleus of the market in Treasury bills. The market became in the war years a major channel through which public sector short-term borrowing flowed. Finally, beginning gradually in the 1920's and establishing the practice in the thirties, the discount houses became important operators in short-term bonds in which they acted as jobbers conveniencing the Bank of England in its work of national debt administration. Throughout these stages the market progressively established itself as intermediary between the central bank and the clearing banks as the channel through which central bank replenishment of the monetary supply flowed and as the prime mover in the chain reaction through which short-term interest rates were made effective. In its evolution through these four phases the discount market has survived a number of changes, each of which, for a time at least, threatened its existence: the decline and near disappearance of the domestic bill; the great contraction in the use of the commercial bill; the rigour of depression with the cheap money which it brought; and the return in 1951 of a new monetary policy with new problems, in particular very widely varying interest rates, which had inimical effects on its bond jobbing and brought new problems to its participation in the Treasury bill tender. All these the market has survived. It has adapted itself to changing conditions and consolidated its capital position by amalgamations and the retirement of smaller and weaker firms.

In its present position the discount market has two sets of problems: the changes which may take place in the market itself arising from institutional changes and changes in the forms of paper in which it deals; and structural changes arising from policy changes by the monetary authority. The first set of problems poses no immediate threat. The decline of the commercial bill appears to have run its course and at the moment there is hope that the recent renewal of commercial bill dealing in the 1960's may continue to augment the market's bill turnover. Since the return of a varying bank rate and a pattern of short-term rates moving in sympathy with bank rate the discount houses have been making a profit on their bill business. Although there has been a fall in discount market holdings of

Treasury bills[1] throughout the sixties, largely due to the demand for Treasury bills from outside financial institutions, this has not alarmed the market. Bill portfolios on the whole have been smaller since 1951 but bill dealing has been profitable, at times profitable enough to offset losses on bonds when they occurred. So far as bond dealing is concerned it is impossible to predict the part it will play in the discount houses' future. Bond business in the fifties was sometimes profitable but depreciation of bond portfolios, especially in 1955, was heavy, heavy enough at times to imperil stability. How far bond dealing will contribute to profits in future will depend upon the frequency and timing of bank rate changes. Such changes when they are made are in response to general economic considerations and are often made quickly and under the duress of events. Although the discount houses are becoming experienced in conducting their business in the general climate of what we have come to call the 'stop-go' policy and of accommodating themselves to frequent changes in bank rate, the impact of sudden changes on their bond portfolios can be severe. A series of unfortunately timed 'package deals' in the later sixties could have detrimental effects. On balance, however, the discount houses can, especially if their commercial bill business is sustained, look forward to a continuance in the foreseeable future of the moderately profitable business of the past decade. Risks, whether on bonds or bills, are a usual and normal feature of their business.

The second set of discount market problems, those arising from changes in monetary policy—either changes in policies themselves or major changes in the ways in which the monetary authorities—the Treasury and the Bank of England—wish to implement them, are imponderable. That they are vital is obvious from the record. The switch to cheap money in 1932, which was such a policy change, changed the whole milieu in which the discount houses had to operate and threatened their very being. The return to active interest rate policies in 1951 changed it yet again with beneficial results. Clearly long-run monetary policy is a prime conditioner of the market's prosperity.

There seems little likelihood in the foreseeable future of a return to cheap money. Flexible interest rates and frequent changes of bank rate were used by the Conservative government from 1951 onwards. The Labour Party on its accession to power in 1964 took over the same mechanisms and has used them persistently. They show no disposition to return to the Dalton philosophy of cheap and neutral money with fiscal policy as the main regulator of the economy. As long as there are free and active interest rates the discount houses will be assured of a margin on their bill business. (Mobile rates increase dealing risks and dealers bid for

[1] A fall of approximately 50 per cent at the end of 1967.

bills only at rates higher than the call rate.) Moreover, their *raison d'être* within the monetary system is assured. In order to rely on market forces, that is on variations of rates of interest, there must be an efficient market. The discount houses provide that market. It is their main justification.

A possible threat to the discount market's future might come from any extension of the tendency of recent years for the Bank of England to regulate the money supply directly through the clearing banks and not through the intermediary of the discount houses. In view of the continual support which the houses have had from the Bank of England this seems unlikely. It is clear that the Bank still values indirectness. Certainly the clearing banks do. The examples of direct dealing which we have had in recent years are not regarded as the start of a general movement towards directness and simplification of the monetary system. Treasury Deposit Receipts, a non-marketable form of paper, were an expediency of the war years. The aid given to the clearing banks by the special buyer when he takes their maturities in order to replenish their cash is a convenience to enable the Bank of England to phase its smoothing operations correctly. It carries, it would seem, no immediate menace to the traditional intermediate rôle of the discount market.

A more insidious change in the climate of monetary policy is the change which has taken place in recent years in the view of the interest rate as a regulator and on the part played by changes in the quantity of money. Until the late fifties we believed that changes in short-term interest rates and changes in bank cash would serve to alter both the price and quantity of credit. The Radcliffe Committee changed this view, focusing our attention on the whole supply of liquid assets to the banks. We have now come to regard the short-term interest rate as a less potent weapon. We now see that in restrictive monetary situations a sale of bills to the market by the Bank does not bring about a contraction of credit, because the shrunken cash ratio of the banks can be quickly increased by calling in money market loans—that is, a switch within the liquid assets structure. This switch in its turn can be fed by the funds obtained by the market at the Bank of England under its last resort privilege. What cannot be avoided is the rise in interest rates which is created by the market having to borrow from the Bank at a penal rate, which, of course, it passes on in its own discounting, and in the rate quoted at subsequent Treasury bill tenders. Open-market operations in bills, therefore, only raise the price of credit: they do not necessarily restrict its amount.[1] It is indeed arguable

[1] They will restrict it, however, if the total number of bills is reduced by the rise in short-term rates. This may happen in either or both of two ways: either by the cost of commercial bills in discount curtailing the number being drawn and therefore the number

that since effective credit control necessitates a check on any tendency for the clearing banks to become over-liquid the state itself should refrain from excessive use of Treasury bills as a medium of borrowing and should finance itself as far as possible by long-term borrowing, leaving Treasury bills as a means only of meeting seasonal disparities between revenue and expenditure. For the State to reduce its dependence on Treasury bills for financing it must borrow more on medium- and long-term and this raises the whole question of the long-term rate of interest and how it may be used and conditioned—a topic far outside our present scope. The lesson for the discount houses in all this, however, is that any future government with pretensions to monetary sophistication is likely to keep a tight rein on its Treasury bill borrowing. There is evidence in recent years that the authorities have learnt this lesson. It is probable in the coming years that with fluctuating interest rates the market will make profit margins on their Treasury Bill dealing: it is, however, unlikely that these margins will be accompanied by large Treasury bill port- folios. A drop in turnover has had to be accepted and may be expected to continue.

This brings us to another aspect of the market in Treasury bills: the present method of issue through the tender and the restrictive practice on the part of the discount houses and their syndicated bid, which is tolerated by the authorities in return for the market's willingness to cover the whole tender, taking up, if necessary, all the bills that are issued. This prepared- ness to underwrite the weekly Treasury bill issue is one of the claims the market makes to utility. But is this claim not based almost entirely on the once-held view that the cash ratio of the banks determines the money supply and that it is the money supply—not the general level of liquidity— which is important? Given the validity of this view it would be essential that all Treasury bills should be taken at the tender. If they were not, the Treasury's unsatisfied borrowing needs would have to be met by Ways and Means Advances. This borrowing from the Bank of England would create cash in the commercial banks and thus prove the basis for an expan- sion of credit. This view is, as we have seen, outmoded. There would be no marked increase in the liquid assets held by the banking system—more cash, less bills and less call money. The additional cash in the system would, in such circumstances, be temporarily absorbed by a rise in the demand of non-financial groups for cash to hold as money balances

eventually available to the banks; and/or by the high yield on Treasury bills drawing large outside bids at the tender and depriving the banking system of Treasury bills. In this sense reducing the number of bills has reduced overall bank liquidity which cannot be replenished save by a switch from earning assets, probably Advances. This would be a true restrictive effect.

pending an anticipated rise in interest rates.[1] There is nothing inflationary in this process. It is an untidiness, a slackness in the system which the present complete coverage of the tender by the discount market prevents.

Let us carry the argument a little further. As long as the Treasury knows that the market covers the tender it can choose its own time for bank rate changes, making them at such times as are convenient for balance of payments or general economic considerations. Its bills will always be sold at a rate which is related to current bank rate—although it may often be influenced also by the market's anticipations of what bank rate will be during the currency of the bills which are being tendered for. The Bank of England can in fact time its bank rate changes without much thought for the Treasury bill market. If on the other hand the discount houses were able to abstain from the tender, if and when they wished, they would most probably do so at a time when a rise in bank rate was thought to be pending. In such a case either: (a) the authorities would be forced to resort to Ways and Means Advances to meet their needs, doing this either until bank rate had been raised or until lenders had been convinced that it was not going to be raised; or (b) if it was considered necessary not to raise bank rate the Bank would have to create money in the market which would be used in buying bills; or (c) bank rate would have to be raised immediately. These are alternatives which, in the working of monetary policy, are better dispensed with. The timing of bank rate changes, particularly for balance of payments needs, is important and the Bank should have freedom to choose its moment untrammelled by any of the above considerations. The discount market coverage of the tender gives that freedom and it gives also smoother and more gradual changes of short-term interest rates, since changes are usually anticipated by the market and allowed for in Treasury bill tenders in advance of the actual change. The syndicated bid by the market and the concomitant agreement to cover the tender is, therefore, a small price to pay for the Bank of England's freedom in its interest rate operations.

III

It is time to draw the threads together. Let us first quickly summarise the uses of the discount market as we now see it.

First, it provides a very efficient short loan market—efficient in the sense that it is drawn tight with no spare and idle balances in the system.

---

[1] It is when a rise in interest rates is expected that the tender would not be covered. In such circumstances there is an incentive to firms and institutions to defer their bid until interest rates have risen.

Banks need hold no surplus cash since they can replenish reserves quickly from the market. Banks do not need to lend to or borrow from one another nor do they require to borrow directly from the Bank of England. The efficiency of this short loan market was, until recently, an attraction and convenience to overseas banks and others who hold balances in sterling. For the overseas banks this market has, however, now been superseded by the more lucrative inter-bank loan market.

Second, it provides a channel for injection of cash by the central bank into the monetary system: either voluntarily by the Bank if it wishes to replenish cash for smoothing operations or on the initiative of the outside world, working through the market and its relation with the Bank of England as its lender of last resort.

Third, it enables the Bank of England to make bank rate effective and control short-term interest rates with more delicacy than would otherwise be possible.

Fourth, it acts as a special mechanism for Treasury bill finance—in particular as a shock absorber to even out interest rate changes and flows of funds.

Fifth, it acts as a shock absorber in the short bond market.

Finally, it maintains a vestigial commercial business which is at least a convenience and is of increasing utility if the commercial bill revival continues.

These are substantial claims. Against them we must set two qualifications of note. The first lies in the change in monetary emphasis from the cash to the liquidity ratio. There is no doubt that the abdication of the cash ratio as sovereign ruler of the monetary situation in favour of the liquidity ratio has altered and reduced the monetary policy significance of the market. In the days when it was thought that control came through changes in the cash holdings of the banks the position of the discount market in the monetary policy chain of command was absolutely strategic. It is now much less so. The lines of cause and effect by which the Bank of England must work on the liquidity ratio are more complex. Some of them pass through the discount market, some do not.

The second qualification is more general. The shift of interest in monetary policy from the short-term rate of interest to the medium- and long-term rates moves the centre of gravity of the system a little. As we have seen the short-term rate is still important and cannot be ignored. In its influence and control the discount market plays a significant part. Whether it is just as significant to the whole picture of the changing monetary scene as was formerly thought is hard to justify.

A more minor deterioration in the discount houses' position in the scheme of things is the ramification of the once unified market in call

R

loans into three distinct markets, in only one of which the discount houses operate. This is not a serious deterioration but some minds in the discount market are troubled by it. They regret the heavy dependence on the clearing banks into which they are now pressed.

There are few fields in which prediction is so unwise as in economics. In the light of the discount market's history, its flexibility and adaptability and the British genius for allowing events to mould institutions so that they often become most useful at the moment when they appear most redundant, it would be foolhardy indeed to venture a forecast as to its longevity. That it has many uses this book has been at pains to point out. That it is dispensable is admitted, but only at the cost of its work being done elsewhere and probably at greater expense. It is far more likely in the writer's opinion that this book is a running commentary on the discount market than that it is a prelude to its obituary notice.

BIBLIOGRAPHICAL NOTE

The literature of the discount market is not large. There are only a very few works devoted solely to it and most of the available information has to be sought in books on various aspects of the monetary system in which the discount market gets passing reference. The Reports and Evidence of the Macmillan and Radcliffe Committees gave valuable descriptions of the market of their day. Articles in the financial journals have provided a sporadic commentary on market developments over the years.

The following is a list of the principal sources which the author has used.

1. W. King, *History of the London Discount Market*, London, 1936.
2. Institute of Bankers, *The London Discount Market Today*, London, 1962.
3. Gillett Brothers, *The Bill on London*, 2nd Edition, London, 1959.
4. R. S. Sayers, *Modern Banking*, 6th Edition, Oxford, 1964, 7th Edition, 1967.
5. N. Macrae, *The London Capital Market*, London, 1955.
6. W. M. Dacey, *The British Banking Mechanism*, London, 1962.
7. F. Lavington, *The English Capital Market*, London, 1934.
8. P. Ferris, *The City*, London, 1960.
9. T. Balogh, *Studies in Financial Organisation*, London, 1947.
10. R. J. Truptel, *British Banks and The London Money Market*, London, 1936.
11. W. Newlyn, *The Theory of Money*, Oxford, 1962.
12. American Economic Association, *Readings in Monetary Theory*, Illinois, 1951.
13. American Economic Association and Royal Economic Society, *Surveys of Economic Theory, Volume I—Money, Interest and Welfare*, London, 1965.
14. Paul Samuelson, *Economics, Seventh Edition*, New York, 1967.
15. D. A. L. Smout, *Chalmers on Bills of Exchange*, 13th Edition, London, 1964.
16. R. de Roover, *L'Evolution de la lettre de change*, Paris, 1953.
17. Sir John Clapham, *Economic History of Modern Britain*, Cambridge, 1930.
18. Sir John Clapham, *The Bank of England: A History*, Cambridge, 1944.
19. R. S. Sayers, *Bank of England Operations, 1890–1914*, London, 1936.
20. R. S. Sayers, *Central Banking After Bagehot*, Oxford, 1957.
21. R. S. Sayers, *Financial Policy, 1939–45*, London, 1956.
22. R. S. Ashton and R. Sayers, *Papers in English Monetary History*, Oxford, 1953.
23. E. V. Morgan, *The Theory and Practice of Central Banking, 1797–1913*, Cambridge, 1943.
24. E. V. Morgan, *A History of Money*, London, 1965.
25. E. V. Morgan, *Studies in British Financial Policy, 1914–25*, London, 1957.
26. E. Wood, *English Theories of Central Bank Control, 1819–58*, Cambridge, Mass., 1939.
27. J. K. Horsfield, *English Monetary Experiments, 1650–1710*, London, 1960.
28. R. D. Richards, *The Early History of Banking in England*, London, 1929.
29. R. Ashton, *The Crown and the Money Market, 1603–40*, Oxford, 1960.
30. L. S. Pressnel, *Country Banking in the Industrial Revolution*, Oxford, 1956.
31. A. W. Kirkcaldy, *British Finance 1914–21*, London, 1921.
32. R. H. Tawney, *Thomas Wilson's 'Discourse upon Usury'*, London, 1925.
33. H. Pirenne, *Economic and Social History of Medieval Europe*, London, 1936.
34. W. A. Morton, *British Finance 1930–40*, Madison, 1943.

35. F. Paish, *The Postwar Financial Problem and Other Essays*, London, 1950.
36. E. Nevin, *The Mechanism of Cheap Money*, Cardiff, 1955.
37. W. A. Brown, Junior, *The International Gold Standard Reinterpreted, 1914–34*. Vol. I, New York, 1934.
38. W. R. Bisschop, *The Rise of the London Money Market, 1640–1926*, London, 1926.
39. T. E. Gregory, *British Banking Statutes and Reports, 1852–1928*, London, 1929.
40. W. E. Beach, *British International Gold Movements and Banking Policy, 1881–1913*, Harvard, 1935.
41. F. C. Benham, *British Monetary Policy*, London, 1932.
42. F. W. Fetter, *Development of British Monetary Orthodoxy, 1797–1875*, Harvard, 1965.
43. A. Feaveryear, *The Pound Sterling*, 2nd Edition revised and updated by E. V. Morgan, Oxford, 1963.
44. W. Bagehot, *Lombard Street*, 14th Edition, London, 1915.
45. H. Pirenne, *Medieval Cities*, Princeton, 1925.
46. Henry Clay, *Lord Norman*, London, 1957.

Two government reports provide important information and comment:

The Report of the Committee on Finance and Industry (The Macmillan Report). Cmd. 3897 of 1931;

The Report of the Committee on the Working of the Monetary System (The Radcliffe Report). Cmnd. 827 of 1959.

The Principal Memoranda and Minutes of Evidence to the Radcliffe Committee (4 vols.) is a mine of information on all British monetary institutions in the late fifties.

The best day to day reports on the London discount market are those of *The Times*. These, supplemented by the weekly reports in the *Economist*, give a good running commentary on the changing state of the market.

In addition to the above books a large number of articles in journals and magazines and in the daily press have been consulted. Among many articles consulted in *The Banker*, *The Banker's Magazine*, *Economist*, *Economic Journal*, *Economica*, etc., the following have proved useful:

H. G. Johnson, 'Some Implications of Secular Changes in Bank Assets and Liabilities in Great Britain', *Economic Journal*, September 1951.
R. S. Sayers, 'Twentieth Century Trends in English Banking', *Transactions of Manchester Statistical Society*, 1953–4.
W. T. C. King, 'The Changing Discount Market', *The Banker*, March 1947.
— — 'What Pattern for Money Rates', *The Banker*, September and October 1954.
— — 'The Extent of the London Discount Market', *Economica*, August 1935.
Richard Lane, 'The Resurgence of the Commerical Bill', *The Bankers' Magazine*, December 1965.
— — 'The London Discount Market: Some Historical Notes'. *Bank of England Quarterly Bulletin*, July 1967.
— — 'The Treasury Bill: An Economist's Invention', *Midland Bank Review*, February 1961.
— — 'The Management of Money Day-by-Day', *Bank of England Quarterly Bulletin*, March 1963.

INDEX